DUTY TO WARN

DUTY TO WARN

CHARLOTTE GRIEVE

Published in Australia and New Zealand in 2026
by Hachette Australia
(an imprint of Hachette Australia Pty Limited)
Gadigal Country, Level 17, 207 Kent Street, Sydney, NSW 2000
www.hachette.com.au

Hachette Australia acknowledges and pays our respects to the past and present Traditional Owners and Custodians of Country throughout Australia, and recognises the continuation of cultural, spiritual and educational practices of Aboriginal and Torres Strait Islander peoples. Our head office is located on the lands of the Gadigal people of the Eora Nation.

Copyright © Charlotte Grieve 2026

This book is copyright. Apart from any fair dealing for the purposes of private study, research, criticism or review permitted under the *Copyright Act 1968*, no part may be stored or reproduced by any process without prior written permission. Enquiries should be made to the publisher.

 A catalogue record for this work is available from the National Library of Australia

The authorised representative in the EEA is Hachette Ireland,
8 Castlecourt Centre, Dublin 15, D15 XTP3, Ireland (email: info@hbgi.ie)

ISBN: 978 0 7336 5379 7 (paperback)

Cover design by Luke Causby/Blue Cork
Cover photographs courtesy of: Tim Bauer, *Good Weekend* (front cover); AAP (back cover, right, photo of Dr Al Muderis and Sue Chrysanthou); Charlotte Grieve (back cover, left, photo of Donald Grieve; and middle photo of Tom Steinfort, Mark Urquhart and Charlotte Grieve)
Author photo by Sam Jonscher
Internal photographs courtesy of: *Sydney Morning Herald*/Steven Siewert (photo of Dr Al Muderis and legal team heading to court, p133); *Sydney Morning Herald*/Dion Georgopoulos (photo of Charlotte Grieve and lawyer Marlia Saunders outside the Federal Court, p231); photo of Donald Grieve, age 15, (p3) and Charlotte Grieve with Dad, Mum and sister Tess (p357) supplied by the author
Typeset in Adobe Garamond Pro by Kirby Jones
Printed and bound in Great Britain by Clays Ltd, Elcograf S.p.A.

To my family,
for your unwavering support

Beware of false knowledge; it is more dangerous than ignorance

George Bernard Shaw

CONTENTS

Prologue		1
PART ONE		3
Chapter 1	Dad	5
Chapter 2	Munjed	21
Chapter 3	The Story	36
Chapter 4	On the Record	52
Chapter 5	Insiders	74
Chapter 6	The Reaction	94
Chapter 7	The Lawsuit is Filed	116
PART TWO		133
Chapter 8	The Trial Begins	135
Chapter 9	Taking the Stand	148
Chapter 10	The Doctor is Called	162
Chapter 11	Facts not Feelings	182
Chapter 12	Kindred Spirits	200
Chapter 13	The Battle for Confidentiality	219
PART THREE		231
Chapter 14	Abuse of Process	233
Chapter 15	Truth Begins	249
Chapter 16	International Patients	274
Chapter 17	The Good Doctors	289
Chapter 18	Sandip's Bootcamp	305

| Chapter 19 | The Longest Cross-examination | 318 |
| Chapter 20 | Case Closed | 344 |

PART FOUR 357
| Chapter 21 | The Long Wait for Judgment | 359 |
| Chapter 22 | What Next? | 374 |

Author's note 383
Acknowledgements 385

Prologue

My father's accident is not something we really speak about. The collective story we've told ourselves is that he is fine, lucky – which is in many ways true. But it's not the full story. No-one could possibly have imagined it at the time, but his accident in 1963 would set in train a dramatic series of events that carried through to today. It would be a needle in the haystack of the $20 million defamation trial brought by surgeon Munjed Al Muderis against myself, my employer and my colleagues. My father, Donald Grieve, would be a witness in the trial, and I would be cross-examined for six long days, defending the truth of our investigation, which put serious concerns about the celebrated doctor on the public record for the first time. Thirty-five of Dr Al Muderis's patients and their families, and dozens of doctors, surgeons and health professionals would take the stand, defending their stories, their lives, their truths. The behaviour I observed during the trial was so shocking it fundamentally changed the way I understand law, the media and healthcare, and also, people. There were tears, sleepless nights, outbursts, tough conversations and endless meetings. But there also were moments of joy. In our pursuit of justice, we set important precedents for investigative journalism in Australia, and patients felt empowered.

To write this book, I needed to know more about that needle that started it all. The sliding-doors moment that got us to where we are today. I had heard snippets about my father's accident throughout my life – that combined to form a glitchy, patchwork version of what happened. But really, I knew only a few details. I knew nothing of how it impacted him and made him who he is today. I knew these would be difficult conversations, for both of us.

After the trial wrapped up, but before the judgment was delivered, I flew from Melbourne to Noosa, a Queensland holiday town that my family has visited every year since I was born. For a few days, my mother and sister returned to Sydney for work while I stayed with Dad to read, swim and ask questions about his past.

Our first day together happened to be the 61st anniversary of his accident. Each year on this day, there is a heaviness in his body and a weariness in his face. I didn't notice this as a child, but it's something I became more attuned to as an adult. The journalist in me knew this was the perfect time to revisit the accident, when feelings are raw, but the daughter in me kept pulling back. Some things are better left unsaid. I had received my family's blessing to write this book so, eventually, I mustered the courage to begin the conversation. To my surprise, Dad became animated as he recalled the events of that long ago day. It was as if he were recounting a book he had just read, or a conversation he'd just had. There are certain experiences in life that leave an imprint so deep, the details never fade. The accident, along with his fleeting interactions with Dr Al Muderis more than five decades later, are two events that his memory cast in stone.

PART ONE

Motor Cyclist's Leg Amputated

A motor cyclist who had to have part of a leg amputated after an accident in the city on Wednesday was in a satisfactory condition in the Royal Adelaide Hospital yesterday.

He is Donald Grieve, 18, of Blythwood road, Torrens Park.

He was injured when his motorcycle and a car collided at the intersection of Gilles and Hanson streets.

CHAPTER 1

Dad

The day my father almost died, he was 18 years old. He was tall and slim, with a mop of blond curls, thick glasses and big ears. Ever since he was a child, Dad has had a quick temper and a serious demeanour. He was accident-prone, and known to lash out at inanimate objects that caused him grief. His sister tells of him as a small child shouting at the pavement – 'you darned thing' – for getting in the way of his feet before a fall. He found solace in jazz, soundproofing his childhood bedroom with egg cartons to blast Charlie Parker and play his trumpet into the night. Those close to him say he was, and still is, somewhat hard to decipher – a creature of habit, often in his own world, but with a sharp intellect, a quick wit and the ability to command a room. His four siblings all agree he was always the favourite.

After finishing school, he was awarded a Commonwealth scholarship to complete a Bachelor of Law at the University of Adelaide. He wasn't particularly enthused about the prospect of becoming a lawyer, but decided it was the least-worst option on the list of degrees that could get him a job.

Almost immediately, he was bored. He couldn't see how the dense readings and abstract theories could apply to the real world. So instead of focusing on his studies, he drank beer, got a girlfriend and skipped class. For these sins, he flunked philosophy and spent his first summer break studying and working, packing shelves at a warehouse in downtown Adelaide.

He was born in Sydney but his father moved the family to Adelaide in 1957, where they lived in Mitcham, in a large house perched on top of a hill overlooking the growing city to one side, and the Brown Hill River to the other. His father built the two-storey house with cubicles in the toilets to accommodate for the many residents – the parents, five children and an aunt, Nancy.

The seven-bedroom home was, at that time, on the outskirts of the city, in a semi-suburban-semi-rural area. There were chickens in the backyard, and Dad's younger brother rode a horse to a nearby dairy to collect milk. The bus trip into town was unreliable and involved hiking up a steep hill. The family owned a car, but it was in high demand among the many residents of the home. So, one morning over breakfast, my father announced his plan to buy a motorbike. Never mind that he had never ridden one before. 'The folly of youth,' he tells me all these years later, with a shrug and a smile.

In 1963, the year of the accident, Adelaide was a city of less than 700,000. Australia's mining boom hadn't yet begun – the primary industry was agriculture. It was a time before Indigenous Australians were counted in the census, before women had access to the contraceptive pill, and before the White Australia Policy had been abolished. It was also a time when driver's licences were a mere formality – no tests were required, just a brief discussion of road rules and shuffling of papers at the local police station.

It was against this backdrop that my teenaged father marched into a car dealership in downtown Adelaide and handed over $80 for a second-hand BSA Bantam, a two-stroke motorcycle – without any idea how to ride it. At first, he mounted the bike carefully and drove slowly down the few streets to the warehouse where he worked. The bike was small, but he could tell it had power. He was cautious.

Dad's shift finished around 5 pm. The sun was still firmly in the summer sky when my father got back on his bike to return home. This time, he tore off down Hutt Street, the wind in his hair, newfound independence in his veins, his life just beginning, when he approached a T-intersection. He tried to slow the bike to a stop, but instead of pulling the handle toward him to brake, he accidentally pushed it forward. The bike accelerated out of control and crashed into the side of a parked truck.

The 180-kilogram bike collided with the truck's steel footstep, cutting into my father's flesh and crushing his bones, before it spun out and crashed onto the road. Dad was hurled onto the bitumen. Everything was suddenly upside down. His breath quickened as he looked down and saw his leg, protruding at a violent angle, covered in blood. The limb had been severed almost entirely in two, his arteries and veins cut in half. He lay on the ground, unable to move, blood gushing onto the road. Years later, he described this moment as somewhat peaceful. He approached death without fear. He was calm. He called out for help, but there was no-one around, except for a young boy, who spotted him and used a payphone to call the ambulance. My father never found out the boy's identity, but always wished he could thank him.

He doesn't remember much about the journey to the hospital, except for the wide eyes of the paramedics, who said if they'd been a minute later, he'd be gone. He came to as he was being rushed into emergency surgery. They would do everything they could, doctors assured him, but there was a 50/50 chance he would lose the leg. When he woke up, there were bloodied stitches and white bandages wrapped around his limb. As he lurched forward in the bed, he realised his centre of gravity was off – something was different. The leg was gone from below the left knee.

That first night in hospital was one of the worst of his life. He screamed, vomited and cried as excruciating pain shot from his freshly amputated limb up through his body. No amount of painkillers could help. 'That was the most horrific night of my life,' he says. 'I had no real understanding of what happened, until dawn broke and I saw half my leg was cut off. The psychological reality of that was almost incomprehensible.'

Visitors came in waves – family, friends and his then-girlfriend, who was 'horrified by what I'd done to myself'. A mixture of sympathy, sadness and terror flashed across the faces of those who came. He was told there could be a secondary haemorrhage that could force the surgical wounds to break open in an explosion of blood. A rubber tube hung at the end of the bed in case a tourniquet was required.

Back home, the family was shattered. It was the first seriously distressing event they had endured together. This was at a time when emotions were rarely discussed, trauma not at all understood. The family did not have words to describe the collective pain that gripped them. 'Sheer tragedy,' his sister Jenny says. 'It was an experience that made him mature a bit. But Don was always a mature fellow.' His brother Steve still chokes up when reflecting on the memory. 'What really gets me, I hate the image of him on the road, alone, no-one around, thinking he was going to die.'

Their father, Sidney Grieve, was a Scottish man who manufactured white goods. He ate lamb chops for breakfast, exclusively voted conservative, and went to church every Sunday. He dropped out of school at fifteen to get a job when his father struggled to get work as a cabinetmaker, and prioritised hard work and frugality above all else from then on. Old Sid was typically reserved, but in the weeks and months after the accident, he was seen weeping in the family's loungeroom. He felt responsible for his son's predicament, for not doing more to stop him getting on that bike.

Dad spent two weeks in hospital, taking elephant-sized painkillers and coming to grips with his new reality. In the bed next to my father was an elderly man in his seventies or eighties who had just had his second leg amputated, leaving him a bilateral above-knee amputee. He lay there with bandages around his wounds, always calm, quiet and kind. 'He was obviously in as much agony or more as I was, yet he dealt with it with an extraordinary degree of courage and stoicism. I got to know him quite well in the fortnight I was there. He was a great inspiration in terms of dealing with the problem with which I was confronted. He didn't say anything specific, but just by example. Through talking with him, I saw life would go on.'

Losing a limb is a complicated experience, to say the least. There is a finality to it: you've lost a part of your body, part of your life, part of yourself, and that can never be undone. Your life will forever be different. On top of the physical pain, the emotional experience can be just as all-consuming as amputees grapple with this permanent, irreversible loss. For a period after the accident, my father briefly returned to Christianity – something I find hard to believe now, given he has been a staunch atheist for my entire life. 'I had this feeling that God was on my side. That he saved me and he would get me through. After about six months, I realised that was a great big load of bloody rubbish. I realised it was just me, and I had to get through it myself.'

After two weeks, he was discharged in a wheelchair. He lived at home, weaning himself off pain medication. 'I can still see him rocking in pain on the sofa. Just rocking. It was very sad,' says Jenny. His brain and body short-circuited as it came to grips with this new reality. Sometimes his foot would suddenly burn with an intense itch, but when he went to scratch it, the foot simply wasn't there. Other times he would momentarily forget about the amputation and go to stand up, only to go crashing down onto the floor.

Then came the first bouts of phantom pain, the sensation of daggers cleaving into his missing limb and electric shocks pulsing through his body. Throughout all this, he began daily trips to the rehabilitation centre, to start the task of learning to walk again. Most people don't realise how much they lean forward as they walk. When your leg is missing, every instinct tells you to lean backward to avoid falling. Amputees must learn to work against these instincts, to overrule their body's warnings and lean into the fear in order to walk. Day by day, the stitches still not fully healed, Dad pushed back against these instincts and, eventually, took his first steps. He was fitted with his first prosthetic – a plaster cup strapped to his thigh with leather buckles, attached to a simple wooden leg. Slowly, painfully, he began to walk again.

By March, he was back at university. Adelaide was a small town where gossip thrived, and news travelled quickly. Upon his return to university, a lecturer called Horst Lucke reached out to offer my father a job as his research assistant. Horst was born in Cologne just before the Nazi Party came to power, and narrowly avoided being conscripted into the Hitler Youth. Bitterly ashamed of Germany's history, he immigrated to Australia for love, bringing with him degrees from Cologne University and New York University.

He was offered a tutorship at the University of Adelaide but needed to complete a local degree before he could start climbing the academic ladder. Horst finished the degree in record time, with distinctions in every subject, and was eventually given a job teaching contract law. My father regarded him as one of the greatest academics in the country, and quickly accepted the offer to work for him. 'He may have had the feeling the job would give me a sense of encouragement or purpose. He was a very admirable man.'

Each week, Horst gave my father a list of cases to find in the library, then read and discuss with him. During this time, Dad helped Horst publish a paper in the *Adelaide Law Review* that scrutinised the doctrines of quasi-contracts – in other words, how payment is determined in handshake deals that go wrong. Horst would later become Head of the Law School. The paper they wrote together was relied upon in a High Court judgment that changed the way building contracts worked in Australia, giving greater power to workers.

The experience of working with Horst moved my father. He became more interested in the career he had chosen, compelled to understand how words carry power. The law is not set in stone, he realised – it is static, something that can be debated, argued and changed, with tangible consequences for real people. Horst helped him see both the beauty and the fallibility of law, and the way it can be altered through sound arguments, using ethics and reason, for the betterment of society. If there was a quasi-contract with Horst, the pay-off was a new lease on life for my father.

After finishing university, he moved back to Sydney. Old Sid gave him $2000, which he spent on a ramshackle house in Forest Lodge. With the help of his Aunt Nancy, he cleared the debris, applied a fresh lick of paint, and patched holes in the walls. 'He was going up and down ladders, doing the most precarious things,' says Jenny. By this point, he was able to walk on the false leg, but something wasn't quite right. The surgeon who performed the amputation had cut the tibia, the dominant calf bone, two centimetres shorter than the fibula – the exact opposite of how the surgery is supposed to be performed. This meant the smaller bone bore the brunt of his weight, making each step painful. My father was daunted by the prospect of another surgery to correct the mistake, so resolved to get on with his life. He walked with a limp and ignored the pain.

As his new home came together, he fired off more than 30 letters to solicitors' firms and eventually landed a job.

Most of his early legal work involved insolvency cases, and he observed, time and time again, how many accountants put fees before the interests of their clients. This didn't sit right. When he switched from solicitor to barrister at 28 years old, Dad's first rule of business was to always put clients first. He developed a reputation for pushing the boundaries of law, taking punts on creative yet strategic cases. Some worked, many didn't. He took cases to the High Court, set precedents, got companies off the hook, and achieved just outcomes for everyday people. His quick temper translated into boisterous courtroom appearances, heated clashes with opponents, and what would become known as his signature 'Force 10' letters – missives sent to enemies with cyclonic impact.

One day in the late 1970s, my father was briefed to advise Ampol on a takeover bid by Howard Smith. The petrol giant's board and legal team arrived at his chambers for a meeting, but his room was so small they couldn't fit. The gaggle of suited men took taxis back to Ampol's head office for the meeting, but the experience sparked an idea for my father. He decided to open his own chambers, with larger rooms and greater opportunities.

Harry Seidler's MLC Centre had just been built on Martin Place and there were a few floors still available. He caught the lift to Level 62, which had wraparound views of the glistening Sydney Harbour. Amazed by the spectacle, Dad teamed up with fellow barristers David Levine and John Garnsey, and together they signed an 18-year lease, with an option to renew for another 18 years. 'I was 38 at the time. I thought 36 years? That should see me out,' he says.

Over beers at the Surry Hotel, the three men tossed around names. They settled on Blackstone Chambers, after an English legal academic best known for delivering the famous dicta: 'It's better that ten guilty persons escape than one innocent suffer.' Blackstone was also known for his arguments in favour of a free press. They enlisted architects to design the floor, creating a beehive of window offices, each with spectacular views, and a massive boardroom in the centre.

It was a bold move for an up-and-coming barrister to leave his spot at the sought-after Selborne Chambers and open a rival floor. Rumours swirled in legal circles, and within Dad's own family, that the venture was a high-risk, disruptive move. 'I remember he called me at the time and told me he'd signed the lease,' his brother Steve says. 'I said, "What the hell? How are you going to do that?" He said, "It'll be right. I just need to find 20 other barristers now to help pay the rent." He was always a great risk-taker.'

The summer before they moved into the chambers, my father decided, 18 years after his accident, that it was time to see a surgeon about the pain in his residual limb. Walking had become too difficult and he had to face the fact it was never going to improve until it was fixed. 'I knew how horrible it was going to be to have the revision surgery, but it was a question of the lesser of two evils.' He booked an appointment with orthopaedic surgeon Bill Marsden, who took one look at the X-rays and was stunned that he'd been walking on the leg in that state all this time. Dr Marsden told my father what he already knew: the fibula needed to be cut back, the leg amputated once more.

'It won't be as bad as the first time,' he promised.

'How would *you* know?' my father shot back.

Despite the doctor's assurances, the pain *was* just as bad. No operation where bone is cut, or removed, is for the faint-hearted. A 2016 paper published by Oxford University lists limb amputation as one of the most severe pains in the human experience.

'I didn't have the psychological element this time,' says Dad, 'but physically, it was very painful.' To make matters worse, Marsden had developed a theory that post-operative swelling could be forcibly suppressed by wrapping the residual limb in a tight plaster soon after the surgery. After a few days in hospital, my father was discharged with the stitched-up limb covered in hard plaster, only to come back screaming in agony, begging for it to be removed. He still shudders when he recalls that pain. The plaster was removed and, over the next six months, the swelling came down and the stitches healed. Once again, my father walked, but this time, with much more comfort.

Blackstone Chambers would come to be regarded as one of Sydney's most prominent chambers, home to a suite of high-profile legal minds, former attorney-general Tom Hughes among them. They attracted new recruits by axing the high entry fees common at the legacy floors. As more barristers joined, Blackstone gained credibility.

'Flutter as legal eagles leave roost,' wrote the *Sydney Morning Herald*'s gossip column in 1991. 'Although Wentworth and Selborne confer instant status, many barristers resent the $270,000 it costs to buy shares entitling them to a tiny single room.'

My father's office was the first room next to the entrance and lobby. It had olive green walls, still-life art and an ashtray filled with Marlboro Red butts on the large, wooden desk. In the room next door was David Levine, a fellow founding member and a friend of my father's since they were classmates at Canterbury Boys' High School in southwest Sydney. The two men's lives would go on to have uncanny similarities: their sons attended the same preschool, and later, as elderly men, they lived on the same street in Paddington.

Admitted to the bar in 1971, Levine became known as one of the country's leading defamation barristers, then judges. He started out as a publisher's advocate, representing Fairfax, the ABC and Channels 7 and 10, and was passionate about press freedoms, while cautious of the unbridled power of the media. At Blackstone, he was responsible for developing the floor's small yet significant defamation division, attracting barristers keen to specialise in the laws of slander and sensation.

As a judge, he was appointed to the defamation list of the Supreme Court of NSW and presided over many high-profile cases, including Australia's longest defamation trial, John Marsden versus Channel 7. In the early 2000s, he happened to hire a young law graduate named Sue Chrysanthou as tipstaff, who then went on to join Blackstone Chambers as a barrister. Even then, the 'baby barrister' was filled with ambition, confidence and a determined work ethic.

Her booming voice and wild cackle were equal parts loved and loathed, and her style of advocacy became defined by brute force and boundless conviction. Years later, she and I would find ourselves setting the record for the longest cross-examination of an Australian journalist when she interrogated me over six long days.

Barristers are a peculiar breed of professionals. They are self-employed, meaning uncertain workflow and overheads. They are lone wolves, often left to come up with legal strategies, identify weaknesses in their opponent's cases, and advise clients on whether to fight, settle or capitulate. They must make a series of rolling judgments – on witnesses' credibility, on interpretations of laws, on logic and fact. Much like chess, law is a game of strategy – there's no singular way to approach a case, and decisions are often made in grey areas, under pressure and based on gut feeling. The courts can be like pigs hunting for truffles, sniffing out lies and unearthing facts. The best barristers place the truth, fairness and justice above all else. There can be the temptation to give advice that prioritises a barrister's fees and fame over the interests of their clients. This was not the path my father chose, often returning briefs he thought hopeless, no matter how much money was on the table. He was prickly at times, downright terrifying at others, but he developed a reputation as a barrister of integrity. He was made silk at 39 years old, among the youngest to be recognised in this way at the time.

Blackstone Chambers would also hold significance for another reason. In the mid-1980s, a young woman was informed that a spare room had become available. Having grown up on the cotton fields near Goondiwindi, she had long cherished water views, and decided to put in an application. By that point, positions were sought-after and she was forced to endure meeting after meeting with male barristers, who sized her up to determine whether she was the right fit. Eventually, she passed and became the sole female barrister on the floor. Having grown up with four brothers, she was prepared to deal with the boys' club, blithely fending off sleazy comments and even an unprompted marriage proposal in her office from a man she hardly knew. 'Nice tits,' a male colleague once told her. 'Only men with small dicks say things like that,' she replied, knowing the Bar Association wouldn't take him on.

Having passed the New York Bar exam, she split her time between Sydney and New York City, having fun and living life all while running cases, and delivering university lectures on emerging areas of law like surrogacy. But then, she met a man who brought her back to Australia for good – my father.

'If it weren't for Blackstone, I would never have married your father. Or had you or your sister,' my mother, Dixie Coulton, tells me now.

I was born in 1993, my father's fifth and final child, behind Madeleine, Hugo, Fergus and Tess. The chambers became the backdrop to many of my childhood memories. The walls of my mother's office were hung with photographs of me and my sister as newborns and paintings we did at school. I would overdose on Tim Tams stolen from the office kitchen, and lay on the floor in Mum's office as she battled with clients over the phone. Every Christmas, John Garnsey dressed up as Santa and doled out wrapped gifts to the children while the adults drank wine and exchanged courtroom stories from the year. Our family home in Elizabeth Bay hosted celebrations for barristers who made silk. The law, that floor, and my father's disability were all normal features of my childhood.

The enduring problem for amputees, including my father, is a poorly fitted socket. Too big, and the residual limb jostles and chafes in the socket, creating blisters. Too small, and the socket cuts into the skin, choking blood flow. Up until the 1990s, my father relied on government services for his prosthesis. These were often basic wooden legs that allowed him to walk short distances only. There was little innovation in prosthetics in Australia at the time, and public subsidies for top-shelf options were limited. As a result, amputees often dealt with uncomfortable sockets, causing them to rely on crutches or give up on walking altogether.

One day, my father read about a new system turning heads in the US. A Minnesotan man named Carl Caspers became a below-knee amputee when he accidentally shot himself in the leg at 18 years old. No sockets fitted his residual limb, and he endured surgery after surgery as doctors tried but failed to find a solution. Exhausted, Caspers decided to take matters into his own hands. He trained in prosthetics, and later started a company that invested in research and development to improve socket technology. He eventually launched a new system that used a vacuum pump to create a tight seal between the limb and the socket. This innovation promised to drastically improve the experience of walking for amputees.

After trying and failing to access Caspers' new system from Australia, my father booked a flight to Minnesota to meet the man himself. 'He was a jovial, friendly man who was obviously very keen on his product, which was quite justified in my view. It was a great breakthrough.'

Within an hour, the amputee-turned-entrepreneur had fitted my father with a new leg, and he was amazed by the results. It was like no other prosthesis he had ever used. The pain of walking was greatly reduced, and he had vastly more control. The prosthesis cost him $US20,000, an eye-watering sum, and reflective of the divide between the haves and have-nots among people living with disabilities.

Upon returning to Australia, my father connected with a new prosthetist, David Howells, who wanted to know more about the American system. Howells became a prosthetist somewhat by accident. At 16 years old, he applied for a casual holiday job at a Sydney woodwork studio after seeing an ad in the newspaper. He arrived on his first day expecting to craft furniture, but was instead put to work sanding timber prosthetic legs – the beginning of a lifelong career and passion in amputee care. He has since become one of the most prolific prosthetists in the country, celebrated for his work in making cutting-edge prostheses for Australia's Paralympians. He's been known to spend hours on the field with these athletes, patiently adjusting the design to maximise comfort and speed.

'The bond we share with an athlete could actually be stronger than the one they have with their coach because we're making the part of the body that helps them win medals and break records,' Howells told journalist Bevan Shields at the *Canberra Times* in 2012.

At his clinic in Sydney's west, the walls are lined with photographs of the bendy pieces of metal that propel these athletes down tracks at record speeds. The designs have evolved so rapidly that there is now debate about whether the artificial limbs might be better than the real thing.

Despite having no medical training, Howells has a unique ability to watch the way an amputee walks and pinpoint the cause of the problem. Countless times over the years, my father has driven to 'the leg factory', where Howells chisels and tinkers away, adjusting the prosthesis until it is just right. With this help, my father has been able to live an active, independent life. Every Sunday since I can remember, he has risen before sunrise to play 18 holes of golf. Only in the last five years has he started using a buggy for the last nine holes. As a young family, we travelled the world. Dad often led the charge, map in hand, outpacing us all, as we walked the streets of Paris, London, New York City,

Beijing. When we climbed to the top of St Peter's Dome in the Vatican, my father and I boasted about how easy and exciting the experience was, while my mother and sister hyperventilated in the cramped and never-ending staircase. Each summer on family holidays, he was the first to suggest driving a boat down the Noosa River, which inevitably saw him knee-deep in water, pushing the boat off a sandbank. He's built houses, run a small cattle property, hiked the Himalayas. In many respects, there has been no limit to what he has been able to achieve.

But there has been one, constant problem that Howells cannot help with – phantom pain. My father's bouts of phantom pain can last anywhere from a few minutes to an entire day. When it comes, unannounced and unwelcome, his body tenses and jolts, and he sharply inhales and grabs at his knee. It comes in waves, shocking his limb. While there is a growing body of evidence showing that phantom pain is both neuropathic and psychological, a 2011 paper by Subedi and Grossberg concluded that the phenomenon 'remains a poorly understood and difficult to treat medical condition' and 'there is still no one unifying theory' for treatment. In 2022, researchers Culp and Abdi described phantom pain as a 'difficult-to-treat' condition and found there 'remains no single therapeutic regimen accepted as the gold standard', with existing treatments, while promising, having limited research and may be exposed to placebo effect.

One afternoon, during my time in Noosa after the trial, I returned to the unit to hear my mother speaking loudly on the phone. It was around 1 pm, and my father had been dealing with a severe phantom pain attack since dawn.

'No, he does not need to go to hospital. He's been an amputee for 60 years. He needs to see a doctor for a script,' she said, her sentences punctuated with frustration.

Many general practitioners have never heard of phantom pain, let alone non-medical staff in regional clinics. I reached for my phone and set up a telehealth appointment for him. When the phone rang, I handed it to my father and before the doctor could ask a single question, he delivered the facts, as if back in court: 'I've been an amputee for 62 years. This morning and throughout today, I've had recurrent phantom pains of a very extraordinary kind. What I need is a nerve painkiller. I've had them prescribed once before, it's been effective, but I've forgotten the name of the medication.'

The conversation was over in four minutes. As we waited for the doctor to send through the promised prescription, Dad tried to take his mind off the pain by reading a book. Every few seconds, he'd jolt forward and groan. 'Shit,' he whispered. 'Oh no.' With each shock, my chest would tighten; I hate hearing him suffer.

The script eventually arrived. My father has resisted pain medication most of his life. But as he has gotten older, he has decided it's sometimes simply not worth pushing through. Phantom pain is a debilitating condition for which he has always sought a solution.

CHAPTER 2

Munjed

The first time my father met Munjed Al Muderis was at The Australian Club on Macquarie Street in Sydney's CBD. It's one of the country's oldest male-only clubs, and counts former prime ministers, politicians, judges and businessmen as members. Women are permitted to enter the building as guests, but are prohibited from becoming members. By all accounts, it's an outdated, stuffy institution where men wear ties, waiters wear suits and a great big painting of King Charles hangs at the entrance. But for some, it's a place to socialise, exchange stories and attend events, such as talks given by people with interesting perspectives or stories to tell.

Dr Al Muderis was one such speaker. Members of the club were invited to hear him speak on 5 June 2018. The room was packed full that night. By this point, Dr Al Muderis had published his first memoir, *Walking Free*, which tracked his journey growing up in Iraq before becoming a refugee and then a celebrated surgeon. His story had been republished by every mainstream media outlet in the country, across television, radio and print. It's an inspiring and captivating narrative of bravery, survival, ambition and, ultimately, achievement, the culmination of which would see him crowned the NSW Australian of the

Year in 2020. But for many in the room that night, this was the first time they had heard his name, let alone his story.

Dr Al Muderis was born in Baghdad on 25 June 1972, an only child born into a well-connected family. His mother was a schoolteacher, his father a judge. He went to the best schools, regularly travelled overseas and grew up with a 'silver spoon' in his mouth, by his own admission, attended by chauffeurs and servants. From early in his life, he knew he wanted to become a doctor and had plans to study abroad. He was accepted to study at New York University, but his plans were brought to an abrupt end when Iraq invaded Kuwait on 2 August 1990.

This invasion marked the beginning of the Gulf War, one of the most intensive air bombardments in military history. Over two years, thousands of civilians were killed under the pretence of liberating Kuwait. Dr Al Muderis didn't want to leave his family during the war, he writes, so he finished his studies in Iraq. As a trainee doctor, he treated injured civilians in under-resourced hospitals and witnessed the horrors of war.

His reasons for leaving Iraq are set out in his memoir, and have been repeated by journalist after journalist over the years. At 27 years old, he was working at a hospital in Baghdad when the morning was interrupted by the arrival of military police. They had brought three busloads of army deserters, and instructed the doctors to amputate their ears, using local or general anaesthetic. He says the officers were heading toward the operating theatres when one man objected.

> The most senior doctor in the operating theatre refused their instructions. He told the officers he had taken a solemn medical oath to do no harm to his patients. Straight away, he was marched to the hospital car park, briefly interrogated, and then shot in front of a number of medical staff.

Dr Al Muderis said the same 'military thugs' returned and told the remaining doctors: 'If anyone shares his view, step forward. Otherwise carry on.' Dr Al Muderis believed he had three options: follow the orders, refuse and face 'almost certain death' or hide. He went with the third option. He hid in a cubicle in the women's change room for hours before slinking out undetected. Dr Al Muderis was certain he would be tracked down and punished for dodging the orders, so that day, he decided to flee the country. 'There was no contingency plan. I would either escape,' he wrote, 'or face execution.'

His mother gave him $US12,000 to get out of the country. Doctors were prohibited from leaving Iraq at that time, so he had the occupation on his passport changed from 'doctor' to 'handyman' and crossed the border to Jordan. He reached Amman and quickly discovered it would be difficult to get a medical job there, so booked a flight to Malaysia, one of the few countries that allowed Iraqis to enter on a tourist visa. There, he met people smugglers and ended up on a boat to Australia.

The leaky fishing boat was overcrowded with men, women and children. Almost everyone became seasick, and Dr Al Muderis treated them for dehydration. Passengers sat, covered in urine and vomit, some of them unconscious, as they crossed the high seas. After 36 hours, the boat was intercepted by the Australian Federal Police. The year was 1999 – the peak of John Howard's Australia. Asylum seekers who arrived by boat had been demonised as 'queue jumpers' and faced cruel and inhumane treatment, including mandatory detention. Political discourse around immigration policy was heating up at the time; two years later, Howard would deliver the now-famous line: 'We will decide who comes to this country and the circumstances in which they come.' Never mind that Australia had been an active participant of the coalition that bombed Iraq, and would later invade the country on false pretences, in a disastrous military exercise that killed hundreds of thousands more civilians.

Dr Al Muderis and the other asylum seekers spent a few nights on Christmas Island before being transferred to the newly opened Curtin Immigration Detention Centre, in the middle of the West Australian desert, 2500 kilometres north-east of Perth. Isolated in the middle of the outback, the detention centre was nothing more than a collection of demountables and plastic marquees surrounded by barbed wire, electric fences, floodlights and surveillance cameras. The ground was red soil, and temperatures regularly soared above 40 degrees Celsius. Deadly snakes slithered into the bathrooms and bedrooms, and each night, guards would search the rooms with flashlights, waking the detainees while stomping dirty shoes across areas reserved for prayer. The media would eventually describe it as Australia's most notorious detention centre, a real-life 'hellhole'.

The food was basic and there was nothing to do. Dr Al Muderis said he spent most of his time studying a small medical book he'd brought from home, while agitating for better conditions. The detainees weren't told how long they would be held there, and the months dragged on. Desperation grew. Some detainees went on a hunger strike. Others sewed their lips together in protest. Self-harm was common.

Eventually, frustrations boiled over at Curtin. A faction of the detainees cut the perimeter wires and walked into the desert, demanding to be released. It didn't work. The escapees were captured and returned to the camp. Dr Al Muderis claims he wasn't part of the break-out and didn't even leave the compound, but he was mistakenly identified as a ringleader and charged by police.

The first time Dr Al Muderis's name appeared in the Australian media was in a short news article published by the *Courier-Mail* on 25 June 2000. He was described as an 'illegal immigrant' who had been charged over the break-out, and explains his reason for leaving Iraq on the public record for the first time.

Al Muderis, 28 ... said he had been forced to flee Iraq because he feared the harsh penalties after refusing to cut off the ears and feet of draft dodgers. "A lot of my colleagues, doctors, they suffered from this," he said. "Some of them, I've heard, I'm not sure, have been executed".

From prison while awaiting trial, he wrote letters to the media and human rights groups. This time, journalists were interested. 'The letters I wrote from jail also triggered a dramatic change in my fortunes,' he writes in his memoir. This was the beginning of a mutually beneficial relationship between Dr Al Muderis and the media that would stretch decades. He connected with an immigration agent and legal team, who ran his defence and processed his asylum claim. Eventually, Dr Al Muderis was found not guilty over the break-out, and was given a visa to live and work in Australia. After ten months in detention, he was free.

He moved to Melbourne, married a woman he had met in Curtin and started applying for jobs. Much to his surprise, he was offered two positions at regional Victorian hospitals, and quickly got to work. Life was coming together. He had become a key source for the media since the detention centre break-out and appeared on mainstream programs about refugees who arrive by boat. Within five years, he had passed the surgical fellowship and moved to Sydney. Some who trained alongside him were surprised at his rise in the profession. One colleague from his early days in Canberra said he gained the nickname 'often wrong, never in doubt'.

An ambitious high achiever, Dr Al Muderis grew concerned his career was turning stale after a few years. He liked complex, challenging cases, and wanted to perform more than bread-and-butter surgeries. According to his memoir, he had long been fascinated with the movie *The Terminator*, a science fiction hit about a cyborg assassin. He wanted to help amputees by making the half-man, half-machine storyline a reality. He'd heard of osseointegration, the novel surgical technique for amputees, and arranged to undergo training in Berlin.

Osseointegration is a term used to describe the process where titanium fuses with bone. It was first used on humans in the 1960s, when a Swedish doctor drilled titanium pins into a jawbone to better connect false teeth. Osseointegration in amputees involves a titanium rod being implanted into the residual bone that protrudes through the skin to connect to a prosthetic limb. The procedure creates a direct skeletal attachment between the amputee's bone and the prosthetic, which can improve mobility and control. The system eliminates the problems with sockets, but also creates a permanent open wound, which must be carefully managed for life. Like all implants that protrude through the skin, infection is an ever-present risk. There is no long-term, comprehensive data covering the lifetime of osseointegrated amputees. There is no credible evidence to show the surgery has any impact on phantom pain.

For as long as the technique has been around, it has been controversial for its uncertain success rates and severe complications. It has been performed on clusters of amputees in specialist clinics around the world since the 1990s, but over the past decade, Dr Al Muderis has become the face of osseointegration globally. He co-designed and patented a new osseointegration implant, and cut the surgery from two stages to one, reducing the hospital and recovery time for patients. He's now performed the procedure on over 1000 patients all over the world – more than any other surgeon.

Upon returning from his studies in Berlin, Dr Al Muderis went about opening a one-stop shop for osseointegration in Sydney. He assembled a multidisciplinary team of psychologists, prosthetists, pain and rehabilitation specialists to assess patients for suitability and monitor their recovery. He pledged to give his mobile number to every single patient, an on-call surgeon ready to meet their every need. In those early days, he was selective with his patients, carefully choosing those he was confident would thrive. The list of contraindications – things that make patients ineligible for surgery – was long. He turned people away.

For those who were selected, the experience could be truly miraculous. People who had long thought they'd be confined to a wheelchair were suddenly able to walk. Emotional scenes occurred as patients seemingly defied all odds and took their first steps. Tears of joy were common in Dr Al Muderis's clinic.

'It really opened my eyes to what was possible,' said one doctor who worked with Dr Al Muderis in the early days. 'I had a patient from Tasmania who never walked, she burned both her legs in a bathtub accident as a child. We did the surgery. To see her walk brought tears to my eyes. In the right patients, it's a great operation.'

The patient success stories hit the Australian media around 2011 and quickly became catnip for commercial news. The first prominent splash was about a woman named Marny Cringle, who lost her left leg after being hit by a train in London. Her femur was too short for a socket prosthesis, so she'd spent 16 years using crutches or a wheelchair. She'd never given up on the possibility of walking and then, one day, she found Dr Al Muderis. After a few consultations, they came up with a plan to lengthen her femur and perform osseointegration.

The procedure was an incredible success. Marny was able to walk, unaided, for the first time in 16 years. 'Ready to be standing on her own two feet,' was the headline in the *Newcastle Herald* in 2012. 'Amputee "growing" new leg,' wrote the *Daily Telegraph*. Marny was able to return to her job as a nurse, and became an inspirational speaker, praising the surgery and the transformational impact it had on her life.

The following year, another story emerged, about a man named Jamie Bertoux who flew from London for osseointegration after losing both of his legs in a car crash. By chance, he met

Dr Al Muderis in Sydney while having his prosthesis re-fitted. 'I take it as fate really,' he said. 'I've known about this operation for nine years … and Munjed is the fastest I've come across. He has a 100 per cent success rate and it might be on the other side of the world but hey, there's sunshine and the doctors are brilliant.'

A few months later, another story praising the wonders of osseointegration appeared in the *Sunshine Coast Daily*: 'I had never heard of anything like it,' said patient Miranda Cashin. 'It would completely revolutionise the way I walked, give me a more natural gait and eliminate the pain I suffered on a day-to-day basis. I thought of it as the stuff of science fiction – I would essentially become a "cyborg".' Miranda, like many others, was under the false impression that Dr Al Muderis was 'the only surgeon who performed the operation in Australia', so she signed up on the day of her first assessment. 'In a way I had been waiting for this moment my entire life. To walk without pain. To walk as close as possible to an able-bodied person.'

These early news stories all featured smiling photos of patients, and made passing references to Dr Al Muderis and his journey fleeing Iraq. The first in-depth feature about Dr Al Muderis specifically was published by *The Australian Women's Weekly* in 2013, a profile written by journalist Clair Weaver headlined 'From penniless prisoner to bionic surgeon'.

'He's a miracle worker who fits amputees with radical robotic limbs. Yet just how did Dr Munjed Al Muderis escape his life in war-torn Iraq to become a Porsche-driving surgeon?'

Weaver's story covered the orders from Saddam Hussein's 'henchman', Al Muderis's time in Curtin, his start in regional hospitals, and the current day, where he had 'all the trappings of Australia's most successful medical elite'. The journalist interviewed devoted patients and described osseointegration in glowing terms. 'The resulting bionic leg,' Weaver wrote, 'allows patients almost the same range of motion and movement as an able-bodied person.' There was no mention of a single risk or potential complication in the article.

Dr Al Muderis's profile grew dramatically after his first memoir, *Walking Free*, was published in 2014. He toured the country to promote the book, which received glowing reviews from all sides of the press. And as his star rose, more people learned about osseointegration and the patient request forms came flooding in.

'As a doctor, his community contribution has been inspiring,' a review by *The Australian* said.

'Munjed Al Muderis' story is worthy of a Hollywood biopic treatment,' wrote the *Sydney Morning Herald*.

'He makes a powerful case as to why our politicians need to come up with smarter, more humane solutions to the refugee crisis,' wrote *The Age*.

The steady stream of ensuing articles took a similar tone. The salvation of Dr Al Muderis and his patients were interwoven to create a miracle, an act of fate, destiny. 'One man lost his legs and the other lost his freedom. Both dreamed of making a new life,' read the tagline for another feature in 2014. These articles never included failure rates or risks and routinely disparaged non-invasive alternatives. 'The sockets date from the 15th century and they haven't changed much, but we are changing things now,' Dr Al Muderis said.

Over the years, the media's celebration of Dr Al Muderis and the surgery would become increasingly effusive. These articles emphasised the positives of osseointegration, while omitting any negatives. Dr Al Muderis was described as 'world-renowned', a 'remarkable surgeon', 'pioneer', 'hero', 'miracle worker', 'human rights advocate'.

His profile turned global in 2015, when Prince Harry visited his clinic during a tour of duty with the Australian Defence Force. The prince attended Macquarie University Hospital in Sydney's west and met some of Dr Al Muderis's patients.

Speaking to reporters, Prince Harry heaped praise on the surgery and on Dr Al Muderis personally. 'What they are doing here is absolutely amazing. Osseointegration, as far as I can see it, is the way forward for single amputees or double amputees above the knee.'

Dr Al Muderis featured prominently in a campaign for better refugee rights in 2016. His face was plastered across tram and bus stops in major cities, under the banner: *I came by boat*. He hired a public relations specialist, who helped promote his image. He appeared on the ABC's hit show *Anh's Brush With Fame*. He became an ambassador for the Red Cross and delivered a speech on human rights for Amnesty International. He hired a speakers' agency and charged tens of thousands of dollars for appearances. He delivered a TEDx Talk at the Sydney Opera House, where he shed tears on stage while talking about the life-changing impacts of his surgery. He travelled overseas to perform osseointegration on patients in Cambodia and Iraq, followed by film crews from the ABC and Channel Nine.

Dr Al Muderis became more than a surgeon. He was a political figure, a humanitarian, the face of cutting-edge medical innovation. Everyday people wrote to major newspapers citing his name in the push for greater compassion toward refugees. In 2018, Labor candidate Ali France ran in the seat of Dickson for the first time against then Minister for Home Affairs, Peter Dutton. France had lost her leg in a horrific car crash, but later regained her mobility through osseointegration performed by Dr Al Muderis. She wrote an open letter about her surgeon 'who came by boat' which went viral online. The aspiring politician used Dr Al Muderis's story to advocate for better treatment of asylum seekers on the campaign trail. His name, his narrative, had taken on a life of its own.

He even became the subject of gossip columns, with Emerald City in the *Sydney Morning Herald* detailing his record-breaking penthouse purchase of $10.5 million. He was named *GQ* Man of the Year in 2019. At the awards, the presenter told the room: 'I heard his story. He was forced to flee Iraq as a young surgeon. His life was threatened at gunpoint ... When he was eventually granted entry into Australia, he was forced to entirely requalify for his medical degree ... This surgery helps people use limbs that they think they've lost forever.'

There are several aspects of Dr Al Muderis's media profile that sit uneasily today. Primarily, the way he allowed the public to be fed unrealistic portrayals of osseointegration. If risks were mentioned at all, they were brushed over quickly, before he returned to the marvels of the surgery. As I researched his story, I became bewildered by the way he conflates osseointegration surgery with bionic prosthetics and robotic technology. He was branded as a 'robot doctor' performing 'sci-fi surgery' but the truth is, osseointegration is an easy-to-perform procedure that has nothing to do with robots. It merely allows for the connection of a prosthesis, which can be basic or high-end, the best of which are designed and sold by global companies for a high price to osseointegration patients and socket-users alike.

The captivating videos he plays to audiences, where amputees use 'mind control' to wiggle the fingers of their false arm, is also not unique to osseointegration. The same technology is available to socket wearers – specialists hook up sensor pads that detect muscle movements through the skin and feed instructions to the electric arm. Dr Al Muderis paints the prosthetic industry as stuck in the past, and himself as the sole brave saviour taking amputees into the modern world, but this also could not be further from reality. There have been enormous leaps forward in prosthetic technologies that do not involve invasive surgery and lifelong risks of infection, such as the work completed by Caspers, Howells and dedicated research teams at top universities around the world today. Dr Al Muderis portrayed osseointegration as the future for all amputees, rather than a high-risk and uncertain solution for those who can't use sockets. He even went as far as combining amputation with osseointegration in a single surgery for some, thereby denying patients any ability to trial less-invasive prostheses. In retrospect, the media's entirely uncritical view of this experimental surgery was, at its worst, dangerous.

As I scrutinised his rise in Australia's public consciousness, I began to notice small but significant inconsistencies in his story. Saddam Hussein's regime introduced a decree in 1994 to amputate the ears of army deserters, but this was declared 'null and void' in 1996 – three years before Dr Al Muderis claims to have been given the same instructions in Baghdad. None of his public statements mention this, and as his account morphed over time, it became increasingly dramatic – from his first media interview in 2000, where he merely 'heard' that doctors were being executed, to becoming an eye-witness to execution. Then: 'His life was threatened at gunpoint,' the presenter said at the *GQ* Awards. Dr Al Muderis never sought to correct the embellishments in how his story was told. He only seemed to lean further in.

However, back in 2018, when Dr Al Muderis addressed members at The Australian Club, I didn't know any of this. Toward the end of his speech, he touched on his osseointegration practice. My father's ears pricked up and, as the crowd was dispersing, he approached the doctor.

'Does osseointegration help with phantom pain?' he asked.

'You betcha,' my father recalls the doctor telling him. 'Come and see me.'

My father emailed me after the event. I was living in Melbourne at the time, and this was the primary way we kept in touch. He had just finished reading *Walking Free* and shared an overview of the doctor's life story – his studies in Iraq, the ear-cutting orders, the senior surgeon who was 'taken into the car park where he was summarily executed', and his subsequent escape to Australia.

'I had read of his achievements but came to read the book as a consequence of attending a function in The Australian Club last Tuesday where he gave a profoundly interesting address to the members present,' he wrote.

'In short, he vehemently condemned the Australian government's approach to refugees. To do that in such a Tory institution as The Australian Club was rather amusing! But I should hasten to add that his condemnation of our immigration policy was eloquent and entirely persuasive.

'I had a particular interest in going to the function [as an amputee]. Dr Al Muderis has developed an orthopaedic technique known as osseointegration.'

He told me the procedure 'effectively replaces the amputee's lost limb with a prosthesis which is an extension of his actual leg'.

A few days later, I responded: 'Wow that sounds like an incredible book and speech. I just quickly googled him and I recognised his face from a billboard campaign in Melbourne that put a spotlight on refugees who have made enormous contributions to society ... To get the osseointegration would be fantastic. Have you reached out to arrange a time? Are there any risks involved?'

My father didn't respond directly to that last question, but went on to book an appointment. There, Dr Al Muderis looked at his stump, looked at the scans, and declared my father to be an excellent candidate. He then sketched a line graph on the back of the bone density scan package. It was a literal back-of the-envelope explanation, but its meaning could not be clearer. There were two lines representing two different directions for my father's mobility. With the surgery, one line shot diagonally upward to his pre-accident levels – back to almost the same level of mobility he had when he was 18 years old. Without the surgery, his mobility would fall off a cliff, and he would be confined to a wheelchair by the time he was 80 years old.

Dad was 75 at the time, so according to Dr Al Muderis, he had five years of mobility left. This is a shocking prognosis for anyone to hear, let alone someone who has spent their life fighting to stay mobile. When Dad returned home, he told my mother that he was getting the surgery, in the same forthright manner he'd used when telling his family he planned to buy a motorbike. 'He was freaked out about being in a wheelchair,' she says. 'That really shook him.'

My parents have lived together for more than 35 years. My mother has an almost telepathic ability to identify tripping hazards, clearing electrical cords, shoes and socks from his path. When they were first married in 1991, she introduced him to Noosa and was surprised to learn that he didn't own shorts. She bought him a pair, and helped him feel confident showing the prosthesis. When they went for a swim, he took off his leg and hopped down to the water. She encouraged him to ask Howells to make him a special leg so he could go swimming more easily. She has nursed him when dealing with phantom pain and gone out of her way to make sure he's safe. She has always been attuned to his health and mobility, so when he came home declaring that he needed this surgery immediately or he would lose his ability to walk – something did not sit right.

'He's never needed a wheelchair the whole time we've been married. Never,' she said. 'He was fixated. Something had changed in him. He was hell-bent on getting this surgery. Quickly.'

My mother encouraged him to get a second opinion. He followed her advice and was warned that Dr Al Muderis underestimated both the risks and the failures of osseointegration. He learned of patients who had become addicted to heavy pain medications and left to languish without the promised fairytale ending. My father was told not to get the surgery. He had lived his whole life being able to walk unaided, and there was no reason to believe that would change anytime soon. The benefits, particularly at his age, simply did not outweigh the risks.

All these years later, I tried to understand what had made him so determined after that initial appointment. I asked what it would mean to him to go back to his pre-injury level of mobility, whether he still wishes things had turned out differently. At first, he dodged the questions. He said he doesn't hold any regret about the accident, and couldn't even entertain the possibility of reversing the injury. 'You know it's just not possible,' he said. 'It would be wonderful if it did, but it's not possible.'

I pushed the point, asking *why* it would be wonderful. I wanted to get inside his head, to understand his motivations. He paused, and his gaze fixed on me.

'I'm always conscious of the fact I'm an amputee. The limitations are there, always. You know you've always got to have a prosthesis on hand. Even if you just go to the toilet in the middle of the night, you've got to put on a prosthesis. You've got to look at the ground, you've got to be careful. You can't just assume the surface is fine. I don't think most people look at the ground all the time. But I can't afford not to.'

Ultimately, he decided against the surgery and hardly spoke of the doctor again. But the experience stuck in the back of my mind. In 2018, I greatly admired Dr Al Muderis's work. He had helped many amputees live better lives, and his advocacy in calling for more humane treatment for refugees was desperately needed. The doctor was bold in condemning politicians who put their careers before what is right. He challenged expectations of what a successful surgeon looks like in this country. He *was* extraordinary.

But my father's experience had raised questions for me. Was the public getting the full story? Was Dr Al Muderis underestimating the risks of osseointegration? Was there an underclass of patients who felt abandoned by the doctor? And if my father, someone I had always thought had been a lucky amputee, was so sensitive to Dr Al Muderis's warnings and promises, what hope did more vulnerable people have?

CHAPTER 3

The Story

I didn't always want to be a journalist, or write a book. I was a shy child, and English was never my strongest subject. In university, I took classes in human rights, social justice and global politics. On the manicured lawns and in university bars, I debated the day's lectures with friends and came up with schemes to save the world. I wanted to do something that challenged the institutions behind society's greatest harms, fight the good fight and change the world. Privileged and idealistic, I had a pin on my backpack with the words *Unfuck the world* – a true reflection of my life plan. In my early twenties, I prioritised travel over starting a career, working pub shifts to fund trips each year across Asia, Africa, Europe and elsewhere. I wanted to learn about the world by being in it, and I was lucky enough to do just that.

On one of these trips, I wanted to test whether journalism might be a career I could pursue. I moved to Ulaanbaatar for two months and volunteered at the *Mongol Messenger*, Mongolia's state-owned English newspaper. The newsroom was in the heart of the city, an almost dystopian collection of blue-glass skyrises and clapped-out office buildings surrounded by a landscape that looked like Mars. It was a country still in the early stages of embracing capitalism, where locals wore t-shirts that proudly displayed Western brands and the recent opening of a Pizza Hut made national news.

I started my first week at the newspaper helping to subedit articles. English is not widely spoken in Mongolia, and my colleagues were thrilled to have a native speaker on board. The editor was a chain-smoking, sharp-writing, suit-wearing woman who kept her political beliefs to herself – until after a round of vodkas, when she'd let rip her true feelings. We got to know each other over karaoke after work, and in my second week on the job, she asked if I wanted to cover an international conference on population growth that was passing through Mongolia.

'Absolutely,' I responded.

She handed me a torn piece of paper with the address, and I rushed outside to hail a car. All motorists in Mongolia doubled as unofficial taxis long before Uber entered the scene. I arrived at a conference room filled with chandeliers and suited men drinking Coca-Cola from plastic cups. Headsets were handed out so speeches could be translated into your language of choice in real-time. Solutions for big problems were tabled and debated. I was given a name tag that said 'Press' and could not have been happier. In that moment, I knew this job was for me. For the rest of my time in Mongolia, I covered all sorts of stories – mining, ancient fighting, horseracing, and even the country's first watermelon farm (big news in a country of largely barren land).

I returned to Australia, enrolled in a Master of Journalism and started volunteering at community newspaper *The City Hub*. Each week, editor Lawrence Gibbons stood before the rag-tag group of student journalists and delivered a passionate address: 'This is the most important thing you will do all week,' he bellowed. 'Publish or perish.' Born in America, the land of roughly 6000 weekly newspapers, Lawrence deeply believed in the importance of local news. Working out of an office with an overflowing bin and paint-chipped walls, he has run inner Sydney's only independent newspaper for three decades. He instilled in us the importance of holding the powerful to account, but also not taking yourself too seriously. Have fun with the job, he said, but strike when it matters. These were important lessons.

Through my journalism degree, I was selected to participate in a two-week reporting trip to Jordan, an all-expenses-paid opportunity to have stories published by SBS. I packed a few cotton shirts and crammed the rest of the suitcase with microphones, cameras, tripods. 'All the gear, no idea,' I posted to social media. Through chasing stories, I met incredible people, learned about the country and experimented with new mediums for telling stories, all from picturesque hotels. We met journalists in Jordan who spoke of colleagues who'd been killed for simply reporting the news. From these conversations, I grew more determined to do the job as well as I could.

One night in Amman, I sat with a few other students on a balcony overlooking the cobbled, limestone streets, smoking sheeshas with Professor Andrew Dodd, who partly organised the trip. As we talked about the different ways of teaching journalism, Professor Dodd suggested I move to Melbourne to finish my degree. That conversation would set in train a series of events that saw me move cities and secure a job with *The Age* as one of five trainees in 2018.

My first 'round' in the traineeship was five weeks in business – an area of the world I had never been exposed to. One of my first tasks was to read a report about the technologies changing the telecommunications industry and write a short piece for the next day's paper. The report was almost 50 pages long, on a dense topic I knew nothing about and the clock was ticking. I flicked between the pages, trying to speed read, digest, and pull out the key points. Nothing was jumping out and the hours were flying by like minutes.

I walked out of the building, sat on the grass and called my friend. 'I don't think I can do this,' I told him. But somehow, I got through it, and the story was published in the newspaper the next day, with a whole heap of editing help from then-business editor Mathew Dunckley. The experience was exhilarating. I loved the pressure to understand new topics quickly, the feeling of producing something and seeing it in print the next day. It was like magic. I was addicted.

In that first year, I quickly found I was most energised when looking for stories beyond the news cycle, digging deeper, exposing wrongdoing. I published investigations on real estate fraudsters, collapsed tech darlings, dodgy builders. I was drawn to stories that scrutinised institutional failings, power imbalances, systemic problems.

When I completed my traineeship, I spent two years of the coronavirus pandemic working as a national business reporter for *The Age* and the *Sydney Morning Herald* from the kitchen table of two different share-houses in Melbourne. As the city underwent the world's longest lockdowns, I covered the financial results of big banks, insurers and investment firms as they navigated the rallies and retreats resulting from attempts to contain the virus – all while wearing trackpants and hunched over a laptop. I was one of those people who always thought the end of lockdowns was just around the corner so never committed to buying a monitor, keypad or mouse.

Over those two years, I largely dodged reporting on the pandemic itself, and instead pursued investigations into so-called ethical superannuation funds jam-packed with fossil fuel stocks, executives misusing workers' money, false promises made by entrepreneurs, white-collar criminals, international fraudsters, money laundering – the list went on. I loved learning the language of finance, and being underestimated by the male, pale business world. But I also knew business wasn't my endgame. I was there to learn, grow, build contacts and then move on. So, when an internal advertisement for positions in *The Age*'s coveted investigations team came up toward the end of 2021, I jumped at the opportunity.

After an interview process, I was given a six-month secondment starting in mid-2022. Before it began, I met then-investigations editor Michael Bachelard, fondly known in the newsroom as Bach, to discuss my vision for the role. We sat in a Japanese cafe at the bottom of *The Age*'s office in the Docklands on a typical grey, cold Melbourne day. I had written a list of ten ideas and raced through each – lobbying in Canberra, China's influence in the Solomon Islands, the private companies running Australia's onshore immigration detention network.

When I reached the idea about the surgeon, 'Al Muderis – patients and complications', I paused. 'Now, this is a story about a high-profile surgeon in Sydney,' I explained, bracing for a lack of interest – this was, after all, for a Victorian newspaper. But Bach has reported on human rights abuses around the world; the kinds of issues that click-hungry editors are often keen to ignore. Parochial is not in his vocabulary. He was interested.

As we munched on sushi and noodles, I explained to Bach that my father is an amputee who once consulted with Dr Al Muderis. I told him about the speech at The Australian Club, the initial appointment, the failure to warn of potential risks, and everything that followed. He paused, thought about it, and then said there was no conflict. If my father had gone ahead with the surgery and it had gone horribly wrong, that might have caused a problem. But this was different. With this encouragement, I got started on multiple ideas at once.

I was rushing around the cafes of Melbourne building contacts during the day, while speed-reading Dr Al Muderis's two biographies at night. As I read his life story, I took note of names I might be able to contact, avenues to explore. I joined a few Facebook groups that appeared to be support groups for osseointegration patients and reached out to some members, asking them if they'd be willing to speak with me. I kept my initial messages vague, saying I was a journalist interested in osseointegration and looking to speak to as many people as possible.

The first patient who responded was Blythe Warland. He sent a short, direct reply less than an hour after I reached out. 'I will give you a call in the morning,' Blythe said.

When he called, we spoke for more than two hours. Blythe is a no-nonsense, intelligent man in his sixties who gives the impression he's lived a thousand lives. A teacher, a tradie, a coal miner, Blythe has been an amputee for three decades. He was riding a motorcycle in the outback town of Katherine in 1987 when he was hit by a road train and lost his leg below the knee.

Blythe explained that disability is all a matter of perspective. He's a man without a leg, and only disabled when he can't walk. When he's wearing a prosthesis that works, he's a man with a leg, and therefore not disabled. He lived most of his adult life using traditional socket prosthetics, and while there were difficulties, he lived a full life. He became an athlete, worked at universities, got married, started businesses, travelled the country.

The troubles began when he was living in Darwin, where the constant heat of the tropics made wearing a socket prosthesis difficult. He was sweating all the time, causing his stump to fluctuate in size. His socket was either cutting into his leg or chafing at his thigh, and he had to make constant trips to the prosthetist. Next came the neuromas – excruciating nerve balls that often require surgical removal. Blythe underwent dozens of operations to remove the neuromas, but they just kept coming back. He was in and out of hospital, reliant on wheelchairs or crutches for long periods of time. He required heavy pain medications that made it difficult to think straight, let alone work.

Blythe had been an amputee for many decades before he considered osseointegration. He devoured all the information he could find online about the novel surgical technique. He scoured the Facebook support group, speaking with dozens of patients before he set up a meeting with the man who had performed the most osseointegration procedures in the world. In 2017, Dr Al Muderis performed osseointegration on him.

'What's the verdict?' I asked.

'It's horses for courses,' Blythe said in that first conversation. 'There are two types of people out there. There are the ones that think Munjed is the new messiah, the Munjed groupies, and that's cool. Things worked well for them. Then there are the ones where things did not go as well. And this is where him and I have respectfully clashed. I stick with being objective about it all. It's not for everyone. There are risks associated with this and people need to weigh up all the pros and cons before you just blithely go, "Oh yes I'll get it done".'

Blythe's osseointegration journey had been mixed. He said the feeling of wind on his stump as he walked in shorts, a sensation not possible with sockets, was incredible. It's something that's hard to appreciate if you're not an amputee, he told me, but it brings immense joy. The neuromas had stopped growing, and he noticed an improvement in his osseoperception – the phenomenon where amputees can better determine the texture of the ground they're walking on. Tick, tick, tick.

But, at the same time, new problems had emerged. He suffered a major infection every six months, he said, sometimes so severe he ended up in hospital on an antibiotics drip. He had developed a new condition, Complex Regional Pain Syndrome (CRPS), which, in short, had ruined his life – a side effect of osseointegration he was never warned about. When an episode of CRPS kicked in, it was as if he was reliving the pain he'd felt during his motorcycle accident – specifically, the feeling of his toes being ground off, or 'degloved', as he called it. It was a severe, all-consuming pain that left him reliant on heavy pain medications, which fogged his brain and made it impossible to work – exactly the issue he'd been trying to resolve. 'I wanted to get osseointegration to get off pain medication, and now I'm on more than I ever have been.'

Every time he turned to the Facebook support group for help, he was ridiculed, attacked and accused of spreading negativity. When he turned to Dr Al Muderis, he felt dismissed or ignored.

In that first phone call, Blythe shared invaluable insights and experiences, and cut through the noise of the celebrity surgeon halo that surrounded Dr Al Muderis's practice. Blythe was concerned about patients going into the procedure with unrealistic expectations, and tried to bring balance to the decision when talking with prospective patients. He said people shouldn't go into the surgery thinking it would be like having their limb back. It's not.

Blythe felt he did his research to the best of his ability, but realises now that there was much he didn't know about the procedure before going into it, particularly for a below-knee amputee, where the complication rate is higher, the benefits less acute, the research less comprehensive. Once he became Dr Al Muderis's patient, Blythe didn't like the way the doctor treated people. He felt Dr Al Muderis routinely ignored problems, and promoted only the positives of the surgery to the amputee community.

Before hanging up, I asked Blythe if he would ever consider going on the record. He said he'd think about it and mentioned that he would be in Sydney the following week. I suggested we meet in person, and he agreed. When I hung up, I rushed across the newsroom to Bach's desk and excitedly relayed the conversation. It felt like Blythe had confirmed that my instincts were right, that there was more to this story. I told Bach about Blythe's experience, the unexpected complications, the shutting down of criticism, the feeling patients weren't being fully informed of the risks. 'That's all very interesting,' Bach told me, before laying out exactly what we would need to get this story anywhere near considered for publication. 'You'll need multiple patients on the record, and at least one independent expert to review the patient medical records.'

I kept digging.

Back at my desk, I typed the doctor's name into various databases, searching for court cases and corporate records. I came across two key cases that strengthened my suspicion I was on the right track.

The first involved a man named Kerry Ford, a very sick man with obesity, dementia, heart problems, incontinence, chronic leg ulcers, septic arthritis and renal failure who had lost his leg from out-of-control diabetes. Kerry learned about Dr Al Muderis's miracle surgery after seeing him on the television. He wanted the procedure, but his insurer refused to pay for it, so he ended up in court, where a judge had to decide whether osseointegration was necessary, or suitable, for Kerry.

A group of experts were given Kerry's medical information and asked to provide an opinion. The result was a sharp divergence in views. On one side, two surgeons said the surgery was wildly inappropriate, insisting Kerry was so unwell that the operation itself could kill him. On the other side were Dr Al Muderis and his Brisbane operating partner, Dr Kevin Tetsworth, who said the only medical option for Kerry, other than osseointegration, was euthanasia.

The judge considered the evidence and sided with the initial two surgeons, ruling that Kerry should not have the surgery – the risks did not outweigh the rewards. As I read through the ruling, I paused and thought, *How can these surgeons be so divided?* The judge said Dr Al Muderis and Dr Tetsworth saw the surgery as Kerry's 'only shot' at walking and, as such, had become blind to the risks. *Was this an isolated case,* I thought, *or symptomatic of their approach to all patients? Were there broader splits in the medical fraternity about the safety of this procedure?* There was something worrying about Dr Tetsworth's assertion that euthanasia was an option for Kerry, something the patient hadn't even considered, and Dr Tetsworth's refusal to even read the other expert reports, dismissing them as lacking expertise, which even the judge said she had 'real difficulty' with. I kept going.

I started reaching out to orthopaedic surgeons who had experience working in osseointegration, and quickly discovered a cagey group of individuals who spoke as if they had almost been waiting for the call. By this point, I soon discovered, a handful of surgeons had tried to raise concerns about Dr Al Muderis through official channels but these complaints had gone nowhere. Dr Al Muderis had a lawyer on retainer and a reputation for threatening, and pursuing, legal action against those who challenged his business. He had built a feverish online following, largely comprising patients for whom the surgery had been successful, who attacked anyone who had a different experience or view. For the private hospitals he worked in, Dr Al Muderis was a rainmaker. Complaints about his conduct were ignored. 'Everybody knows it's wrong, but they feel powerless to stop him,' one confidential source told me.

Like my messages to patients in this early stage of the investigation, I kept my initial approaches to surgeons vague.

> Hi,
> I'm a journalist with *The Age* and *Sydney Morning Herald* currently researching osseointegration.
> I would like to speak with [surgeon X] about some technical matters related to this surgery.
> I'm happy to speak with him on or off the record.
> Can you please ask him to call me on the number below?
> Regards,
> Charlotte

Eleven minutes later, this surgeon personally responded, confirming he would be happy to talk off the record. That afternoon, I had my first conversation with this person, who would become a key and confidential source. The surgeon was immediately suspicious of my request to speak about 'technical matters' and chose his words carefully as he sussed me out, just as I was doing the same to him. Could he trust I would keep his name in confidence? Could I trust he would keep my investigation in confidence?

I gave him my iron-clad guarantee the conversation would be off the record, assuring him that source protection lies at the heart of what an investigative journalist does. I'd be out of the job if I went around breaking those kinds of promises. The surgeon relaxed, and launched straight into his honest opinion.

'There's a lot of us in the community who are …' his voice trailed off. 'Frustrated. The person we're talking about is very litigious. He's gone after colleagues. It's gone on for a long time. There's a colleague of mine who has a whole database of people who have been left in dire circumstances because of what has happened. It's not something that should be done as liberally as it is. There is a person who had maggots coming out of his legs for five years and nothing was done. It's not just this procedure, the deeper you dig, you uncover certain practices that …' His voice trailed off again. 'It will be a snowstorm.'

The surgeon told me about patients who had mortgaged their houses to pay for the miracle surgery, only to have their lives upended by unexpected complications. Dr Al Muderis had developed a new osseointegration implant to use in patients, owned by a company of which he was the sole shareholder. This meant that for every osseointegration surgery Dr Al Muderis performed, he got paid twice – first for his time in the operating theatre, and again for the implant he used. The surgeon felt this created a conflict of interest, an incentive to maximise the number of patients Dr Al Muderis offered osseointegration – consciously or unconsciously influencing his judgment over which patients are suitable for the surgery. Other surgeons would later raise similar concerns about this conflict of interest, as well as about Dr Al Muderis's reluctance to inform patients of other surgeons performing the procedure, other systems available, or less-invasive alternatives.

'It's just not regulated,' he said. 'It was never intended to be done en masse. It's not a first-line therapy.'

I could hear the frustration in his voice as he grappled with the most effective course of action. He believed in the power of the media, but I sensed doubt – he wasn't certain I was up to the task. 'This needs a big *60 Minutes* exposé or something,' he told me, unaware that by that point I had already pitched and produced three stories for the program.

I asked him to provide me with as many contact details as he could, of patients, surgeons, colleagues, anybody with personal experiences or information to share. At 6.14 pm, less than six hours after my initial email to his clinic, the surgeon sent me the mobile numbers for three patients, three surgeons and a raft of other people, as well as copies of documents and emails we had discussed.

'I apologise if we all appear guarded but based on what has transpired in the past, many of us feel like nothing will really change and no-one will really be held accountable,' he wrote.

The first patient on his list was Carol Todd, an elderly woman living in Queensland. I called her and quickly deduced that Carol was someone who hated to complain, tried desperately to see the positive in life, but also knew that what had happened to her was wrong. Carol was born with 'blue baby syndrome', a condition where the baby's skin is blue due to insufficient oxygen in the blood. She required blood transfusions through her ankles, and during one transfusion, a blood clot developed, which later became gangrenous. At six weeks old, Carol's left leg was amputated just below the knee. By two years old, she was fitted with her first prosthetic limb.

Like Blythe, Carol didn't consider herself disabled. She was active and valued her independence. She raised three children on her own, mowed her own grass, grew her own garden, even told me how she would climb onto the roof to clear leaves from the gutters. 'I've always been independent, ever since I could crawl,' she said.

Carol was a go-getter, strong, and fiercely self-sufficient all through her adult life, using sockets. Eventually she met and married a man who worked as a prosthetist. Like many amputees, Carol's sockets gave her blisters, and as she got older, she developed back pain from walking unevenly on her prosthetic limb. For many years, her husband, Geoff, helped her to walk more comfortably by adjusting the socket, chiselling away to make it fit better and get Carol back on her feet. But eventually, Geoff started to notice a tremor in his hands. He went to the doctor, who confirmed the worst – he was diagnosed with Parkinson's disease.

As the disease progressed, it became clear that Carol would soon need to become his primary carer. To do this, she knew she had to be strong, mobile and, importantly, independent. It was around this time that she first heard of osseointegration. Geoff was invited to attend an information session about the new procedure at the Royal Brisbane Hospital in 2013, and Carol tagged along. 'They showed us what they did, it all sounded very interesting. I said this would be a good idea if anything happened to Geoff, I could look after him by getting the osseointegration, and I wouldn't have to worry about all the crap that goes on with it [sockets].'

Intrigued, Carol booked a flight to Sydney to visit Dr Al Muderis's clinic. Carol entered the waiting room and found herself surrounded by patients who had only positive stories to share. They talked about how the surgery had changed their lives, and how fantastic Dr Al Muderis was. *Wow. This is a new way of life for me*, Carol thought. During her first appointment, Carol was assessed as suitable for osseointegration, and encouraged to sign up for surgery on the spot.

'He didn't give us a lot about risks at all,' she told me in that first conversation. 'He'd had so many successful patients, he said you can get an infection, but never went into how bad that infection could be. Maybe I didn't ask enough.' Carol remembers specifically telling the doctor her primary goal was to care for Geoff, that safeguarding her mobility so she could look after him was what was most important to her. Little did Carol know, the surgery would rob her of her independence and transform her from carer to dependant. But on that day, everything moved quickly, and before she knew it, she was scheduled for surgery. She was told that undergoing the amputation as a child meant her bones were not fully formed, so a custom implant would need to be made, meaning there would be a delay. 'He said he had to get a special rod made up,' she told me. 'But when I had the operation, he put the original rod in that everyone else got.'

When Carol woke from that first operation, her nightmare began. She was in excruciating pain. Dr Al Muderis had forced the normal-sized implant into her child-sized bone, causing fractures that he tied together using steel cables. She spent weeks in hospital, and said the wound looked like a shark had bitten her. Afterward, she dealt with infections so pronounced she was hospitalised with an antibiotic drip, time and time again. Her leg oozed with pus and blood and throbbed with pain, which was so severe her husband often woke to comfort her in the middle of the night as she screamed into a pillow. 'It's like having a baby,' she said. 'Only the pain is worse. It's absolutely shocking.'

This pain would come to dictate Carol's life, arriving in bouts that would force her to use a wheelchair, or be admitted to hospital. As her problems mounted, Carol said Dr Al Muderis became less available. Each time she called to ask for help, he turned her away, telling her it was normal, all part of the healing process, and insisting she'd be back to herself in no time. When her problems didn't get better, Carol remembers the doctor becoming frustrated with her. 'He was always brushing me off,' she said.

Carol couldn't name the number of operations she had to deal with the infection, pain and constant oozing that plagued her. She went under the knife time and time again, but nothing seemed to work. Her stump became shorter, further reducing her mobility and prospects for returning to sockets. By the time I spoke with her, Carol needed a wheelchair, and struggled to get around the house, let alone town – a reality she couldn't have imagined before the surgery. 'Going right back to when I first met him, I said, "I don't want you to cut anything off my leg. I want it to stay as it is." But every time I've had an operation, it's got shorter and shorter. Now I have a very short stump,' she said. 'I've had nothing but trouble.'

Carol considered suing for medical negligence, and even saw a lawyer to have her case assessed. But she was told it would be a tough case, and she risked losing everything. 'I was going to have to put my house up to beat him,' she said. 'I just don't know how he can get away with it all these years. He's really wrecked my life. I was hoping I would have no pain and look after my husband. I have to get help in now. I'm such an independent person. I do everything for myself. Always have since I was able to crawl … the things I've gone through, it's unbelievable.'

Carol couldn't bring herself to hate Dr Al Muderis, despite all that had happened, but she couldn't forgive him, either. 'The thing that annoys me is that Munjed goes out and praises himself. Everyone thinks he's god, the ones who have had no trouble. He promotes these people to get out there and promote him. And he promotes himself.'

This was the first of many conversations I had with Carol. Over time, I learned more about her story, and gently encouraged her to go on the record. She wanted to speak publicly, but her family was against it at first. They were worried that the doctor would sue her for defamation, making a bad situation infinitely worse. They could lose the house, their savings, everything.

At one point, Carol asked me if the newspapers could provide any assurance of protection in the event of a lawsuit. I asked my superiors, who gave me news I didn't want to hear. In the normal course of events, I was told, if a media company publishes a defamatory story about an individual, the media company would be sued, rather than the sources. Media companies have deep pockets and, generally, the priority of the person suing is to have the stories removed and an apology issued.

There have been rare exceptions to this, where the defamed person sues the sources as well as the media company. When this has happened in the past, the media company has run the defence for the sources, too. But, as I was informed, if, in this case, the doctor sued the patients and not the media company, they would be on their own. This has never happened before, but that doesn't guarantee it never will. It's a risk, albeit a small one. My superiors informed me we couldn't make any written commitment of legal representation for either scenario because that would constitute an indemnity, which could be seen in court as encouraging the patients to embellish their stories, or even outright lie. The best I could do was explain this to the patients and ask them to trust me. It was a hard pill to swallow.

I wondered if we could make a rare exception, and provide legal indemnity to Carol, an elderly disabled woman with a sick husband who was afraid of losing her house. I understood the strategy behind the decision, but it all seemed a bit tactical and down the track, particularly given that we would run her defence if she was sued anyway. Couldn't we do something to resolve Carol's fears? I escalated the matter to then-editor Gay Alcorn, who considered it, but ultimately decided against it. When I relayed all this to Carol, she said she would think about it but, for now, her answer was no. She would not go on the record.

CHAPTER 4

On the Record

The first patient who did agree to go on the record was Mark Urquhart, who was also on the list of contacts the surgeon had given me. Beneath his name and phone number was the descriptor: *Mark was the gentleman with the maggots from his legs.*

When I first googled Mark's name, I saw a photograph of a man with all his limbs intact, using a wheelchair. I thought, *That can't be the person I'm looking for, he's supposed to be an osseointegration patient.* But I quickly learned Mark was a particularly shocking example of a patient Dr Al Muderis should never have operated on.

I called Mark from my family home in Sydney and explained how I got his number. With military precision, Mark clocked the threat and assessed the battleground. 'He will get into court. People will be afraid to talk. Am I? I'm not afraid to talk, but wary that's what he will do. I'm not scared of him. I've had it out with him. He knows me.'

Mark shared his story. He joined the army as a teenager and was training to become a paratrooper when a routine exercise brought his service to an abrupt end. At 1500 feet in the air, Mark's parachute malfunctioned, sending him hurtling toward the ground. He survived, but his body was badly broken. He underwent 50-odd surgeries over many years, and when a malfunctioning morphine pump damaged his spinal cord, Mark ended up an incomplete paraplegic. This meant he had residual movement in his hips, but his legs were paralysed, and he became a full-time wheelchair user.

The disability hardly slowed him down. Mark competed internationally at an elite level in a range of sports: bobsledding, triathlons, the lot. He made global news in 2016 during the Invictus Games, an international multi-sport event for wounded, injured and sick military personnel, when he pushed a competitor across the finish line to win gold. In the games' closing ceremony, Prince Harry singled out Mark's selflessness. 'What could explain the remarkable sportsmanship of Mark Urquhart in sacrificing gold on the track to push Stephen Simmons into first place?' Prince Harry said, to roaring applause. 'Invictus.'

Of course, the paraplegia brought hardships. Mark said it caused his marriage to break down. He suffered medical problems from the lack of mobility, struggles that devastated his children. He always wanted to walk again.

'I made a promise to my daughter that whenever she got married, I would walk her down the aisle,' he told me. 'Then I met Munjed, and I thought, this is my chance. I'm a very determined person. If I want something, I'll make it happen.'

He attended the doctor's clinic in 2014 for assessment. At first, pain specialist Andrew Paterson knocked him back, saying the surgery would increase Mark's pain to an unbearable degree, that it could lead to painkiller abuse, deteriorating mental health and self-harm. Despite this, after further testing and multiple appointments, a plan was hatched to amputate both of Mark's legs above the knee and insert osseointegration implants into the residual limbs. The hope was to harness the movement in his hips, to move the false limbs and enable Mark to walk. Privately, some of Dr Al Muderis's colleagues thought the plan was wildly experimental and doomed to fail.

'I had the surgery,' Mark told me in that first conversation. 'And look, it was wrong right from the get-go.'

Shortly after the surgery, Mark had a stroke because of a hole in his heart, and he suffered intense full-body spasms from pain. That wasn't the worst of it. Near the protruding titanium was a small piece of exposed bone. 'About the size of your thumbnail,' he told me. 'All the doctors said it shouldn't be like that.'

Over the next few months, he worked at his rehabilitation every day. The pain was intense, like nothing he had ever experienced before. But eventually, it worked. Using all his strength, Mark swung his body from side to side and compelled his metal legs to walk. It was painful, but he did it. He took his first steps.

Mark was thrilled – it was a dream come true. He pledged to do all he could to promote the surgery, and his surgeon. He admired Dr Al Muderis for taking a chance on him, and sent effusive emails singing his praises. Mark gave speeches at hospitals about the benefits of the surgery, and posed for media articles under the tagline: 'The Man With The Golden Legs.' He even proposed to his then-girlfriend on national television, while standing, and credited the surgery for making this possible.

'It's only impossible until it's done,' he told the *Courier-Mail* in 2016. 'Now I hope there will be many more after me.'

Beneath the glowing public narrative, however, there were serious problems. The wounds around the implants never healed. Ooze and blood continuously dripped from Mark's legs. The pain only got worse. Dr Al Muderis tried to treat the exposed bone using skin grafts, but it didn't work. A foul odour started to come from Mark's legs, so bad he was embarrassed to go outside, and stopped inviting people over. The smell was 'like a dead body' and lasted so long Mark said he could eventually taste it in his mouth. It was doing his head in.

One warm day, Mark looked at the wounds around his implants and noticed something moving. He looked closer and saw clusters of live maggots burrowing into his flesh. He jumped in shock, and a shower of small white worms dropped onto the ground. 'I had maggots all through my right stump,' he told me. 'I had to get my 13-year-old son to get a pair of tweezers while I basically pulled my skin back as far as I could.' Mark took a video of the maggots in his legs and posted it to the patient support group on Facebook, asking what to do. His post was swifty deleted, and he was blocked from the group. He went to Dr Al Muderis for help, who was slow in getting back to him. Once again, he felt dismissed. 'He kept saying, "This is normal, you'll be right".'

But eventually, a line was crossed. Mark was in Dr Al Muderis's clinic in November 2019, again complaining about the smell and seeking a solution. Dr Al Muderis's operating partner, Dr Kevin Tetsworth, chimed in with some advice. 'Just spray it with Febreze,' he said. Junior doctors in the room giggled, and something in Mark snapped. He was insulted by the suggestion, and incensed that his doctors were now openly laughing at his expense. This was a serious problem that had consumed Mark's life for years and that his doctors had failed to fix. Furious, he left the room.

Dr Al Muderis later arranged for Tetsworth to text an apology to Mark, but the damage had been done. He sought new surgeons, who were horrified when they saw the state of his legs. After some tests, the worst was confirmed. Mark had osteomyelitis, a chronic infection of the bone. The implants had to come out, or the infection could spread through his whole body. It was a devastating prognosis. But by this point, Mark was no longer walking, and the pain, rolling infections and deathly smell coming from his legs had become too much to bear. Mark was used to dealing with pain, but the pain after the osseointegration was like nothing he had ever experienced before. He described it as being like a welder blowing in his legs. 'They always feel like they're on fire. You can't even explain it. It affects everything. Your brain, your mind. It drives you insane and you can't fix it.' The pain would come in violent episodes, keeping him up at night, and forcing him back onto heavy pain medication. He relapsed into addiction to painkillers, and they fogged his brain.

Mark's story encapsulated many of the same problems that were coming up in my reporting. Poor patient selection. Risks not properly conveyed. Aftercare lacking. Hope exploited. He had put his anger about what happened behind him, and part of him wanted to move on with his life.

'It's been recovery since 2016. I'm tired. I'm tired of the pain. I'm tired of being grumpy because of the pain. It affects your entire life with family and friends. When you're a grumpy person, people don't want to be around you. I've watched too many of my friends kill themselves. I'm not one for that,' Mark told me. 'I'd hate to think about how much money he's made out of the military. He's ruined a lot of lives. And he should be stopped. He's living the dream life while we all suffer.'

Initially, Mark was hesitant to go on the record. He was in the middle of packing up his home in Brisbane to start a new life in Tasmania, where he hoped to find peace. He relied on a military pension for income, and knew Dr Al Muderis could be highly protective of his reputation. But he also knew what had happened to him was wrong.

He said he would be passing through Melbourne soon, and I jumped at the opportunity, suggesting we meet in person. He agreed. Not long after, I walked from *The Age* newsroom in Docklands, through the wind tunnel of glass skyscrapers, past the grey harbour, to the hotel he was staying in. Mark is a broad-chested man, with a tight smile and a knowing look in his eye. I sat with him at the kitchen table for hours that night. He told me more about meeting Dr Al Muderis and everything that followed. He showed me videos of the surgery where his legs were amputated, and photos of the ooze and muck that came out of it. 'This will disgust you,' he said, as he showed me a photo of his leg, with a thick hard wall of cheese-like discharge coming out of it. He pointed to another picture. 'This one is the exposed bone. He did not care about it. Not one bit.'

I told Mark why I thought this could be an important story, how I needed to speak to as many people as possible, and for some to be named. He gave me names and numbers of others to call and, by the end of the night, he had agreed to go on the record. The next day, I excitedly relayed the news to Bach, noting how quickly the story seemed to be coming together. 'Sometimes the door opens easily,' he said.

I arranged for photographer Scott McNaughton to come to the hotel to take Mark's portrait. 'Thank you for your service,' Scott said upon entry. 'Thank you for saying that. Not many people do,' Mark responded. The pair quickly built a rapport, and Scott snapped an incredible photograph of Mark in his chair, a warped reflection bouncing off the television screen to his right. The portrait would later become the key shot in the series, perfectly capturing both Mark's strength and his scars – physical and psychological.

I turned to Facebook to track down other people I thought might be able to help with my investigation, looking for anyone related to Dr Al Muderis's company or osseointegration in Australia. This was how I came across Mitch Grant. I sent him the same vague message I'd sent others, sharing my number, and hoping he might call. 'I'm a journalist researching a story about osseointegration.' Not long after, my phone rang.

'Are you doing a story about the surgeon or the surgery?' Mitch said. 'Because they're two different things.' From the get-go, Mitch was concerned about being involved with any story that cast osseointegration in a bad light. He was 21 years old when a motorcycle accident left him an above-knee amputee. He struggled using sockets for a few years, which robbed him of many of the things a man his age should be able to do. Walking was tough. The chafing and rashes around his thigh made even sitting on a barstool uncomfortable.

Mitch's mother worked at Macquarie University Hospital, where she learned about Dr Al Muderis's small but growing osseointegration practice. Mitch became one of the doctor's earliest patients, leaving him a staunch advocate for the surgery. Osseointegration had changed Mitch's life for the better – so much so that he created a business selling connectors, and was trying to build a team that would help patients get the surgery through the public hospital system. He wanted more people to have access to osseointegration, and was wary of any story that might scare people off. But when it came to the surgeon himself, he knew there was a story there.

In that first conversation, Mitch, like many others, told me about how litigious the doctor could be. Mitch had already received an email from Dr Al Muderis's lawyer, seeking to intimidate him about selling competing osseointegration parts. 'Every man and his dog has got a legal letter from Munjed,' he said. 'Why doesn't he leave the connectors to us?'

Mitch described how carefully Dr Al Muderis protects his reputation. He said the Facebook support group was controlled by people who worked for the doctor. 'You can't mention price, or anything. He calls the admin to block people, kick people off.' He warned me to tread carefully.

The next time I was in Sydney, I met Mitch at the gym he owns with his father. I was greeted by a tall, young man, with big brown eyes and lots of secrets to share. Mitch spoke quickly, at length, and through it all, certain traits became clear. He's close with his family, particularly his mother, who still works in the hospital system. While he would like to make money from osseointegration one day, his main motivation is helping people experience the benefits of the surgery. He is a caring and passionate person with an entrepreneurial spirit. Like with most people I spoke to, I was on the lookout for signs of ill-intention, any indication that he was a person seeking vengeance. But over the several times we met, and spoke, I never detected anything beyond genuine care for amputees.

Over cups of coffee, Mitch told me about his experience with the doctor in greater detail. He was Dr Al Muderis's third patient, and had to beg the doctor to give him the tick of approval. It was 2011, a time when Dr Al Muderis's practice was in its infancy, and he selected patients with great caution, and great care. Mitch's operation was performed over the two-stage procedure, and his recovery was monitored closely. He was blown away by the results: the procedure gave him a level of mobility he had thought gone forever.

'I felt like I had a leg back again,' he told *The Australian Women's Weekly* in 2013. So thrilled by the results, he offered to become a patient advocate. He attended Dr Al Muderis's clinics to share his experience with prospective patients, and made videos for social media promoting his success story. It was advertising that money simply could not buy, and he was doing it voluntarily because he believed in the cause.

Dr Al Muderis started asking Mitch to accompany him to prosthetics conferences around the world, where he became a walking, talking example of the future of amputee care. Back home, the doctor asked Mitch to speak with prospective patients about his experience, from the clinic waiting room, the hospital, his gym or even over the phone. Mitch was happy to spread the good word, but eventually he started to feel used. He was spending all his spare time in clinics, even taking time away from his paid job to speak at conferences, make videos, visit patients. He asked the doctor if his work could be formally recognised and he could be paid a wage, or commission, as an official patient advocate. Mitch says the doctor agreed, and draft agreements were written up, but never signed.

Meanwhile, Mitch was becoming more enmeshed in Dr Al Muderis's personal life. He went to his house for New

Year's Eve parties, became close with his family, his staff. He got a close-up glimpse of the man behind the clinic. Mitch kept asking to be paid for his work, but was brushed off each time, and couldn't shake the feeling he was being strung along. He was also becoming uncomfortable with the way Dr Al Muderis's practice was changing. He noticed that the standard of care was slipping, complaints were piling up, and the doctor was less available. As Dr Al Muderis became more famous, he took on more and more patients. More patients meant more problems that simply weren't being dealt with. The system was buckling under the pressure.

As Mitch's unease grew, aspects of the doctor's practice that he'd initially turned a blind eye to became more of a problem. The doctor yelled at his staff, and Mitch often saw his nurses crying. Mitch felt that the osseointegration practice had become the 'Munjed show', the surgery coming second to the doctor's growing profile.

Then, Mitch attended a dinner that crossed a line. The doctor regularly stated that he wanted to make osseointegration available to everyone living on less than $1 per day. He had been to Cambodia once before, and now there was an opportunity to travel to Iraq, the doctor's home country. The idea was pitched by the Iraqi government, and officials took the doctor, Mitch, and representatives from a large prosthetics company to dinner at a high-end French restaurant in Sydney to discuss logistics. 'Anything you want,' Mitch says the Iraqi officials told the group. 'Business class airfares. Anything.'

To Mitch, this didn't sit right. This man was pitching himself as a humanitarian while receiving the royal treatment on these missions. Then there was the fact that Dr Al Muderis's company owned the patent for the implant he used. He failed to mention that his pledge to expand the procedure to the developing world would make him a very wealthy man.

To make matters worse, when I eventually tracked down patients the doctor had operated on in Iraq, some said he'd left them with half-finished jobs, arms that didn't work, or pain and infections that had them bedbound. When they had tried to contact the doctor, many simply could not get through. 'Can you please help me?' one man asked me in desperation through a translator. 'He needs to come back.'

Mitch didn't want to be involved in the story, but he provided me with the names and numbers of patients who had come to him for help after giving up on Dr Al Muderis. The first person on Mitch's list was Brennan Smith.

Brennan is a straight-talking veteran who has seen the dark side of the military complex. He served in the Australian Army for several years, shuffling weapons and gear around the Middle East and helping control the outbreak of violence in the Solomon Islands. Like many veterans, the horrors he witnessed left him with post-traumatic stress disorder. Back home, he turned to alcohol, which plunged his blues into an all-consuming black. Haunted by memories, he tried to kill himself. That was when he realised something needed to change: with two young children, he knew he had a lot to live for. He booked an appointment with a psychologist but, tragically, had an accident on the way to his first appointment. Much like my father, a split-second decision on a motorbike would change the trajectory of his life – Brennan clipped the side of a car going around a roundabout and went flying over his handlebars.

He spent five months in hospital, dipping in and out of comas, and developed an infection that spread throughout his body and almost killed him. The doctors commenced a series of amputations to stop the infection spreading. In the end, he had 19 amputations, and his left leg was gone from above the knee. The skin that covered his stump was raw, scarred and extremely painful. It made socket use all but impossible, and he often relied on a wheelchair. Brennan took pride in his identity as a strong, tough, military man, but told me the wheelchair made him feel emasculated, ashamed. 'To even have to sit down to pee, it does a lot to your head,' he said. 'Then to have someone telling you they can make you walk again, it's dangerous.'

Brennan first met Dr Al Muderis in a hotel lobby in Brisbane. He was using a wheelchair that day, and feeling particularly determined to take charge of his mobility. He claims Dr Al Muderis showed him photos of amputees running, swimming and riding a dirt bike after surgery, then took one look at his stump, and declared Brennan would be an excellent candidate. Dr Al Muderis promised the procedure would deliver him a new lease on life, pain-free. He was offered a veterans' discount and asked to transfer $10,000 to Dr Al Muderis's bank account to secure his spot. 'What kind of a medical outfit does that?' Brennan said to me.

Soon after, the operation went ahead. At first, it worked. Brennan walked, and with every step, his confidence grew. But, just as quickly, the problems started. The permanent opening in the skin around the implant, known as the stoma, began to throb and burn with pain. This is a complication known as hyper-granulation, one Brennan was never properly warned about, where, as the skin tries to heal, tissue gathers and distorts.

The pain was so intense, Brennan couldn't sleep. He was up all night, screaming into the darkness, crying as his children brought medication and hot water bottles to his bedside. 'No child should have to see their father in that way,' he said. Brennan was told the only way to fix the problem was by burning off the excess flesh with silver nitrate. Every time his stinging flesh was burnt off, he would experience brief relief before the pain returned. He was travelling to doctor's appointments multiple times a week, having to take time off work. It wasn't sustainable, and it wasn't working.

Brennan became so sleep-deprived and so exhausted by the pain that he became consumed by it. One day, he took a kitchen knife to his own leg to cut off the flesh. He filmed himself doing this, recording his voice over the top: 'What kind of aftercare is this?' He sent the clip to Dr Al Muderis.

I asked Brennan to send me the videos, along with any medical records and correspondence, and I asked him to consider going on the record. Like others, Brennan was hesitant. He didn't trust the media and knew how protective Dr Al Muderis was of his reputation. Still, he told me he would think about it. I noticed an intensity within Brennan – it was clear how badly he wanted to protect others. I kept checking in, updating him, still hoping he might go on the record. 'There's power in numbers,' I told him, like I told so many other patients.

In the end, what got Brennan across the line was the doctor's expansion to children and his relationship with the military. He knew Dr Al Muderis was on the Australian Defence Force's list of recommended surgeons, and he believed the doctor saw veterans as a lucrative business opportunity. He also knew how dark life can become post-service, and how desperately amputees want their limbs back. That combination can be lethal, and that's what made Brennan agree to be named.

Having two on-record patients was excellent progress, but there was still a long way to go.

My search for relevant court cases – the one that had led me to Kerry Ford – also turned up another key case that would change the trajectory of my investigation. When I typed the doctor's name into PACER, a database for American court documents, several lawsuits came up, all relating to a man named Fred Hernandez.

I downloaded all the files, scanning the pages. It quickly became clear that this would be a tricky case to navigate, laden with landmines but also brimming with leads. In short, Dr Al Muderis had sued Fred over Facebook posts he made in 2018. In one of the posts, Fred detailed his concerns about the safety of part of the osseointegration implant system, the dual cone, which he claimed was snapping and causing amputees to fall. Fred claimed the doctor's team knew about this risk, but chose not to recall the faulty part because doing so would be too expensive. The information had been suppressed by the company, Fred claimed, in what amounted to a dangerous cover-up.

Dr Al Muderis succeeded in a case against Fred that related to Fred deliberately spreading misinformation about Dr Al Muderis to win business away from him. There are specific anti-compete laws in America that made this legal strategy particularly advantageous for Dr Al Muderis. According to Fred, a combination of hopeless lawyers, disorganisation and the coronavirus pandemic meant he was completely unaware the case had even been brought against him, and he failed to file a defence. A summary judgment was handed down against Fred and he was ordered to pay $US2.7 million to Dr Al Muderis. The bill was calculated on the notion that Fred's posts had lost Dr Al Muderis business – costing him a profit of $US75,000 per American patient.

The second lawsuit Dr Al Muderis brought against Fred alleged that after this judgment was delivered, Fred set up companies and shuffled funds between different businesses to avoid paying the money he owed. Dr Al Muderis's lawyers put surveillance on Fred and his business partner, annexing photographs of his cars and offices to allege that Fred was trying to avoid paying up. I scanned the documents, brow furrowed, as I tried to piece together what had happened. It was clear that Fred was someone with a story to tell. I tracked down his contact details and called him.

Fred is quite the character, a tall man with a handlebar moustache and thick black and silver hair that he sweeps back in an Elvis-style do. He loves whisky, steak, cigars and women, and regularly posts inspirational messages on social media. He's also a meticulous record-keeper. He would eventually send me hundreds of pages of text messages exchanged between himself and Dr Al Muderis's employees, talking about drinking late, sleeping with women and growing the osseointegration business.

These messages did not paint Fred in a particularly flattering light, but he said he was a man with nothing to hide. He wanted the truth to come out, no matter what cost. But, amid all the lawsuits, Fred was also a man with a clear vested interest in bringing the doctor down. I knew I had to remain vigilant.

It didn't seem plausible that a lawsuit could be filed against Fred without his knowledge. When I asked him about this, he gave me documents showing his initial attorney had since been struck off and assured me that he had hired new lawyers to set aside the judgment. It still niggled at me, but I pushed this aside and asked for his back story.

Fred lost his leg in a car crash at 17 years old. He had been a socket-wearer for 28 years before he discovered osseointegration, and became enthralled by the science and the promise of near-perfect mobility. He built a website dedicated to raising awareness about the procedure, and quickly established an online following in the amputee community. However, he couldn't afford to pay for the surgery, so he emailed osseointegration surgeons around the world asking for free surgery in exchange for his promotional services. Dr Al Muderis was the only one who was interested.

'I worked for him for about five years before everything fell apart,' Fred told me in that first conversation. 'To be honest with you, it occurred to me the guy's nothing but a conman. I backed off, started to look for another job. I started writing about the things I knew about. Everything I said was true. It's all verifiable. They're saying because I started working at the competitor when I made those statements, it made me liable.'

I wanted to know more about Dr Al Muderis's practice. I asked if risks were appropriately conveyed, and Fred's answer was clear – they were not. 'In my experience, he hid the complications. Which is part of the reason I decided to leave. There were a lot of other things, but that was a big one.'

Fred confirmed that patient complaints were deliberately scrubbed from the support group on Facebook. He was an admin of the group for a period of time, and said he was routinely asked to delete anything negative about Dr Al Muderis or the procedure. 'If a patient had a complication, he would either ignore it, attack the patient or downplay it as if it were nothing.'

Fred's own surgery was a success. He suffered a few infections and worsening pain, but overall believed in the potential of the surgery, when done correctly. But, like Mitch, Fred started to feel uncomfortable about aspects of Dr Al Muderis's practice. The surgeon started operating on higher-risk patients, like below-knee amputees, at alarming rates. 'He was pumping them out,' Fred said. He operated on younger, older, more disabled, less healthy patients, with lower chances of success.

And it didn't come cheap. For American patients, the operation often cost upward of $80,000. Osseointegration surgery was illegal in the US, so patients had to travel to Australia for the procedure. 'I was selling them on the illusion of Australia, a holiday destination. Get your surgery here at the same time,' he said. 'A lot of people were refinancing their houses, taking loans out, things of that nature. I probably sent 100 patients over there over a five-year period.'

Fred was making money too. For patients he referred to Dr Al Muderis for surgery, Fred received a secret commission of $US1000. I asked about patient feedback, and the answer was mixed. 'Some were happy, others were disgusted,' Fred said. The biggest complaint was how difficult it became to get answers, or assistance, once they were back in America. Patients felt totally alone when things went wrong. Dr Al Muderis sporadically held clinics in the US, but these were costly to attend and legally dubious, given he was not licensed to provide medical services in the US.

Fred was prepared to go on the record. While I knew a story couldn't lean on the say-so of one disgruntled former business partner, Fred could be a useful source of information and I trusted he was telling the truth. I spent hours sifting through the mountain of documents he'd shared, and reached out to every patient he suggested I contact. These people told me of poorly explained risks, unexpected complications, bad communication and high-pressure sales tactics. Then one story went beyond even what now felt like a repeat pattern.

Chris Bruha is a real estate agent with a deep love of the outdoors. It was this passion for nature and adventure that would cruelly cause him to become a double amputee, after a change of wind during a paragliding session in Hawaii saw him crash, break his back and crush both ankles. He spent more than a year trying to heal, but after a bone infection in his left ankle, the prognosis became clear – the feet had to go.

Chris was searching the internet for answers when he came across a video of an amputee mountain biking after osseointegration by Dr Al Muderis. Intrigued, he reached out to the woman, who connected him with Fred Hernandez. Within weeks, Chris was on a flight to Chicago to meet Dr Al Muderis, who was presenting at the Hyatt Regency. Chris attended the conference, then saw Dr Al Muderis for an individual assessment and was quoted $US75,000 per leg. The eye-watering sum completely floored Chris – it was miles higher than he'd expected, and than he could afford.

'Fundraising is one of the ways patients have paid for their surgery,' Dr Al Muderis told Chris.

Chris followed this advice. He held fundraisers, took a loan against his house, borrowed more from people he knew, and eventually scraped together enough to fly to Australia for the surgery. All this time, he was taking OxyContin and Fentanyl to deal with the pain in his legs. Looking back, he regrets making such big life decisions while under the cloud of strong medication and, even at the time, he felt like something was off from the start.

Chris was one of the first patients who combined amputation with osseointegration, and none of the nursing staff seemed to be across the details of his procedure. One nurse casually asked if the amputation would be above the knee. Chris's eyes widened in shock. 'I felt sick. I couldn't believe it. My gut was telling me to get up and run out of that hospital. I should have listened to it.' Instead, he grabbed a thick black texta and drew arrows on his legs pointing down below the knee, hoping this would prevent an amputation higher than planned.

When he woke from the operation, Chris was relieved to see two below-knee osseointegrated limbs, but a few minutes later, waves of pain hit and Chris wondered what on earth had he done. Over the next four weeks, he saw Dr Al Muderis only a few times, and each visit felt rushed. His legs were red around the stitches, and painful. After three rounds of antibiotics, the infection still didn't clear. Chris was put on a plane home with the infection still raging and no instructions for how to care for his wounds. Back in America, he dealt with infection after infection. Ooze and muck dripped from his legs. He tried and failed to get help from Dr Al Muderis. Chris heard the doctor was presenting at an amputee conference in the US, and flew across the country to catch him.

'Show me your leg,' Dr Al Muderis said when they met on the conference sidelines. Chris bent down to pull up his pants, revealing the ooze pouring from his implant. The doctor glanced at it, then smiled. 'It looks fine,' he snapped and walked off.

Chris was having serious, ongoing problems and felt no-one could help him. He took rounds of antibiotics and tried to stay positive. He pushed through the pain and led an active life, even returning to kayaking and hiking. Until one day, he was walking down some steps when he suddenly came crashing down; his prosthetic limb had broken off at the top. The dual cone – the part that Fred tried to warn patients about years later – had snapped. He reached out to another surgeon in the US, who arranged for replacement parts to be sent from Australia.

Chris wasn't the only amputee who had experienced a broken dual cone. Dr Al Muderis's company had noticed a steady increase in patients reporting breakages in the years leading up to 2018. Among the documents Fred shared was a confidential report written by Dr Al Muderis's company, Osseointegration International Pty Ltd, to investigate the breaking parts. The report collated the incidents from the clinic and from prosthetists around the country, which found the parts were breaking not just when amputees were walking but also spontaneously, 'without excessive external forces'. Red, underlined text described the incidents: 'Broke while seated at gym doing shoulder press', 'broke while walking', 'broke while walking dog', 'broke while standing up from bar stool'. The problem was not isolated to a bad batch, but rather was a function of a bad design that had made the part weaker.

The report concluded there was a high probability the dual cones would continue breaking, resulting in a 'high consequence of hazard', including serious injury. For these reasons, the risk of continuing to use the dual cones was deemed 'unacceptably high' and 'immediate action' was recommended, including immediate cessation of use and a voluntary recall.

Despite these recommendations, Dr Al Muderis's team continued to use the faulty parts for almost a year. An anonymous complaint by a 'health professional' was made to the Therapeutic Goods Administration in January 2019 about a dual cone that broke while an amputee was walking. The complaint, which is still publicly available on the TGA's website, claimed the doctor initially sought to initiate a recall of the faulty product, but when the manufacturer refused to cover the costs because it was a design problem, the plans changed. Instead of a recall, patients would be given a new part – but only when it broke. 'The new dual cones are given to the patient in an unsterile package, without any labelling on it. The patients are advised to find a prosthetist to remove the broken dual cone and replace it with a new dual cone at their own expense,' the TGA notice states.

What wasn't publicly available was a complaint by Dr Solon Rosenblatt, a former member of Dr Al Muderis's team, to the national medical regulator AHPRA in December 2018. In it, Rosenblatt claimed the implant part had not gone through sufficient testing before being used. 'Several of the implants have broken … Dr Al Muderis has elected to change the device only when it fails rather than changing it in a general recall. Fortunately, none of the patients who have experienced a broken implant have been severely injured. But it will happen.'

Chris Bruha received a replacement dual cone in the mail. A friend of his, who has no medical experience, replaced the part in a painstaking process that took hours. Afterward, Bruha received an invoice. He had spent more than he could afford on the surgery and had nothing but problems. Now they wanted him to pay for a broken part that could have seriously injured him? He ignored the letter. The clinic never followed up. Still, his problems weren't over. The ooze continued, as did the pain and infections. Eventually Chris went to get tested by new doctors. He too was diagnosed with osteomyelitis and was told the rods had to come out.

Listening to Chris reflect on that moment was heartbreaking. He said he felt stupid for not asking more questions. Guilt and regret weighed heavily on him over the money he had borrowed and spent, only to be back to square one. 'I have no-one to blame but myself,' he said.

What happened to Chris was unsettling but also revealed deeper, structural problems. Complaints were made through official channels, the Therapeutic Goods Administration (TGA) and the Australian Health Practitioner Regulation Agency (AHPRA), but went nowhere. Big institutions were on notice that there was a doctor seemingly cutting corners and patients were being harmed, but no-one did anything. Profit motives got in the way of proper patient care.

When I asked Chris if he would consider going on the record, he said he would consult his attorney and come back to me. I immediately assumed this was a dead end. Australian lawyers are almost entirely risk averse, and rarely advise anyone to speak with the media. But, in the land of the constitutionally enshrined freedom of the press, I was proven wrong. Chris was in, for print and for television.

At the end of every conversation, I asked whoever was on the line to recommend others I should speak to. What started as a trickle turned into a flood. In total, I spoke with more than two dozen of Dr Al Muderis's patients. Most did not want to be named. Some said they felt they had been warned of the potential risks, and that the procedure was the best thing that had ever happened to them. One woman said she was part of a group who described Dr Al Muderis as their 'god'. Others felt they'd had no idea what they were walking into, and regretted the day they ever consented to the surgery.

Over interviews that went for hours, I was told of hospitalisations, serious infections, exploding legs and further amputations. I received so many photographs of severed limbs covered in blood and discharge of green, yellow, white and orange, so inflamed, swollen and raw, it didn't take a medical degree to know something was wrong. Images of rotting flesh, bionic limbs, man-turned-machine gone horribly wrong started entering my dreams. But the problems described to me were not just physical. Severe and chronic pain robbed patients of their lives, their personalities, their independence. Some were plunged into dark psychological states. I spoke with people who were taking antidepressants for the first time in their lives, battling feelings of hopelessness and despair that on more than one occasion led to suicidal thoughts.

One man described feeling like a 'cash cow' after Dr Al Muderis performed surgery after surgery, which turned out to be unnecessary. Others were frustrated by the media coverage, which only promoted the best-case scenarios. Reports of complications were deleted from the Facebook support group. Those who raised problems were hounded out, berated into silence. 'I just can't handle the bullshit on there,' said one patient. 'It's just people blowing smoke up his arse. They've drunk the Kool-Aid and they're selling it.'

Many patients I spoke to had experiences that were not strictly positive or negative, but a blend of both, a rollercoaster of emotions. One such patient stuck with me. She had known Dr Al Muderis since the beginning of his career, and had watched how he had changed over the years. She lived with a complicated combination of disabilities, and was determined to avoid ending up in a wheelchair. Dr Al Muderis performed operation after operation on her that no other surgeon would even contemplate, eventually including amputation and osseointegration. She wasn't where she wanted to be, and some days she looked at her body and thought, *Shit, why did I do this to myself? What am I doing?* Still, she was grateful he gave her a shot.

After one of her early operations, she had been discharged from intensive care to the regular ward, and her leg was hot from pain. Dr Al Muderis came to see her around 6 pm and arranged for the nurses to pack her leg full of ice. He then sat with her for three, maybe four hours, 'just talking shit', she told me. 'I've met a lot of surgeons in my life. I don't know many who would talk to you for so long, to calm you down, to shoot the breeze,' she said, before her voice trailed off. 'He has changed. I've seen a fairly rude side. I won't go into the details but I had to tell him to get out of the room once. When you go to his clinic, the waiting line is halfway down the corridor. He does surgery after surgery after surgery. He doesn't have the time to spend sitting there talking with you. The higher up the ladder, the more ego there is. You start to think you're pretty cool once you get up the top but it's a long way to fall. All in all, I think he is good deep down. I still see that caring bloke who actually wants to make a difference. When I met Munjed, I was looking for someone who was willing to take a chance on me. He was willing to take a chance. Some of the things he did didn't work out. Maybe that's the cowboy in him … but you don't get to where he's got to without trying things. There's not many people willing to go out of their way, to put themselves at risk, to help someone.'

It was conversations like these that made me wrestle with the larger ethical questions of the investigation. Where is the line between risk-taker and reckless? Genius and mad? Innovative and experimental? At what point does a surgeon actually better serve their patient by refusing to operate? I wanted to speak with practitioners who could shed light on these grey areas. In total, I spoke with more than 20 healthcare professionals, including surgeons from around the world, many of whom had treated ex-patients of Dr Al Muderis. Some described disturbing stories – an anorexic woman who Dr Al Muderis gave osseointegration to so she could maintain her pathological addiction to exercise, a schizophrenic veteran found at St Leonard's train station walking around on an infected limb after absconding from hospital. I learned of two patients who had died while in Dr Al Muderis's care.

The more people I spoke to, the more names were recommended. The list of leads seemed endless.

CHAPTER 5

Insiders

Amid this storm, I got in touch with a woman named Shona. She has a kind voice, and a quiet determination to set right from wrong. She was always in a rush, juggling young children and a demanding schedule as she transitioned to her career from nursing to law. The first few times I spoke with Shona, she was adamant that she would never want to be named in any story, too afraid of backlash, too concerned about the impact on her family.

Shona joined Dr Al Muderis's team in 2014 as a nurse. Initially, she was enthralled by the promise of osseointegration, the boundaries being pushed and the energised, inspiring surgeon at the helm. She saw how the surgery could change lives for the better and was in awe of the strength of people she met. But just as others had described, over time, Shona noticed Dr Al Muderis operate on patients who were previously deemed unsafe. 'I can't really remember any that were turned away in the end,' she said. 'Munjed would get bored. He wanted complexity and difficulty. He would say that often. There was one patient in the US who had cancer, who was in so many ways too sick to have the surgery. That was probably the breaking point for me. There was just no way Munjed could operate on this man, he wouldn't survive. But yet I was ordered to get the X-rays, get this, send that, get him ready, get him on board. I thought to myself, "For god's sake, this man is dying".' Shona sounded exasperated.

The discomfort intensified when her role was switched from nurse to salesperson. She was tasked with calling prospective patients to offer them the surgery. If they said no, she would offer to connect them with people who'd had a positive experience to talk through any concerns. If that didn't work, she would keep checking in, promoting the benefits, offering discounts and downplaying the risks. If money was an issue, she would offer payment plans or help them understand how to access their superannuation early. She was instructed to double-book patients on clinic days so they always looked busy, which often meant waiting times blew out by hours. 'The busier the waiting room, the more successful I look,' Dr Al Muderis told her.

Despite the pressure to sign up new patients, problems with existing patients kept piling up. Shona received panicked messages at all hours from patients desperate to know how to stop their wounds from weeping, sending photos of reddened stumps, worried they were infected, or simply asking for Dr Al Muderis to return their calls. 'The messages were coming from all over the world,' she said. 'I had no idea how to respond.'

Shona also helped with managing the clinic's data. In medicine, robust and accurate data is critical to obtaining informed consent – even more so when the procedure is novel. Prospective osseointegration patients relied on research produced by Dr Al Muderis about surgical outcomes when deciding whether to proceed. Disturbingly, Shona said she was pressured to fudge the data to make the procedure look better. 'If Munjed didn't like the figures, he would redo them.'

I was floored when I heard this. 'He would make them up?' I asked.

'I would say so,' she responded. 'I think it's probably the reason I went into law. I just couldn't comprehend how doctors could get away with doing this stuff to people. And it was okay. He's the judge and jury. He had no accountability. They're just not questioned.'

Shona's position became somewhat more complicated when she began having an intimate relationship with Dr Al Muderis. She was attracted to his life of luxury and big-thinking, high-achieving personality, and the affair never strayed beyond casual and consensual. But when he started bullying her in the workplace, it cut deep. He yelled at Shona in front of patients, belittled and mocked her and called her names, like 'monkey' or 'stupid'. He once told her: 'Nobody wanted you, not even your mother' – a particularly searing insult for Shona, who was adopted. She left shortly after that.

While the relationship ended amicably, it put a red flag in the back of my mind. Not because I thought Shona was vengeful, I could tell she was not, but I was conscious of how this might be twisted into accusations of a jaded lover down the track. Shona showed me recent texts with Dr Al Muderis showing they had remained friendly after she quit. I teased these concerns out with my editors, and we ultimately agreed it wasn't an issue.

Much of what Shona had described was also supported by other people. I had seen written complaints about the doctor's bullying and spoke to other people who described similar abuse. I spoke with experts and other surgeons about Dr Al Muderis's approach to research. I learned there are two different ways to produce research about the safety of new procedures. The first is through a clinical trial. This involves ethics approval, rigorous oversight, and meticulous recording of adverse events. It's the gold-standard for reliable research, and has tight guardrails to ensure patients know exactly what they're signing up for. While clinical trials increase the burden of data collection, they also create a much richer, more transparent picture for prospective patients about the full spectrum and likelihood of risks.

The other way to produce research findings exists outside of this system, where private clinics produce research papers for peer-reviewed medical journals. This is the pathway Dr Al Muderis's clinic went down, releasing papers that drew conclusions from a sample of his patients. One expert explained that this approach enabled the clinic to focus only on a certain group of patients, rather than the whole lot. 'In science, it's commonly known as the drawer bias,' one data scientist told me during the initial investigation. 'From a research point of view, it's not fraudulent but it's not honest. You never pretend to provide the whole picture. It's the responsibility of the editor and reviewer to say, you treated 200 patients, why is there only 30 in the cohort you're reporting? Most editors don't do that. There are plenty of little subtleties you can manipulate.'

The research produced by Dr Al Muderis's clinic also often relied on patients self-reporting events like antibiotics use or pain levels. I was told that collecting research like this, rather than a clinical trial, increased the risks of the outcomes being skewed. 'In this case, science becomes a marketing tool rather than the way to present the truth and inform people of the positive and negative.' As a result, it becomes harder for patients to truly provide informed consent, because they simply don't have an accurate understanding of the risks.

By this point, I had spoken with patients who had refused to fill in questionnaires about their mobility after they had fallen out with Dr Al Muderis. I'd seen text messages from inside the clinic with instructions to ensure the results slanted toward the miracle outcome. 'Munjed wants to highlight the fact that most [of] our patients throw out their wheelchair after getting OI,' one researcher wrote.

These pieces of information painted a concerning picture that indicated perhaps patients really were flying blind when it came to this procedure. 'None of us know the true risks,' the data scientist said. 'How do we know if we don't record? Science takes a long time. It's not compatible with the agenda of the patient who wants the solution here and now. He's filling the void by selling the dream.'

Years later, after the trial, this issue would crop up again. Dr Al Muderis published a research paper on whether osseointegration was suitable for patients who lost their limbs from sepsis. The study looked at nine patients over four years and concluded the surgery was 'safe and effective'. However, a surgeon from Melbourne had treated one of Dr Al Muderis's patients who fit this description, but was left out of the study. The surgeon wrote to the scientific publication, outlining seven ways in which he believed the paper risked 'selection bias' – or the drawer problem. He didn't hear back.

While my interviews were combining to paint a horrifying picture, getting people to put their names to the story was tough. Bach's words kept ringing in my mind: *you'll need multiple patients on the record and one independent expert.*

Until one day, another American patient agreed to go on the record – Rachael Ulrich. She was born with a vascular disease and became a below-knee amputee at 27 years old in 2015. She found Dr Al Muderis online, and flew to meet him on the sidelines of a conference in Florida. He was with a nurse, and another woman with osseointegration. 'She is super happy with her osseointegration, let her tell you about it,' Dr Al Muderis said. With a quick scan of Rachel's leg, he said the surgery would be 'no problem' and explained the patented implant system meant 'we will have a connection for life'. Rachael was quoted $US78,000 and Dr Al Muderis told her about fundraising. She launched a GoFundMe page and worked on a cannabis farm for a year to scrape together the money.

When she finally arrived in Sydney, she was gobsmacked by the disorganisation of the clinic. Staff acted like they had no idea who she was, and she had to explain her health history over and over again. After the surgery, she was consumed by an intense, but familiar, pain. The clinic had not given her the blood-thinning medication she had repeatedly requested, and now, she suspected her blood was clotting. 'They told me I was imagining it,' she said in our first interview. 'When I told them I could hardly breathe, then they realised what was happening and they found clots in my lungs. I was rushed into ICU. I was on the verge of death.' Her father flew from America amid the emergency and his concerns turned to anger when he met Dr Al Muderis for the first time. 'He basically acted like nothing had happened,' she said. Her father demanded answers, but Dr Al Muderis sat back in his chair. 'Well, she's alive isn't she?' he said. 'Look Rachael, things happen. This is not my fault. This is just the risk that comes with surgery.' After returning home, Rachael's surgery was a success, allowing her to hike, bike and do strenuous outdoor work. But like others had said, there was a difference between the surgeon and the surgery, and Rachael wanted the public to know that Dr Al Muderis could be reckless. She was in.

I kept checking in with patients I had spoken to earlier too. I called Carol Todd every few weeks, updating her on our investigation and to see how she was going. During this time, her condition worsened. She developed another major infection in her leg, which put her in hospital. The doctors told her the infection appeared to have spread to the bone, and was at risk of spreading further. She told me the doctors had said she would now have to amputate the rest of her leg, or the infection could kill her. If the leg came off, she would be confined to a wheelchair for the rest of her life.

It was a damning prognosis. Here was a woman who wanted to help her sick husband, always putting others first and never wanting to make a fuss, and now, through no fault of her own, her life had been upended. She should never have been operated on. In that call, I could hear her husband Geoff's shaky voice in the background. 'You've got to do something about this, love,' he said. After months of talking, her health steadily deteriorating,

Carol was ready to go on the record. Not for television, but for print. It was great news.

The search for an independent expert was tough. Osseointegration is a small field; one where everyone knows everyone. There are opposing 'camps' defined by which type of implant the surgeon uses, and whether the procedure is performed in a single or double-stage process. In building his practice, Dr Al Muderis was fiercely competitive, and while everyone knew his name, many also feared him.

I reached out to experts in osseointegration around the world. The first person I spoke to was Horst Aschoff, widely regarded as the pioneer of osseointegration in Germany. It was Aschoff who trained Dr Al Muderis in osseointegration two decades earlier, and the German surgeon had since followed his protégé's meteoric rise from a distance, with an even-handed curiosity.

I tracked down his clinic's contact details and sent him an email, asking if he would speak with me about the procedure. To my surprise, I quickly received a response, with Aschoff suggesting a time we could talk. It was in the middle of the night for me, but I eagerly set up the call. I asked him about patient selection criteria, what kinds of red flags make a patient higher risk for surgery, and some general questions about recovery and follow-up care. Aschoff did not criticise Dr Al Muderis as strongly as others I had spoken to, but he did offer this telling observation: 'The difference between me and Dr Al Muderis is that he believes everyone should have osseointegration,' he said. 'Whereas I think they should try sockets first.'

I asked Aschoff about the ethics around a surgeon owning the patent for the implant they use on patients, and whether this creates a conflict of interest. Aschoff paused, then acknowledged it might. 'It means surgeons are not free in their decision-making.'

He told me Dr Al Muderis was, in fact, a businessman, adding drily that this in itself was not necessarily a problem.

'Money makes the world go around,' he said. At the end of our conversation, I asked Aschoff if he would consider being an independent expert in the story. He would be asked to review patient files, and let us know whether the treatment had been normal or not. Nonchalantly, Aschoff said he would, but his availability was uncertain. *Great news,* I thought to myself, and ended the call.

A confidential source gave me the number of another surgeon, Dr John Anstee, who I hoped might be able to provide his expertise. Anstee performed the very first osseointegration procedure in Australia in the 1990s, and has since performed dozens of osseointegration surgeries on carefully selected patients, working with the team at the Alfred Hospital in Melbourne, which, like Dr Al Muderis's team, has a multidisciplinary approach. Where Dr Al Muderis's clinic is a high-profile, money-making machine, the Alfred team flies under the radar, quietly monitoring its small cohort of patients for life. Anstee knows the benefits of osseointegration, but also is acutely aware of the risks.

From *The Age* newsroom, I cold-called his mobile and introduced myself as a journalist researching osseointegration. John's tone hardened. The media had played a terrible role in the promotion of this surgery, he told me, and he wanted no part in another irresponsible puff piece promoting high-risk surgery. I pushed back, quickly and firmly: 'That's not what I'm here to do.'

Anstee backed down, and I convinced him to meet me in person. I knew I needed to look him in the eye. A few days later, I drove to Anstee's house. We sat in the front room of his large, antique-filled house and I shared what I had discovered. I told him about Mark, Brennan, Carol, and one other person whose identity I didn't disclose – my father. I told Dr Anstee that a patient, not mentioning his name or connection to me, had been told he would be wheelchair-bound by the time he turned 80 if he did not proceed with the surgery, adding that he was fast approaching that age and still walking without any problems using a socket. As I told Anstee about my father's predicament, his eyes looked downward. 'Poor bugger,' he said.

When speaking to sources, I was careful not to mention my family connection to Dr Al Muderis, though I couldn't quite explain why. In part, I felt the disclosure might be manipulative – if I mentioned my father was an amputee, patients might feel closer to me in some way. It was also partly an effort to establish boundaries, to be the objective impartial observer our industry demands. There are no written rules in journalism, and often you are guided by a gut instinct on when to press and when to pull back.

Dr Anstee and I spoke for around an hour that night. I explained what I had found, why I believed this story was in the public interest, and how it was crucial to have an independent expert on board. Anstee told me he was very busy, that he didn't need this in his life, but by the end of the hour, he agreed. He laid out what he would need – permission from each of the patients to discuss their cases, and as many of the medical records as we could muster. I shook his hand and left, with a biting feeling inside me – we might actually be able to publish this story.

By that point it felt like I'd been working on the investigation for months, not weeks. I'd spoken with patients, surgeons, prosthetists, rehab specialists, data scientists, nurses and whistleblowers, and collected a huge body of evidence. I knew this story was of national significance, and that the impact would be even greater if it reached a television audience. With that in mind, I put together a pitch to collaborate with *60 Minutes*. We met via Zoom, and made a plan to start filming interviews. Tom Steinfort was assigned as the reporter, and Natalie Clancy as producer. The production quickly kicked into gear.

Over the next month, we criss-crossed the east coast – to Ballarat to interview Mark, then Brisbane to interview Brennan, and Melbourne to interview Dr John Anstee. Tom is an award-winning journalist at the top of his industry, and he quickly put everyone he interviewed at ease. They were impressed by his credentials, and his presence gave the story the professionalism it deserved. Natalie kept everyone on schedule, while the program's executive producer, Kirsty Thomson, eagerly encouraged everyone along. It was a great team.

Less than two months after we first spoke, I was back in John's house, which was now jam-packed with camera gear. While everyone was setting up, my phone started ringing. It was Shona. I stepped outside and updated her on what was going on, and took the opportunity to try my luck again – how was she feeling about going on the record? To my surprise, she'd changed her mind. 'I'll do it,' she said.

I was ecstatic. Shona was an eye-witness to the inside running of Dr Al Muderis's clinic. She'd had firsthand experience of many of the key issues the investigation would expose – problems with patient selection, aftercare, sales tactics, a toxic workplace. Having her on board was a real gamechanger.

While we were on the road filming interviews, I was still digging, and speaking with new sources from hotel rooms. One avenue I was keen to pursue was the patients Dr Al Muderis had operated on during his humanitarian missions to Iraq and Cambodia. I wanted to speak to these patients myself, and started with Cambodia. I tracked down a doctor named Jim Gollogly, who was the point of contact for Dr Al Muderis's patients in Phnom Penh. I called the number and was connected to a gruff-sounding man.

'You want to know about the Cambodian patients?' he barked. 'They're all fine.'

'That's good to know. I'd like to speak with them. Do you have their numbers?'

Much to my surprise, within a few minutes of ending the phone call, I received an email from Jim. It appeared to be a screenshot of a patient database, with contact details of four people, alongside their age, gender and patient ID numbers. *Here you are, Charlotte ... happy hunting ... with a Khmer speaker, as none of them speak English*, he wrote.

I got to work. I posted in *The Age*'s Slack channel, 'Anyone know a Khmer speaker?' and our correspondent in South-East Asia, Chris Barrett, quickly reached out. He sent me the name of a journalist he used for reporting in Cambodia, but stressed that the story couldn't be political, or it could get the journalist into trouble. I called him and explained the story, and he was happy to proceed.

I drafted a script with some background information about me, the project and questions for the Cambodian journalist to ask the patients. He hit the phones. Some of the lines were disconnected, but he got lucky with two of the patients. Just ten days later, he sent me transcripts of his interviews with Eang Srey Da and Pril Sina translated into English. Both described daily ongoing complications – pus, fluid, pain, confusion – and both said they would not recommend the surgery to other amputees.

'They said it would be better after the surgery,' said Eang Srey Da, who was a village fruit seller. 'But I did not know that I would have such a lifelong wound.'

While tracking down the Cambodian patients had been relatively simple, finding the Iraqi patients was another story. I went down some deep rabbit holes attempting to contact orthopaedic surgeons in Baghdad. Eventually, I came across a prosthetist in Iraq who proved to be immensely helpful. We'll call him Ahmed. The line made a series of long beeps as I called his clinic in Baghdad, then no-one answered. I left a voicemail asking for them to return my call, and later that day, I received a WhatsApp message from Ahmed.

Hi, you called our Iraqi number. How can I help you?

I explained that I was an Australian journalist with some questions about surgeries performed in Iraq by Munjed Al Muderis.

Yes, I know him personally, Ahmed responded. He then asked for proof that I was a journalist. *Bcz this issue is so sensitive and I have important information about it.*

Someone in Iraq not only knew Dr Al Muderis, but had something to say. It felt like I'd hit the jackpot. I sent a photo of myself holding my work ID and a link to my online articles. *I want to know how the osseointegration patients are doing.*

Ahmed then told me he had concerns about Dr Al Muderis's work in Iraq. 'Knees was so bad and all of them get faulted because of high temperatures and hard climate in Iraq,' he said. 'The most important thing and the thing that made me reject any deal or cooperation with Munjed was because he never care about his patients. He always care about doing surgery very quickly without any deep investigation before surgery. After surgery he was never ever answer anybody to follow up patients … And this issue was making me so angry because patients contact me and feel hurted to seek a medical help from surgeon who did the surgery.'

I asked Ahmed to connect me with Iraqi patients, and he gave me three numbers. I arranged to hire a professional translator and we got started. I was cold-calling these people, half a world away, to ask about their most intimate medical affairs. I had no idea how it would go. Our first call was to a man named Karar Hydar Yusur. I introduced myself as a journalist, and paused as I waited for my words to be interpreted. Slowly, but surely, I learned that Karar had lost his left leg in a bomb blast while fighting ISIS. The man, then aged 29, met Dr Al Muderis during his mission to Iraq in 2017, and the doctor promised to have him up and walking in no time. Dr Al Muderis performed osseointegration on the left leg and returned a few years later to amputate Karar's right foot and inserted another rod. Despite the promises of perfect mobility, when we spoke, Karar was bedbound. He couldn't walk, let alone work.

Karar said some of his friends had success with the surgery, but he was not so lucky. Over the years, he has struggled with pain, infection and side effects from medication, like vomiting and stomach problems. He said he knows people who have travelled to Iran to try to have the implants removed, feeling they had nowhere else to go. Like many others, Karar's main problem was the lack of information and aftercare provided. 'I can't get in contact with him,' he said.

On 10 August, I received an email from a marketing and communications specialist named Kate Reddin Johns, saying she worked with 'Munjed' and had heard I was working on a story. She invited me to the clinic to 'see the team in action' and offered to connect me with 'many great patients'. She was aware of my interest in patient selection, and tellingly, noted: 'Potentially you have some personal experience with this process.'

This wasn't the first time I'd received a pre-emptive effort to sanitise a story ahead of publication. Kate knew the lines of inquiry I was pursuing, and made clear Dr Al Muderis knew who my father was and shared this with his spinner, breaching patient confidentiality and laying the groundwork for a 'conflict of interest' allegation. Toward the end of the email, Kate warned of 'vested interests' and wrote: 'Undoubtedly in your conversations you've discovered the osseo world is small and can be complicated as a result.' This was the earliest iteration of the 'concoction theory' that would rear its head in the trial.

Within ten minutes of receiving the email, I forwarded it to my colleagues. 'FYI – Al Muderis has now hired a strategic comms firm. Will no doubt be the point of contact for when we ask for an interview.'

My response to Kate was brief: I told her it was great to have her details and I'd be in touch soon.

Kate sent another email asking to 'schedule a call' or have 'an old-fashioned coffee meeting?' and signed off with a smiley emoji. I didn't respond. A week later, she sent another email:

'Can you please let me know what the angle of the story is?' I didn't respond again. But the repeated emails provided a window into the chaos that I would learn was descending on the clinic as Dr Al Muderis began calling some of my sources, asking if they knew what was going on. I started receiving stacks of unsolicited emails from a number of Dr Al Muderis's patients, saying they had heard I was working on a story, and offering interviews.

His team was encouraging certain patients to come forward, and I set up phone conversations with a handful, to hear their stories. I already knew the benefits of this surgery but listening to the individual stories was powerful. Each experience was compelling, heartfelt and raw. Like those who featured on the news, these people had been through hell before meeting Dr Al Muderis, and all told me he gave them a fresh start through his revolutionary procedure. The surgery really can make a difference, and Dr Al Muderis can be caring, attentive and thorough, these patients insisted to me en masse.

'I honestly cannot put into words how much this amazing team has meant to me,' said one patient. 'Munjed and the team have brought me back to life. I will be forever grateful.'

As I collected these stories, and spoke to more people who emailed, I kept grappling with the same questions over and over. Is it unfair to focus on surgical complications, when the majority of patients *are* happy? Could a story about the risks of osseointegration dissuade people who might benefit from getting it? I called Nine's in-house lawyer for the newspapers, Larina Alick, to see what she thought.

Larina is a high energy, fast-talking, no-nonsense straight-shooter. She spends most of her days assessing stories ahead of publication for legal risks, delivering bad news to journalists in her trademark brutal-yet-cheerful style, or working with editors to get the stories across the line. 'Charlotte,' she told me. 'One case of medical negligence is not justified by a million positive cases.' Her words gave me the confidence to stay on track.

After the call, I reflected on how this logic applied to other areas of society. If someone was accused of murder, would a journalist be obliged to interview and publish the testimonies of the many people in the accused's life who were not murdered? The more severe the allegation, the less important it is to give equal weight to 'positive' and 'negative' stories. The job is to ensure the allegations are correct, and there is public interest in exposing a pattern of behaviour. This story was not just about the 'negative' experiences of some patients, it was to present evidence I had gathered about Dr Al Muderis's routine failure to warn patients of the full spectrum of risks involved in the procedure. It was about his failure to care for patients when things went wrong. It was about his deliberate and extensive efforts to promote only the good side of the surgery, to the media, his patients and the public at large. This was an unrealistic portrayal, and no amount of happy patients could change that.

Amid the onslaught of these messages, one jumped out at me. Cindy Asch-Martin wrote that she was a 'complex amputee' who flew from America to Australia for osseointegration surgery because 'none of the US doctors could deal with my level of complexity'. I arranged a time to speak with Cindy, and we spoke for hours. She agreed to be part of the *60 Minutes* documentary, so we arranged for a crew to visit her home in Washington and film her working out using her osseointegration leg. We wanted to include Cindy's full-throated defence of Dr Al Muderis, and showcase the active lifestyle she now lives as a result of his treatment.

After most of the interviews had been filmed, Tom Steinfort took the lead in organising the interview with Dr Al Muderis. He sent a list of broad topics we wanted to discuss, and Kate Reddin Johns responded with a long list of research papers for Tom to read. This was one of the few times I didn't prepare a 'briefing doc' for Tom's interview, giving him background information, timelines and suggested questions. By this point, he had interviewed several patients and whistleblowers, and we had chatted at length about the story, its merits and its weaknesses on the road. Tom had devoured medical papers, leaked documents and emails that exposed the inside of the clinic. He knew what he was doing.

The night before the interview, Tom asked me to arrange consent videos from the patients. We knew that Dr Al Muderis would say he could not comment on individual cases due to patient confidentiality, and wanted to provide a way around this. Tom thought the simplest way to do this would be to arrange short videos of the patients giving Dr Al Muderis permission to discuss their cases on television. I arranged the videos and sent them to Tom.

I wore a blazer to the interview in Castle Hill that day, on 6 September 2022. I felt nervous but confident. I arrived before Dr Al Muderis and had a few minutes to discuss key points one last time with Natalie and Tom. The room was large, two seats in the centre surrounded by cameras and lights. Dr Al Muderis arrived with Kate Reddin Johns, and I introduced myself and shook their hands. We made small talk before Natalie guided them into the room and the cameras started rolling.

'Thank you very much for sitting down with us, I was going to say Munjed. I should call you Dr Al Muderis,' Tom said, breaking the ice. I watched on from the sidelines, heart pounding.

'Munjed is fine.'

'Okay, thank you. Look, I know you said before you're not the man who created osseointegration, but you've had a huge role in developing it in Australia and I guess around the world, particularly where you've come from and what you've achieved. I mean, your life really does read a bit like a movie script …'

'Look, I don't look at it that way. I mean every individual has their own stories and we all have our struggles and my life continues … So I never take things for granted.'

Throughout the interview, Natalie and I were vigorously texting Tom with questions. As Tom was asking about how patients can afford Dr Al Muderis's expensive surgery, I texted: *Ask about fundraising.*

'Have you encouraged your staff to teach people how to fundraise?' Tom asked.

'That ... They ... No,' he stumbled, before collecting his thoughts. 'That's never happened. I'm actually, as a matter of fact, I'm very strongly against that, GoFundMe and these things. We don't allow it.'

Tom asked again, 'To be very clear, you've never encouraged your staff to teach patients how to fundraise?'

'Definitely not the case. Definitely never encouraged any of the staff or any person. As a matter of fact, I'm philosophically opposed to anyone raising money or using GoFundMe to pay for their surgery. This is not my practice. This is not what I would do. This never happened in the past and would never happen in the future.'

This was one of the many times throughout the two-hour interview where I knew we had exposed a lie. I had seen an email in which Dr Al Muderis had specifically told his employees to teach patients how to fundraise. I had spoken to patients, like Chris Bruha and Rachael Ulrich, who said the doctor encouraged them to do so. The fundraising website he had referenced, gofundme.com, was stacked full of people asking friends and family members to donate so they could receive Dr Al Muderis's life-saving treatment.

The interview went on, as Tom skilfully switched between casual inquirer and ruthless interrogator, exposing revelations and facts that Dr Al Muderis could not wriggle out of. As we had expected, he refused to talk about individual patients, but even his answers to general questions about patient care came off as callous, dishonest and self-serving. His position was that the majority of his patients are happy, and we must have spoken to the 'handful' who were 'disgruntled'. He pointed out that all surgeries come with risks and complications, and said he does his best to explain these to patients. But at the end of the day, he maintained there was a difference between 'facts and feelings'. While some patients might *feel* they have been hard done by, the *facts* were that he did all he could. Tom went through all the patients who felt abandoned, the maggots, the pain, the suffering that his patients complained of, and then toward the end, he asked: 'Do you have any regrets?'

'Look, I'm very satisfied and content with what I've done in my life,' Dr Al Muderis said, before launching into a spiel about how he would like to spread the technology to more people in developing countries.

'Don't you think this is kind of the problem?' Tom responded. 'I just asked you if you have any regrets and you couldn't acknowledge that you've done anything wrong or made any missteps along the way.'

Only then did Dr Al Muderis finally concede that he had made mistakes, that his patients have experienced complications. 'I feel for every single patient who's disgruntled,' he said. 'I truly do, but I can't carry it with me because it's unfair for the next patient that I'm looking after. And I openly admit if I made a mistake to a patient, I openly apologise to the patient. I always honour my complications and I always work to the best of my ability to fix the problem.'

When the cameras stopped rolling, Al Muderis turned to Tom. 'Gosh that was hard, Tom,' he said.

We assembled on the sidelines as the camera gear was packed down. I thanked Dr Al Muderis for sitting down for the interview, and he quickly made a comment about my 'personal connection' to the story. He probed me for information, asking where the story came from. He blamed Fred Hernandez, the sockets industry, the world at large – anything but the shortcomings in his clinic, as expressed by his own patients and colleagues. I stood my ground. 'This is journalism,' I said, before explaining the Kerry Ford case, and how divided Australia's medical community appeared to be about osseointegration, and who it is suited to.

Despite saying during the interview that he could not discuss his patients, when the cameras stopped rolling, he denigrated the very same people, including Mark Urquhart, who he wrote off as mentally unstable. He showed me videos of other patients he claimed were doing well. During the interview, Tom had asked about the allegations Dr Al Muderis had sexual relationships with staff, and a complaint that was made to the regulator alleging a dysfunctional workplace culture. On camera, Dr Al Muderis issued a vigorous denial but on the sidelines, he described the claims as 'below the belt' and there were no denials.

By the end of this chat, it became clear that Dr Al Muderis thought he'd won us over. He said none of the questions surprised him, and even confessed that he'd parked his luxury car around the corner to avoid our cameras. Then he said something that stuck in my mind: 'If I had to do hips and knees for the rest of my life, I'd be so bored I'd scratch my eyes out.' This was the closest I came to understanding what I believe drives Dr Al Muderis, which was a question we debated at length before publishing the investigation. Many of his patients assumed he was driven by riches and fame. But this comment, and other scraps of insights I had gathered, made me think it was something more compulsive. He had just told us there was a core part of him that was restless and wanted to be challenged. He was a high achiever prepared to work long hours, and was drawn to complicated cases. It seemed he wanted to be praised for pushing boundaries, for changing the world, for being the brave doctor who always said yes. It was a certain type of notoriety that Dr Al Muderis coveted – he wanted to be celebrated as an entrepreneur, a fearless innovator, a visionary surgeon who made his mark on the world. The money certainly didn't hurt.

The interview with Dr Al Muderis was the last piece of the puzzle we needed for the story to go ahead. Back in the North Sydney office, Tom spent hours in the editing suite, picking out the best quotes, refining the script and re-cutting the documentary to ensure Dr Al Muderis's position was fairly represented. Every denial, every response was included. Executive producer Kirsty Thomson, supervising producer Stephen Taylor, Natalie, Tom and I crammed into a small room for a screening. Printed scripts were handed out, so we could mark up any changes as it played. 'Sorry to be nit-picky, but this doesn't seem quite right,' I said at one point. 'This is the time to be nit-picky,' Kirsty said back with a grin.

We were in the weeds, debating the minutiae. We smoothed out the rough edges, snipped off problematic words, phrases and claims, and tweaked others to make the script clearer, tighter, punchier. It felt good.

Finally, we were ready to go. But there would be one last hiccup.

The promos started rolling throughout the week, kicking off a social media storm. This all came to a screeching halt when, on 8 September 2022, Queen Elizabeth II died. This was the biggest story imaginable, sending shockwaves around the world. Our investigation would have to wait. The promos were pulled down, the broadcast date pushed back. I was devastated, but Kirsty assured me we would get it out soon.

The Queen's death would take up the full *60 Minutes* program the week we were scheduled to broadcast, but the following week, Kirsty said they could get by with just a short one-section package on the Queen's funeral. We had to shave about five minutes off our feature-length documentary, but we were finally ready.

CHAPTER 6

The Reaction

I was sitting with two friends on my couch with a glass of wine and bowl of pasta when the show aired. By this point, I had already seen the documentary countless times, but my heart still thumped against my rib cage as hundreds of thousands of Australians saw it for the first time. I watched my friends' faces turn to horror when Mark's maggot-infested limb flashed up on the screen.

At the same time as the program aired, the print articles were published by *The Age* and *Sydney Morning Herald* online. We embedded a 'tip jar' into the stories – a small digital box that asks readers to submit any information they have about the story. Almost immediately, the tip jar started filling up. New patients described simple operations that went 'horribly wrong' and others wrote about serious infections that were ignored, and lives destroyed.

> 'This is the tip of the iceberg for Munjed's dodgy clinical management. His joint replacement practice is a bigger scandal ... He often operates on needless joints that are not yet completely worn and always instils a sense of urgency, telling these patients we need to get on and do

this now before it's too late. How are these surgeons still operating?'

'There were multiple bullying complaints lodged by hospital staff.'

'I used to work for Al Muderis and quit because I felt as though treatment of patients and female staff and practices were unacceptable.'

'He operated on my elderly mother and we felt that the surgery done was too intrusive for someone of her age. My mum also felt abandoned once surgery was done.'

'He doesn't care he's rude and arrogant and tries to scare you about going elsewhere. I'm not even half the person I used to be. I'm so glad he's been exposed.'

'I made the first documentary on Munjed Al Muderis … Perhaps there is something for the media to learn in this.'

The sheer volume of tips we received was something I had never experienced before. As I read these new messages, I felt the patients, surgeons and whistleblowers who'd spoken out had been vindicated. Our reporting had been vindicated. We had not simply spoken to one-off disgruntled patients, as Dr Al Muderis had claimed: there was a clear pattern. There was also a larger, more sinister, story emerging of a profit-driven hospital system that covered up problems to keep the cash flowing. Insiders encouraged us to keep digging.

Still, not all the tips were supportive. Some were keen to defend Dr Al Muderis.

'Shame on you. If we interviewed everyone you have written a story [about] – what percentage would say you were an imbecile and what percentage would say you were a great journalist? Surgery is difficult at the best of times. Very simple – fewer surgeons will offer the Osseointegration and more handicapped people will remain handicapped. That is all you have achieved.'

'Please stop harassing this incredibly talented surgeon and allow the proper medical channels to investigate the alleged misconduct before spreading such slander in the community.'

'Get a real job Charlotte. I have more respect for a toilet bowl.'

A public campaign was mounted in Dr Al Muderis's defence. A group of his patients started using the hashtag #IStandBehindMunjedAlMuderis on social media. Dr Kevin Tetsworth, who told Mark Urquhart to spray Febreze on his legs and would later become a star character in the trial, tweeted his support.

Cindy Asch-Martin, the woman we filmed in America, posted: 'I am outraged! The promo on Prof Al Muderis is false reporting. I too have had maggots. Do your homework to know that maggots have been used for centuries to help? You need to look after your stoma yourself! @60Mins #istandbehindmunjedalmuderis.'

Ali France, the Labor candidate who eventually beat Dutton to become a member of parliament, posted. 'I hear @60Minutes has a piece on my wonderful surgeon & NSW Aus of the Yr @ drmunjed. I wouldnt b walking without him. Osseointegration was my only hope & he was the ONLY surgeon willing 2 do it. I knew the risks, have now been walking 9yrs.'

Social media was plastered with allegations that the reporting was 'gutter journalism at its best', a 'hatchet job'. We received messages accusing us of being 'cretins' executing a 'character assassination'.

Amid the storm online, action was being taken in the real world. The day after our stories went live, Avant, the country's largest medical insurer, suspended Dr Al Muderis's coverage for osseointegration surgeries and launched an investigation. His clinic emailed patients with the news, and we reported the story as it broke. Patients cancelled their surgeries. The NSW healthcare regulator said it had reopened investigations. New complaints were made by patients and colleagues to the regulator, the hospital, the Australian Orthopaedic Association.

We rolled out the follow-up stories we had already planned, about international patients who had been abandoned, about the Type B dual cone that was used in patients despite Dr Al Muderis's team knowing it was faulty. Every time we published a new story, my inbox was again filled with fresh allegations. A surgeon I hadn't spoken to in months called to thank me for getting the stories published. 'Your reporting is literally saving lives,' he said.

I had whiplash from the public reaction, some of which made me feel sick to the stomach. Our sources were attacked and blamed for their suffering. Racist remarks were made about Dr Al Muderis. Members of the public called his clinic to hurl abuse at the receptionist. It was toxic.

His supporter base launched an online petition titled 'Dr Munjed Al Muderis – Avant reinstate his insurance asap' which quickly clocked up more than 1500 signatures. The petition was started by a farmer in the Northern Territory, Gavin Howie, one of Dr Al Muderis's patients.

'*60 Minutes* has gone from being an advocate for the man who gave me my life back, to condemning him! They have been led down the garden path by a group with vendettas and those vying for personal gain.'

Messages of support piled up on the petition website.

'The work this doctor does is groundbreaking. We should all be very proud of his "migrant story" not laying rocks in his way,' wrote one person.

'While I sympathise with the interviewee's story, I don't think *60 Minutes* doing a hit piece on this Dr was ethical. Trial by media AGAIN!' said another.

As I was reading through the petition responses, an email landed in my inbox. Subject: 'Defamation of Dr Munjed Al Muderis'.

I opened it, quickly skimmed the pages, and immediately forwarded it to our in-house lawyers. The attached 41-page document was marked 'URGENT' in thick red letters. It claimed we had engaged in an 'unmeritorious campaign' by publishing stories stacked with false and damaging claims. It was a warning shot, also known as a concerns notice – the legally required first step in initiating defamation proceedings, where the aggrieved party stakes their claim and warns of legal action if no solution is found.

We'd expected this would come. But Dr Al Muderis's request was so far-fetched I couldn't believe it was serious. He wanted the stories immediately taken down and an undertaking that we never publish the allegations again. He also wanted us to write a 'public and sincere apology', published in a prominent position in the newspapers for 14 days, and for Tom Steinfort to read out an agreed statement on-air at the beginning of the next *60 Minutes* episode. I knew Dr Al Muderis was litigious, but I also knew that what we had published was only a very small fraction of the overall allegations against him. A lawsuit would flush out every scrap of damning information I had gathered, under the full privilege of the courts.

'He would be mad to sue,' I told my desk buddy and veteran investigative journalist Ben Schneiders. After decades of holding powerful people to account, Schneiders had been in this scenario many times before. Experience taught him that most concerns letters went nowhere. I felt like I'd been put on notice, but I was also confident that Al Muderis wasn't serious. The stakes were too high – for him.

Amid this whirlwind, I began getting messages from Dr Al Muderis's latest spinner, Peter Wilkinson. Wilkinson had started his career in journalism, working for some of the country's premier investigative journalism outlets – ABC's *Four Corners*, Nine's *60 Minutes* – but had since switched to public relations. He was the chair of a company that specialised in 'crisis management' and had reached out to Dr Al Muderis to offer his services. The Sunday after the investigation broke, Wilkinson spent four hours at Dr Al Muderis's harbourside apartment with barrister Sue Chrysanthou, debating strategy over dinner.

Wilkinson took over from Kate Reddin Johns in handling the press. First, he issued a statement quoting Dr Al Muderis, who said the stories were defamatory, 'demonstrably false' and 'simply untrue'. Next, he devised a 'campaign' to undermine our investigation. He wrote several media lists and contacted hand-picked journalists he thought might be more open to peddling a counter-narrative. He interviewed some of my sources, and sent a copy of the concerns notice to *The Australian*.

At one point, Wilkinson called to give me a heads-up that his team was going to publish a press release outlining four major inaccuracies in my reporting. Up until this point, I had been running on adrenaline. Watching the reactions unfold, weighing up the messages that were coming in, and supporting my sources through the attacks. While it was intense, I felt strongly that the stories were true and important, and that we'd done the right thing. I could handle the social media storm that had engulfed us, and the debate over differing experiences and perspectives. But as soon as I heard the word 'inaccuracies', I felt sick. Getting an error of fact is any journalist's biggest fear. Even the smallest correction can undermine the entire investigation. Four major inaccuracies was a whole different ballgame – and Peter knew it.

'I don't know what they are yet,' I emailed my editors.

I spent the afternoon feeling like I was about to vomit. But as the hours ticked on, no statement came. I followed up with Wilkinson a few times, and then suddenly, something changed. *No statement coming*, Wilkinson texted me. Later that week, Wilkinson informed me he was no longer working for Dr Al Muderis. I was relieved, and then acutely intrigued. What happened? Were there really four inaccuracies? If so, what were they and why wouldn't he tell me? Or was this just a tactic to intimidate me?

Gossip thrives among journalists, and multiple versions of what happened began to circulate. One version was that Wilkinson had told Dr Al Muderis they should handle the crisis 'through the media' rather than through defamation litigation, but this was overruled, so he resigned.

An invoice attached to Dr Al Muderis's subsequent affidavit showed the doctor spent $19,000 on Wilkinson's services that lasted nine days and only dug him further into a hole of his own creation. Later, Wilkinson was replaced by Mark Hawthorne, another journalist-turned-spinner. There is certainly big business in shifting the narratives toward the interests of the rich and powerful. Journalists and the public alike should tread carefully when dealing with information that comes from these people.

Once the immediate storm had settled and the news breaks stopped rolling in, I turned my mind to which stories from the avalanche of new information needed to be published. One post from social media caught my attention of a man responding to posts that criticised the program. '*60 Minutes* have already aired two pieces marvelling at Muderis' work for those patients "who will always thank him",' he wrote. 'It's time we hear from those "few patients who had a bad experience".'

I later spoke to the man, who told me about his father who had died on Dr Al Muderis's operating table. He sent me the coroner's report that listed the cause of death as sepsis, as well as photographs of his father's swollen, pus-filled wounds. He couldn't understand how the operation went ahead with an active infection, but was more concerned about the grip that Dr Al Muderis had on his father. He had refused to let the family question his treatment plans, which became increasingly invasive. What started as a knee replacement escalated to a planned amputation, before he died. I was preparing to write this man's story, alongside those of two other patients who died after surgeries performed by Dr Al Muderis. We arranged to have photographs taken of the grieving family, but they pulled out at the last minute. The pain was still too raw, and the family too scared.

I emailed every person who sent information to the tip jar. I spent hours and hours on the phone, hearing fresh horror stories that spanned not just osseointegration but typical joint replacements. 'Thank you from the bottom of my heart for exposing him,' said one patient, who told me she'd had a hip replacement that went horribly wrong. 'He's a monster.'

A woman from the Australian Defence Force broke down in tears as she relayed what happened to her. 'He took a chunk of my shin, relocated it, screwed it in. Why did he do that? He didn't tell me.'

Another veteran said he was medically discharged after a botched operation with Dr Al Muderis. 'He cost me my career,' he said. 'I couldn't bring myself to watch the *60 Minutes* ... People write about him like he's a hero, a legend. But he's just a surgeon. He's that type of guy that says, "I don't make mistakes".'

Each time I ended these calls, I asked for supporting documents, medical reports, contemporaneous notes, photos, videos, anything to corroborate the claims. I also routinely asked if they had filed a complaint with the medical regulator.

The vast majority had not. Many had never even heard of the regulator, let alone had any idea how to lodge a complaint.

As this new body of evidence started piling up, I spoke with Bach about how to proceed. There was so much material, almost too much, and I simply didn't know what to do with it all. Bach told me there were only so many stories we could publish about a surgery gone wrong, so suggested I pick the ones that reveal broader insights about the system failures.

A few stood out. A young woman named Temperance Gollan had sent through a 12-page Word document that she had written with tears running down her face after watching the *60 Minutes* program. Dr Al Muderis's comment about us speaking to every 'disgruntled' patient really got to her. These were not customers upset about a faulty product. They were human beings dealing with life and death. She thought, *They haven't spoken to me.*

'In August of 2016, my mum, Kim Gollan, went in for what should have been a routine double knee replacement … what came next was five years of agony ultimately leading to her death,' she wrote.

I called Temperance to hear more. Her mother had died only three months earlier, and it was clear the young woman's emotions were raw. Despite her unbridled grief, Temperance spoke concisely and methodically as she explained exactly what had occurred, and where everything had gone wrong.

After that first conversation, I knew that I had to meet Temperance. The topic was too sensitive, her loss too great. I needed to give her, and the story, the respect it deserved. I flew to Sydney and drove to her family's home on the south coast, where I met the quietly spoken, determined young woman and her sister, Morgan, who lives with cystic fibrosis. Before Morgan became unwell, her mother had rallied the government for better public funding of treatments, protesting outside Parliament House and applying pressure through mainstream media. 'Mum was a fighter,' Temperance told me. 'Now it's our turn to fight for her.'

The sisters showed me around the house where Kim spent her final days – the lowered kitchen bench they'd built to accommodate her wheelchair, the garden where she once loved to grow vegetables, the room where she passed away. I could feel the grief in the air as they told me about what happened in more detail.

Kim had worked as a midwife most of her life, a career that required her to be constantly on her feet. She had begun experiencing a dull pain in her knees, and it became harder to walk, and work. She booked in to see Dr Al Muderis after seeing him on the television and was excited to be able to receive such top-quality care. Over a series of appointments, he suggested Kim get both knees replaced at once. She trusted him, and believed the recovery would be manageable. But when she came out of the operating theatre, one of her legs bulged violently from one side. She was in agonising pain.

Dr Al Muderis told her this was normal, and instructed her to walk on the legs. Only later did it emerge that this was the opposite of what she should have been doing. Dr Al Muderis had fractured her bones when he put in the implant and was telling her to walk on a broken leg, each step causing her to cry in pain.

Only after much pleading and begging did Dr Al Muderis finally order an X-ray and discover the break. In that appointment, both sisters recalled that he broke down in tears and acknowledged their mother's pain was his fault. The treatment plan changed course, but things only continued to get worse. Kim developed an infection, which spread into full-blown sepsis. As Temperance recounted her mother's hallucinations, her begging for help, tears ran down her face. 'No daughter should have to see their mother like that,' she said. 'He should have listened to her.'

A trained nurse, Kim Gollan suspected what she was going through was wrong. She began taking notes, and later made inquiries about a medical negligence lawsuit. I wanted those documents. As horrifying as Kim's story was, I needed medical reports, expert opinions, contemporaneous records, to verify what they were telling me. Losing a family member is one of the hardest things anyone can go through in life, and Temperance and Morgan were fresh in the grips of raw grief. I didn't want emotions to get in the way of clear-eyed allegations of wrongdoing.

As a law student, Temperance fully understood my request for evidence, but she was also hamstrung. The case had settled with a chunk of cash and a confidentiality agreement. I had to find ways to verify the claims without breaching that agreement. The last thing the Gollans needed was another lawsuit on their hands.

Over the next few weeks, I obtained reports from experts who had assessed Kim. It was clear that Kim had not been a healthy woman to start with. She was overweight and dealt with arthritis and depression. Some believed these pre-existing conditions meant she would never have returned to work. Others squarely blamed complications from Dr Al Muderis's surgery for her suffering. A lengthy report by an occupational therapist detailed how, prior to the operation, Kim worked three or four shifts each week, loved socialising and was responsible for most of the house-work. But afterwards, she was house-bound, lonely, in pain, and needed help for even the most basic activities. Instead of giving her life back, this operation had taken away her independence, mobility, dignity.

Walkley-award winning photographer Kate Geraghty took the pictures to accompany the story. Kate takes her job of documenting the first draft of history very seriously, and believes in the power of an image to change the world. She took portraits of the grieving sisters standing in front of a wild coastline, hair blowing in the wind in what could have been a perfect metaphor for the uncertainty that had rocked their worlds. The story packed a punch.

THE REACTION

Three days after it was published, I was visiting the home of yet another family who had been traumatised by an operation performed by Dr Al Muderis – the Mooneys. I had earlier received an email from Tim and Leah Mooney, an elderly couple who lived on Sydney's northern beaches, and now had found a time to meet up.

Leah had been Dr Al Muderis's patient more than ten years ago, and suffered chronic bone infection after two unsuccessful operations on a broken leg. The couple spent years in court, successfully suing Dr Al Muderis for negligence. Tim and Leah were anxious to share their story. 'It's a shame he wasn't stopped earlier,' their first email stated.

Over time, I got to know Tim and Leah very well. Their marriage is a true partnership, built on mutual support, love and respect. They share an email and phone number and when you call, they both answer and speak in unison, finishing each other's sentences but never speaking over the other. They married in the seventies and went on to have four sons together. They were a family that loved the outdoors. Leah in particular saw walking as key to her life, and felt energised by being in nature.

In 2011, the family went on a ski trip to Canada. Photographs of the holiday show thick white snow, bright ski jackets and happy faces. But the good times came to an abrupt end when Leah's skis malfunctioned and she crashed. Paramedics quickly discovered her leg was badly broken and she was medically evacuated to Australia for treatment.

Back in Sydney, Leah was transferred from the airport straight to the Sydney Adventist Hospital. The regular orthopaedic surgeon was about to go on holidays, so Leah was handed to a young doctor who introduced himself as a trauma surgeon, Munjed Al Muderis. They would later discover that he had not actually undergone specialist trauma surgeon training, but rather had an interest in challenging cases. He ordered scans, and scheduled Leah for surgery. It was a complicated break, he said, but he was confident he could handle it.

When Leah came out of the operating theatre, her leg jolted violently to one side. Her son remembers asking Dr Al Muderis about it. 'I'm no doctor, but it didn't look right to me,' he said. 'It was literally,' he paused, and made a V-shape with his hands. Dr Al Muderis blamed the manufacturer that had made the plate now in Leah's leg, and promised to fix it. She went in for a second surgery, which Dr Al Muderis would falsely claim was part of a planned two-stage surgery, to rectify the deformity.

But it just kept getting worse. Leah's leg swelled to twice its normal size, throbbed with pain and oozed fluid from the puncture wounds. Dr Al Muderis insisted this was normal. Worried, she sought a second opinion from a sports physician at a nearby clinic. He took one look at her pus-filled, red, swollen limb and suspected an infection. The sports physician ordered blood tests which indicated Leah had a deep tissue or chronic bone infection. When he called Dr Al Muderis to relay these concerns, he encountered an aggressive man who questioned his qualifications and insisted he was wrong.

'Osteomyelitis is a diagnosis we don't like to use in orthopaedic surgery,' Dr Al Muderis wrote in a letter after that call.

Leah was exhausted by the pain and confusion, and saddened by how the injury was dominating her life. At home one night, she stepped outside for some fresh air. It had been raining and the deck was damp. She slipped, went flying, and smashed hip-first into the ground. Tim rushed her to the emergency ward. The nurses took one look at her and were horrified. 'Forget the hip, the leg is the problem,' she was told.

Leah's hip was fractured, but the entire medical team were focused on her left leg, which was stiff, dripping with pus and looked like it was about to explode. They immediately put her on an antibiotic drip and connected her with an infectious disease specialist. In hushed tones, the nurses told Tim to start collecting documents – they could have a medical negligence case on their hands.

As it transpired, Leah did have a raging infection in her leg – one that caused serious damage. She was put on an aggressive antibiotics treatment plan, and had to sleep on a makeshift bed in their kitchen because she could no longer climb the stairs to her bedroom. Specialists came daily to hook Leah up to a PICC line and monitor her symptoms. The pain was unbearable. Tim became Leah's primary carer, cooking her meals, bathing her, hoping and praying she would get better.

Having lost confidence in Dr Al Muderis, the Mooneys saw a new surgeon, Dr Dimitri Papadimitriou. He examined Leah's leg and asked questions about her care. While he didn't encourage Leah to sue, he agreed she had a strong case. By that point, Leah's leg was a mess, and Dr Papadimitriou had to operate once again. When he opened her up, he found the infection was so severe it had eaten away at her bones and locked her knee stiff. He also discovered a broken drill bit in the knee that Dr Al Muderis had left behind. He did all he could to repair the damage and sealed her back up again with bad news. Leah would never return to normal. She would have to deal with the stiffened leg for the rest of her life. This was a damning prognosis for anyone, let alone a woman as active as Leah.

They decided to take their case to court. Experts reviewed the medical records before reaching a finding on Dr Al Muderis's conduct. One of these reports, by surgeon Elton Edwards, found that Dr Al Muderis had negligently performed the first surgery, then lied about his treatment plan to cover up his mistakes. It was a damning assessment that slammed everything from the doctor's surgical ability to his willingness to tell a lie to protect himself and place his interests over the care of his patient. Other experts assessed the level of disability resulting from the surgery. It was a bad break to start with, so the evidence needed to show that Leah's life had been changed because of Dr Al Muderis's negligence, rather than the severity of her initial injury.

As the matter wound its way through the slow wheels of justice, the family was dealt a fresh blow. Tim had served in the Vietnam War as a young man, and had been exposed to Agent Orange poisoning. As a result, he was diagnosed with an aggressive form of blood cancer. He had fought the disease before, but now it was back with a vengeance. With few treatment options available, his prospects weren't great. Tim was dying, and doctors said there was little they could do.

Leah didn't accept this. She pushed and pushed to find new treatments, other options, clinical trials or experimental medicines – anything that could save the love of her life, the father of her sons. As the case wore on, with Dr Al Muderis's insurer fighting it tooth and nail, Tim got sicker and sicker. Tim lost almost half his body weight and spent his days vomiting and reeling from pain, but pushed for an early hearing so he could give evidence while he was still alive. Eventually, Dr Al Muderis's insurers offered the Mooneys a large amount of money and consent judgment in Leah's favour to go away. At this point, the family couldn't handle the stress any longer, and it didn't look like Tim would survive to see the end of the case. He was worried that if they kept fighting and lost, the family would be left financially ruined and he wouldn't be there to protect them. They accepted the offer.

After settling, Leah's dreams came true. She found a clinical trial, and Tim started on a new form of chemotherapy. He endured surgery after surgery, to the point where half his face was cut out, but it was worth it – the treatment worked. Tim beat the cancer. Despite this miracle, the family harboured a niggling regret that they didn't take the case to trial.

I drove to meet Tim and Leah at their family home, a treehouse of wooden beams surrounded by lush rainforest. I sat at the kitchen bench, surrounded by members of the Mooney family. Before launching into what happened, one of their sons turned to me. Protective of his mother, and wearied by their ordeal, he wanted to know whether they could trust me, and whether any of this would be worth it.

'What will be the impact of this? Will he be stopped?' he asked me.

Another son cut in. 'That's not her job,' he said.

I agreed, explaining that all I could do was keep reporting the stories, but that I did feel there was a public interest in examining the healthcare regulator's role in handling complaints about Dr Al Muderis. The consent judgment had found in Leah's favour and awarded her $1.75 million, but this information was not publicly available. Despite the high sum and judgment in their favour, the medical regulator took no action. Dr Al Muderis's AHPRA profile remained squeaky clean. It didn't stack up. I wanted to know more about what had happened and to see the paper trail before I could say what might happen next. I explained that I couldn't make any guarantees about the impact of my reporting, but I believed the media was an important tool in holding institutions accountable. And from what I knew at that point, this seemed like a strong example of institutional failure.

There was fear on all their faces. Leah's accident, and all that followed, had consumed their lives for years. The sons had almost lost both of their parents in the process, and their quest for justice had taken an unthinkable toll on the family. Reopening that wound was hard, and they wanted to make sure it would be worth it.

Leah is a softly spoken woman with a big heart and quiet determination. Standing in her kitchen, surrounded by her boys, her tears fell as she told her story. She felt responsible for the pain that Dr Al Muderis had inflicted on his patients, and choked up when she thought about the suffering of Temperance and Morgan Gollan. 'If I had kept fighting, maybe those girls would still have their mum.' She knew she was being too hard on herself, but she couldn't change the way she felt.

After the family recounted what happened, Leah and Tim brought out a big box of documents from their court case. For a journalist, there is no better sight. I eagerly seized on the neatly ordered box, rifling through its contents page by page, folder by folder, pulling each report out and photographing the contents. One of the key documents was the consent judgment order in their case. To my great pleasure, it stipulated that the only part of the case that could not be disclosed was the settlement sum, a term Al Muderis would later waive during his defamation case. This meant we could report Leah's story with the full weight of expert opinions, contemporaneous notes, letters and other evidence. This was among the clearest-cut cases I'd come across of Dr Al Muderis getting the surgery wrong and the regulator failing to act.

I left that day with a stack of evidence and a heavy heart. As Leah and Tim walked me out, I saw how Leah's stiffened leg caused her to limp and slowed her down. These were honest people who had been failed by the system. How many others had suffered similar experiences but hadn't come forward? This question continued to bug me. When cases are settled before trial, there is no public record that they ever existed. It was almost impossible to know how many other cases had been brought against Dr Al Muderis, or any doctor for that matter, and settled. Why is the public not entitled to know this information?

We published Leah Mooney's story on 30 October 2022. It squarely exposed the broken processes of healthcare regulators that had failed to take action on Leah's case. Professor Elton Edwards, who had provided the medical opinion in Leah's case all those years earlier, agreed to go on the record with his concerns about the Medical Board, which has a history of dismissing complaints that to all intents and purposes appear valid.

'Failure of the Medical Board to act reinforces doctors' reluctance to make reports,' Edwards said. 'The Medical Board has a role here and needs to reconsider its involvement in these cases and responses when complaints are made.'

The final patient story that I would delve into deeply before the trial began was that of Lisa Calan, who lived in Türkiye. The day after Dr Al Muderis's supporters launched a petition in his favour, I received several emails from Lisa. She forwarded correspondence from between 2018 and 2022 that tracked a breakdown in relations between herself and Dr Al Muderis after she'd desperately sought his help with problems with her osseointegration surgery but was ignored.

This trail of emails once again illustrated the pattern that had cropped up time and time again. Unexpected complications. Poor communication. Non-existent aftercare. Hopelessness. Despair. I knew I needed to hear the full story.

Lisa can't speak English, but had a friend in Canada who spoke her dialect of Kurdish and was happy to translate. We set up a videoconference across the three time zones. It was a Sunday afternoon in Melbourne when Lisa's face beamed into my bedroom. Lisa's friend is not a professional translator, so the conversation moved slowly, but piece by piece, I learned her story.

Lisa is a filmmaker and human rights activist who has spent much of her life advocating for Kurdish independence. She was marching the streets of Diyarbakir, the largest Kurdish-majority city in Türkiye, on 5 June 2015, days before the country's general election. Lisa was marching in support of the pro-Kurdish party, the Peoples' Democratic Party (HDP), in a campaign that had already been mired with political violence. She was weaving through the crowd when two bombs went off. Hundreds of people were injured and at least four killed. When Lisa came to, there was dust and debris everywhere. She looked down and saw blood and jagged bone. Her legs had been entirely blown off.

Lisa made it to hospital and narrowly survived. At just 25 years old, she was now a double amputee, with one amputation above the knee, and the other just below. She underwent eight operations, but each time, her residual limbs were shortened and she was no closer to being able to walk using socket prostheses. Defeated, she began preparing for a lifetime in a wheelchair – until she heard of Dr Al Muderis's surgery. The Kurdish community fundraised to pay for the miracle procedure, and she paid $108,151.47 before flying to Australia. She wanted so badly to walk again and return to her normal life.

She underwent the surgery at Macquarie University Hospital on 11 October 2017. Olan Gufer, a member of Sydney's Kurdish community, told me she visited the hospital that day and saw Dr Al Muderis, who told them everything went well, that Lisa would be walking within three days. Olan was relieved, but when they returned the next day, Lisa's pain was far more intense than anticipated. 'She was literally shaking in her bed in extreme pain,' Olan said. Lisa was discharged first to a Meriton hotel room, then to the Hills Rehabilitation Centre, where Olan said she received little assistance. The wounds around the implants were oozing with blood and discharge, but none of the staff knew how to help her.

'Dr Al Muderis literally did not see her at all. He was doing phone consultations at the beginning saying, "You will be fine." But the look of the thing was terrible. It was making me feel sick to see it like that. The part of her body, the meat … The flesh was coming out from her implant. It was growing and growing and he wasn't doing anything about it.'

Over the next few weeks, Lisa's journey was rocky. 'My wound was very open, my legs very deformed,' Lisa told me. She spent almost a month in the rehabilitation centre, and slowly, she was able to walk. She was thrilled, and participated in interviews with mainstream media outlets, including my own newspapers, praising the surgery as a miracle. Still, something wasn't right.

She was in agony. Her wounds were warm to the touch, red and pus-filled, and she had a fever. She was prescribed intravenous antibiotics and given an emergency ketamine infusion by other doctors. Despite all this, Dr Al Muderis wrote in his own records 'a considerable amount of her pain and discomfort is psychological' and she 'simply needs ... to get out and about and see some of Australia'.

As the expiry of her visa approached, she asked whether she should apply to extend her stay so Dr Al Muderis could monitor her recovery, but he pushed back on this, aggressively. He was worried she would apply for asylum, getting him in trouble with the immigration department. Lisa was offended by this suggestion, but he assured her that he would connect her with doctors in Türkiye who were skilled in osseointegration. If anything went wrong, these doctors would take care of her, he insisted. He would also be on-call for any support.

Reassured by these promises, combined with a feeling she had burnt through a lot of goodwill from the local Kurdish community, she returned to Türkiye. The flight would turn out to be one of the hardest experiences of her life. Her legs were swollen and throbbing with pain, pouring pus all over the plane seats. The air stewards were so concerned, they cleared a row so she could lie down. When she eventually made it home, she continued to deteriorate. Panicked, she started contacting the surgeons Dr Al Muderis had recommended. Each person she called said they had no idea about this novel surgery, or why they were on the list, and turned her away. Nobody could help her.

Eventually, she ended up in an emergency ward, in excruciating pain and desperate for answers. She called Dr Al Muderis repeatedly, to no avail. Texts and calls went unanswered, or were sparingly responded to. The local doctors had no experience in osseointegration, but admitted her to surgery and removed the flesh protruding around the implants.

This turned out to be the wrong course of action. Lisa almost died in that operation due to loss of blood.

For years, Lisa tried and failed to get help for the excruciating pain in her legs. In early 2018, Dr Al Muderis was planning a trip to Iraq and suggested that she meet him in Baghdad. If Lisa harboured any hope that her surgeon cared about her welfare, this comment snuffed it out. 'This was impossible for me. First of all, I'm a victim of an ISIS bombing. Second, the state I was in, I couldn't travel. Munjed knew this very well. I don't know why he proposed it to me. After I told him that was impossible, he didn't respond. I asked what other options there are, he didn't respond.'

She travelled to Europe in search of specialists who understood osseointegration. Some were helpful, many weren't. She spent all of her savings, and borrowed more from friends and family, desperate for a solution. She felt hopeless. 'Because of Munjed, I entered into a deep depression,' she said. 'Yes he helped me walk. But the situation afterwards was awful.'

Months after the initial surgery, she had given up on Dr Al Muderis and was still dealing with problems, when she received an email from his personal assistant. Subject: 'A/Prof Al Muderis – second book'.

'As per my previous email Munjed is writing a second book and his ghost writer Patrick Weaver would like to mention you in the book. He would be very happy to speak with you or alternatively get feedback on the attached story. I look forward to hearing from you.'

Attached was a one-page document that described the bomb blast that injured Lisa, and her journey to Australia. 'The operation was a complete success and before she left Australia, Lisa was walking on her new robotic legs,' the draft passage stated.

Lisa was taken aback. 'How after such a long time of not treating me, not doing anything, you come to me and ask me to be in his book?' Angry and confused, she did not give permission to be named.

Lisa decided to speak to me on the record because of her commitment to exposing human rights abuses, rather than anger toward Dr Al Muderis. She couldn't understand why he had treated her this way. Was it because she didn't have any money? Was he racist? How could he claim to promote refugee rights while acting that way? She became exasperated as she grappled with these unanswered questions. After the call, Lisa's friend sent me screenshots of messages she had sent to Dr Al Muderis on Lisa's behalf. WhatsApp logs that showed a series of unanswered calls and increasingly desperate texts. *This is getting ridiculous ... Is there anything that can be done?* No response.

As I was corroborating each story and getting them published, the wheels of justice were turning in the background. On 31 October 2022, Dr Al Muderis lodged a Statement of Claim with the Federal Court of Australia. This made his lawsuit official. We were being sued.

CHAPTER 7

The Lawsuit is Filed

It was still dark when my alarm went off on 30 March 2023. Ordinarily a deep sleeper, I was already awake when the electric bells began clanging. I stumbled into my swimmers and drove to Bondi Beach. As I arrived at the car park in front of the Pavilion, the sun had just started to peek over Flat Rock. The sand was cool under my feet as I propelled myself into the ocean, feeling the rush of cold saltwater over my head. These sunrise swims became somewhat of a ritual in the early days of the lawsuit, a way to calm my nerves and energise me for the day.

Over the past few months, I'd been in the depths of the discovery process – capturing every scrap of written material I had that might be relevant to the case. At the beginning, this seemed like an impossible task. Tidy notes are not my forte, and I'd spoken to almost 100 people all over the world. I sent the lawyers 600 pages of notes spread across multiple documents, thousands of emails and messages from WhatsApp, Instagram, Messenger, Proton Mail, Gmail, Slack, the list goes on. At one point, I had to hand over my phone to a forensic IT specialist for the day while he scraped all my text and WhatsApp messages. It was a huge, cumbersome, invasive process – and no doubt a horrible task for whoever was on the receiving end, trying to make sense of it all.

After the dawn swim, I put on a suit and went to the offices of Level 22 Chambers at Sydney's Martin Place to meet barrister Lyndelle Barnett and solicitor Samantha McGeoch. Thomson Geer had been engaged to defend us, led by partners Marlia Saunders and John-Paul Cashen, who had assembled a team that was already working full-steam. Lyndelle has a reputation as a whip-smart junior in major defamation cases, having taken on the likes of Geoffrey Rush to Ben Roberts-Smith. She had come head-to-head with Sue Chrysanthou before, who had been briefed to represent Dr Al Muderis.

'Sue told me the last time she saw you, you were this high running around Blackstone Chambers,' Lyndelle said, her hand at her waistline. I trawled through my mind for memories of Chrysanthou's time working at Blackstone, my parents' chambers, but drew a blank. I wondered if this was an early effort to discredit me, but laughed, changed the subject and we got to work.

Dr Al Muderis's statement of claim had drawn the battle lines for what lay ahead. The document ran to more than 100 pages, starting with a long list of Dr Al Muderis's achievements – his awards, the charities he represented, the medical papers he had written, his international medical missions, the many hospitals he worked at. He was suing not just the media companies, the Nine Network, the *Sydney Morning Herald* and *The Age*, but the journalists personally – myself, Tom and Natalie. Practically, this makes little difference to the case, but is often used as a tactic to intimidate the journalists. The bulk of the document contained a laundry list of imputations – meanings Dr Al Muderis said the articles conveyed.

> 'Al Muderis has ignored patients with maggots in their wounds.

> 'Al Muderis has negligently left patients mutilated, addicted to pain medication and antidepressants.

'Al Muderis employs high pressure sales tactics to the detriment of his patients in order to grow his business at all costs.

'Al Muderis' practice of osseointegration surgery is unethical and dangerous.'

The list went on and on. The document also cited all the subsequent articles we had published – a leaked recording capturing Dr Al Muderis joking about maggots at a conference, the use of the faulty part, his troubles with the insurer, Kim Gollan, Leah Mooney, Lisa Calan – describing them as 'sensationalist and tabloid' and compounding his hurt. Dr Al Muderis outlined the damage he had already suffered, which included surgeries cancelled and the end of his paid speaking invitations. A law firm that specialised in personal injury was now offering free initial consultations for impacted patients. The Australian Orthopaedic Association had denied his application for a fellowship. In the document, he argued we had misled him about the nature of the *60 Minutes* interview, and not fairly represented his responses.

The statement of claim also gave an early indication of the path Dr Al Muderis would take – discredit the witnesses at every opportunity. Al Muderis claimed his former nurse, Shona, was only involved because she wanted to solicit clients for a class action against him (despite the fact she had only just finished her law degree). More insulting, he pointed to Mark Urquhart's diagnosis of post-traumatic stress disorder, suggesting this meant Mark was not to be believed. It was clear he was prepared to fight dirty, slinging mud at people who had suffered genuine harm.

In all, he claimed we had embarked on a 'campaign of denigration' using 'sensational, emotive' language. He singled out the most despised words from the publications: *oozing*, *horrified, unethical, abusive, rotting flesh, infested by maggots, smelt like a dead body*. No matter that these were words that had been used by his own patients, colleagues, staff, and even by Dr Al Muderis himself.

Once the statement of claim was filed, we had to issue a defence – a document that outlined the legal defences we intended to deploy, the people who would give evidence to support these defences, and the overarching case theory we would present.

The Australian media industry is packed full of scoundrels who cut corners in search of a scoop, whether it's to sell newspapers, drive political agendas or pursue biases. There is an understandably low level of public trust in the profession, and it is important that there are safety nets for those who find themselves unfairly at the pointy end of a journalist's pen. The laws of defamation have long grappled with how to strike a balance between keeping the media industry honest, without stifling a free press. But somewhere along the way, Australia has managed to get that balance horribly out of whack. Sydney has become known as 'the defamation capital of the world', where suing for defamation is a sport among society's elite. Firing off a concerns notice can be an easy way to settle for a hefty sum, or to scare editors into avoiding certain topics altogether.

You often hear people say, 'It's not defamation if it's true', which, at its core, is correct. But proving that something is true to a legally acceptable standard is an exhausting, gruelling and often impossible process. I've worked on investigations where dozens of people have made the exact same allegation against an individual, but the story has been spiked because no-one is prepared to go on the record, let alone testify in court. I've seen colleagues lose defamation cases because they were in possession of key confidential documents that meant nothing in court without a witness to vouch for their authenticity. Stories and facts we know to be true are held back from publication every single day, because they can't be proven in court.

Despite the challenge, the first defence we planned to deploy was truth. This meant that, for the imputations we agreed were conveyed, we had to present evidence that proved they were true. The most severe of the imputations was that Dr Al Muderis is a negligent doctor who does not deserve his glittering reputation. Proving this was true meant the case took on a whole new life beyond the words that had been printed. We needed patients to give evidence about their treatment, and experts to analyse Dr Al Muderis's standard of care. The more patients, the better, regardless of whether their stories had been published.

In the end, the trial would become a series of quasi-medical negligence cases dressed up as a defamation case. This raised the stakes for Dr Al Muderis. Up until that point, his public record had been entirely clear. Medical negligence cases had been brought against him, but they had been settled behind closed doors. Patients had complained about Dr Al Muderis to the medical regulators and professional associations, but these too had been settled without a trace. The major hospitals he worked at were prepared to go to extraordinary lengths to protect him. As a result, his public record remained completely clean. In pursuing this litigation, asking the court to make a finding on whether he was a negligent doctor, he was tempting fate.

This is the risk that powerful people take when they sue for defamation. Two recent examples put this in stark terms: Ben Roberts-Smith and Bruce Lehrmann. Both men were accused in the media of committing heinous crimes – the former, war crimes, and the latter, rape. But, on paper, they were innocent. Both sued the media companies in an attempt to clear their names and rehabilitate their reputations. However, in defending the stories, the media companies proved to the presiding judges the allegations were true.

In the Roberts-Smith case, soldier after soldier was compelled to come to court and answer questions, under oath, about what they had witnessed in Afghanistan. Soldiers who had stayed silent were now on the stand, describing in detail the war crimes they'd seen perpetrated by the country's most decorated war hero. It was hard to believe this was a case that Roberts-Smith had initiated himself.

It was the same for Lehrmann, who escaped a criminal trial due to juror misconduct only to plunge himself voluntarily into litigation that exposed his cocaine and sex worker habits, and teased out in excruciating detail the inconsistencies in his account of what occurred the night of the alleged rape. Both Roberts-Smith and Lehrmann lost their cases, leaving all media outlets free to openly call Roberts-Smith a war criminal and Lehrmann a rapist.

I was sitting in *The Age*'s newsroom when the Roberts-Smith judgment was livestreamed on television. The entire newsroom waited with bated breath for the result. As it became clear that the case had been dismissed, tears welled in eyes all around me, and laughter and cheers erupted. It had been a long, painful and expensive journey but, finally, truth had won.

The claims Dr Al Muderis was disputing were of an entirely different nature, but the cases had some similarities. Among the most damning allegations we published were questionable patient selection and poor aftercare. Neither of these were crimes. And, as we later discovered, Dr Al Muderis's insurer had already paid $1.75 million to Leah Mooney after a judge upheld her claim for medical negligence, and $1.2 million to Kim Gollan on a 'no admissions basis' – both on the upper end of payments made to patients who'd been harmed by doctors. I couldn't shake the feeling that right from the get-go, this seemed like a ludicrous case. But for our truth defence to go anywhere, we needed patients to become witnesses. This included those who had featured in the stories, and anyone else who'd experienced similar problems with Dr Al Muderis.

John-Paul Cashen, known as JP, a tall man with a penchant for making bets, was one of the main solicitors on the case. He became a partner of Thomson Geer young and quickly became known as one of the country's best media lawyers. When you google him, an old interview pops up: 'Anyone who's needed a lawyer in their life will know how much you need that person to be on your side.' Over the next two years in the trenches together, I never doubted JP was firmly on my side.

In one of our early conversations, he wanted me to help set up conferences with each of the patients named in the stories so he could begin the process of understanding their cases and asking them to give evidence. Some had known this was a possibility when they decided to speak with me, but others were completely blindsided. Most of the people I had interviewed had never spoken to a journalist before, let alone understood what happens when that journalist gets sued. At that stage, I barely knew the process myself.

JP told me that all witnesses in the case needed to be quarantined from each other, to avoid allegations of contaminating evidence by people 'getting their story straight'. 'As you might be a witness in the proceeding, that includes you,' he said. 'It also means that when we interview them, you won't be able to listen in. You can still be on a call at the beginning to introduce everyone, but when we get down to business, you would need to drop off.'

JP gave me the names of more than a dozen patients he wanted to speak with first. I spent the rest of that afternoon calling each person. At that stage, my understanding was that the lawyers just wanted to explain the process, and it was up to them to decide if they wanted to get involved. Most were happy to speak with the lawyers. They wanted the truth to come out, justice to be served. Others were guarded, still scared Dr Al Muderis would sue them for even speaking to a lawyer.

The commencement of these conferences was the first of many times I felt my control over the situation slipping. Who was talking, what they were saying, how the situation was being handled was no longer up to me. I had to find a delicate balance between trusting in the process, handing over authority to JP and the team, and keeping a watchful eye over events to ensure my sources were protected. I felt like I was walking through a battlefield blindfolded, desperately trying to figure out how to avoid being blown up.

While I had to stay at arm's length from the preparation of the truth defence, I was right in the centre of our second main defence – public interest. This was a new defence introduced in 2021, which aimed to rebalance the scales by giving greater protections to media companies and journalists.

The public interest defence recognised the difficulties in producing investigative journalism. Journalism is a peculiar job. We gather information without any formal powers and with few protections. Our primary trade is speaking to people who have sensitive information that powerful people want withheld. Trust must be built on a shared sense of justice, righting wrongs, serving the public. We're often asking people to take action that is not in their best interests, or that squarely puts them at risk. Once we have the information, we must carefully corroborate and verify it to the best of our ability, before assembling it in a way that informs readers of important issues not already in the public domain.

The public interest defence acknowledges the precarious nature of newsgathering, and allows for minor errors of fact, if the journalists can prove they reasonably believed the stories were true and in the public interest. For the defence to succeed, the journalists' conduct and motivations must be proven to be objectively reasonable. This opens them up to an unprecedented amount of scrutiny. 'It's like a royal commission into your work,' solicitor Sam McGeoch told me once. 'This will set a precedent.'

The defence had only been taken to trial once before, unsuccessfully. It was a case brought by veteran Heston Russell against the ABC over reports that he alleged portrayed him as a war criminal. The evidence in the case was thin and nobody was surprised when the ABC lost and was ordered to pay up and apologise.

This case felt different. We had spoken to almost 100 people, gathered a tranche of thousands of internal documents and spent months testing and verifying claims. When I couldn't access medical records, I had to rely on the memories of patients. The trauma of the experience, combined with the fact that some of the operations had occurred many years ago, meant errors were bound to surface after records were subpoenaed. The legal team was confident this would not shake the public interest defence.

For this defence to go ahead, I had to become a witness. Much like the patients, this meant I had to write an affidavit and be cross-examined on its contents. My meeting in Lyndelle's chambers that Thursday in March 2023 was to discuss this part of the case. We ordered sandwiches to the desk and worked nine hours straight. At one point, Larina, who has been executive counsel for the newspapers since 2017, called to deliver an important message.

A strategic thinker, Larina is always five steps ahead. While she can rub journalists the wrong way for spiking their stories or killing their darlings, there is no doubt that she is in our corner. She deeply believes in investigative journalism, and once she's confident in your process, she'll do everything in her power to back you. She also deeply cares about the welfare of her journalists, and their sources. It was in this vein that she beamed into Lyndelle's room via video link that day.

'Charlotte, this is going to be tough. You will have to give evidence. This means cross-examination. We don't like putting our journalists on the stand. We usually do everything we can to avoid it. You will be exposed. If at *any* point, you don't want to do this, or you don't feel comfortable, you tell me. And I'll pull the defence.'

Journalists hate getting in the box because it exposes them to a barrage of attacks, from both lawyers and rival media outlets. A bad performance in the witness box can forever taint a journalist's reputation and career, let alone a judgment that finds they acted unreasonably. I was nervous about what lay ahead, but also felt that if the patients had to endure cross-examination, so should I.

In writing the affidavit, I had to retrace all my steps in painstaking detail, from those early conversations with my father five years earlier, to my meetings with Bach, speaking with patients, whistleblowers and surgeons. I had to document every single phone call I took, email I sent, text message I received. Everything had to be accounted for, down to voicemails and handwritten notes scribbled on paper.

Lyndelle was thrilled that I had taken so many notes during the interviews I'd conducted. Over the course of the investigation, my notes document had grown so large it froze each time I opened it. They'd been typed while I was on the phone, either at my computer or on the move, so the bursts of text were jagged, stacked with typos – to the point of complete incomprehensibility at some points.

As I would come to deeply regret, there was no mention of any dates when the calls took place, or whether I considered each source a confidential source. There was, however, plenty of information in there that never saw the light of day. I had a gnawing fear that these notes could become a problem if the other side cherrypicked certain lines and twisted the words left on the cutting-room floor into something sinister. Cases have been won or lost off the back of a single line in a journalist's possession that has been weaponised by the other side.

Some of my colleagues delete all their notes after the story is published, or avoid taking notes altogether, for this reason. Their thinking is when you get into a dispute, the courts must rely on the journalist's word, and confidential sources are afforded greater protection. Lyndelle saw it differently. She saw the notes as being one of the most comprehensive contemporaneous records she had ever seen. Memories fade quickly, and notes can provide a useful record when there is a dispute. She was also amazed by the sheer number of people I had spoken to. This was no slap-dash investigation; she was confident it was a well-researched piece of public interest journalism.

I left that first meeting feeling ever so slightly more confident, but I also knew we had an enormous job ahead of us. After a full day's work, we had barely scratched the surface, and everyone was exhausted. Leaving that meeting, my affidavit was only 17 pages. The final version would run to 254 pages, which I jokingly referred to as my first novel. It truly did feel like Sisyphus pushing the boulder up that hill. Each time it felt like we were making some progress, I would get bogged down in trying to find out exactly what time I had called or texted someone, or exactly where I had obtained their phone number. It was an unforgiving task, one that seemed to go on for a lifetime. Sam McGeoch became my key partner in finishing the affidavit. Sam is a polite, caring solicitor who does things by the book and doesn't put a foot wrong. She's always prepared to go the extra mile to get the best result. We became like detectives on the hunt for the most minute details – exact dates when conversations took place, or details about how I got so-and-so's number. Sam and I worked around the clock, and our phone conversations lasted hours. At times, I had Sam on loudspeaker with my computer on top of my doona, as I lay in bed for meetings that stretched into the early hours of the morning.

The next step was to figure out how to deal with confidential sources. A large number of surgeons, doctors, prosthetists, experts and patients had spoken to me 'off the record'. They'd done so for a variety of reasons. Most were scared Dr Al Muderis would come after them. There are legal protections given to journalists that allow them to maintain the confidentiality of sources. This is the court's way of recognising, through somewhat gritted teeth, that the work journalists do is important. But the overall sentiment from the courts toward the press is not friendly. Lawyers think journalists operate in the wild west, printing allegations willy-nilly without the weight of evidence required to establish facts in the cold, hard justice system. Judges have a tendency to look down on journalists as naïve, self-serving actors, loose on facts and thick on sleaze. For this reason, courts rarely uphold journalist privilege when it comes to source protection.

But still, the privilege exists and we needed to deploy it. In the first instance, JP wanted me to ask if my confidential sources would consider voluntarily waiving confidentiality and going on the record. This would mean handing over unredacted versions of our notes and correspondence, but didn't necessarily mean they had to become witnesses. Some sources had told me that if push came to shove, they would give evidence in court, so I felt hopeful some might agree.

Initially, I wrote up a list of all the confidential sources I had spoken to – 23 people in total – and cleared the day to hit the phones. These were going to be difficult conversations. I was essentially retracting a promise, asking people who I had assured could remain confidential to reveal their names and become involved in a very public, very aggressive defamation battle. It was not an easy sell, and it went against every instinct to go back on my word, but I knew I had to try. The more people on the record – particularly surgeons – the greater the chance we had of winning.

In phone call after phone call, these sources said they didn't want to be named. Some were so spooked by the prospect, they began melting down. Some did agree to waive their confidentiality – including surgeons Elton Edwards and Andrew Ellis – but most did not. This meant that large chunks of my affidavit included references to conversations I'd had with people we could not identify. Whether the courts would allow us to use this evidence and maintain these confidences was a question for a later date. If the court compelled me to reveal their identities, I would refuse – placing me in contempt of court, a crime which, in the worst of outcomes, carries a prison sentence.

While my affidavit was coming together, JP and the team had been busily working on filing the defence. This set out our case in granular detail – the identities of our witnesses, what they would say, the evidence we had, which defences we would deploy and how. As JP had previously flagged, I had been kept largely in the dark as they put this together. But after a back-breaking effort over many months, the results were in. More than 30 patients had voluntarily agreed to testify for us. For each patient, we hired at least two independent experts to review their medical files and make a finding on whether Dr Al Muderis's conduct was negligent. Fred Hernandez, Shona Stewart, Mitch Grant and Dr John Anstee would all testify, along with a string of other surgeons who would speak publicly for the first time about their long-held concerns with Dr Al Muderis's practice. Some I had spoken to before, others I had never even heard of.

Annexed to the defence was a document outlining the 'particulars of justification' or, in plain English, the facts our case would rely upon. It described osseointegration as 'relatively new and the surgery is performed by very few groups' before quoting flyers published by Dr Al Muderis's team that contained 'misleading representations' about the surgery including it would be a 'perfect fit every time', resulting in 'complete comfort' and a 'small amount of discharge', where the 'risk of infection is very low'.

The document also pointed out that what these flyers didn't say was equally misleading: they failed to warn of any of the potential negative outcomes, which so many patients had experienced – more pain, maggots, constant ooze, bleeding, further amputations, greater disability. The defence particulars detailed how Dr Al Muderis arranged for patients with successful outcomes to speak to prospective patients. How he broadened his patient selection criteria over time to operate on more vulnerable people. How Dr Al Muderis's decision to operate prevailed, even when others disagreed. As Dr Al Muderis's profile grew, the lawyers wrote, he had less time to deal with the higher volume of patients he was taking on. The document cited emails where Al Muderis's team, and Dr Al Muderis himself, actively encouraged patients to fundraise for the surgery. The illegal clinics he operated from US hotel rooms. The secret cash commissions paid to Fred Hernandez for new patients. The bullying and humiliation of his employees.

The document ran to almost 200 pages. In clinical terms, it stated how Dr Al Muderis had acted negligently, and how his patients' lives had been permanently damaged as a result. On State of Origin night, 31 May 2023, I was at a Fitzroy pub with friends when my phone started ringing. It was JP. The amended defence had been filed, he told me, with 12 new patients who had agreed to be witnesses. Some of these stories were truly harrowing. At the same time, word was going around that Chrysanthou was cold-calling surgeons asking if they had spoken with me, trying to sniff out our confidential sources. She wasn't getting anywhere.

'I'm feeling good,' JP said. 'We don't want to get too confident, but I'm happy with where we're at.'

A few months later, JP gave the doctor an opportunity to bow out. The stage was set, and it didn't look good for Dr Al Muderis.

In a letter sent 22 August 2023, JP offered to split costs and walk away. He said Dr Al Muderis's treatment of some patients was 'indefensible' and 'it is hard to see how his reputation and practice can survive' if the matter proceeds to judgment. Six days later, the doctor's lawyers responded, rejecting the offer. His white-haired solicitor, Nicholas Pullen, wrote that it was now 'abundantly clear' the evidence was against us, claiming that our public interest defence was 'hopeless'.

'Our client has incurred over $1.1 million in legal costs, and this amount is increasing at an exponential rate as the trial approaches,' Pullen wrote. He reiterated that Dr Al Muderis would only drop his case if we deleted all the publications, apologised and agreed to never write about him again. They gave us an eight-day deadline, but JP responded in two – rejecting the offer in the strongest terms possible. Again, JP said patient stories ranged from 'distressing to heartbreaking' and reminded him these people had no motivation other than telling their stories.

'We are instructed that our clients will not dishonour the brave former patients who came forward to give accounts of how their lives have been diminished by reason of their interactions with your client, and who are prepared to stand by those accounts at trial, by falsely asserting that their allegations are incorrect.'

JP said the stories were 'meticulously and professionally prepared and presented' and our public interest defence was 'impregnable' given the reports were 'manifestly in the public interest and the interest of public safety'.

'Against that, your client's position, as we understand it is, in effect, that all of his former patients to be called at trial – from Australia, the United States, Türkiye and Cambodia – are lying or confused; and that he knows better than all of the many medical experts the respondents will call at trial.'

He reiterated the backlash for Dr Al Muderis should he choose to proceed. 'No person would want to be treated by a surgeon who shows such little respect for his former patients' honest and heartfelt expressions of what it was actually like to be in his care.'

This time JP made a less generous settlement offer – you pay our costs and we walk away. He said this would save the enormous costs involved, relieve patients of the trauma of cross-examination, and spare Dr Al Muderis of the 'unedifying prospect of testifying against his own former patients'.

The offer was ignored. We were going to court.

The night before the trial began I was sent a list of Dr Al Muderis's witnesses. When I opened the email, my stomach turned. There were more names on that list than I had expected. Surgeons, nurses, doctors, all prepared to defend the humanitarian hero in court. It was Father's Day, and we went to Silvas in Sydney's inner west for dinner. By this point, an enormous amount of work had gone into preparing for the trial, and, in an uncomfortable collision of personal and professional, my father was set to be a witness. I was managing all this alongside my demanding job as an investigative journalist. I projected an image of control but, on the inside, I was terrified. That night, as we dined on chicken and fresh fish and discussed the news of the day – the Voice to Parliament, the Ukraine war – I tried to think of other things, but my mind kept straying back to the case.

The witness list was a stark reminder: this was going to be a battle. Nothing was certain.

PART TWO

CHAPTER 8

The Trial Begins

My eyes were already open when my alarm went off on 4 September 2023, the first day of the trial. I got up and went for a run along the waters' edge of Rushcutters Bay, then back up the windy streets to my parents' house in Paddington, where I was staying. I had just spent two weeks in Thailand with my partner, where I'd had my nails painted fluorescent yellow. My plan was to scrub the polish off after the run, but when I went to apply the remover, the polish wouldn't budge. I realised I had been given Shellac, which can only be removed with a trip to the salon.

This seemingly small detail got under my skin. A large part of Dr Al Muderis's case against us was that I'm an inexperienced journalist. Five years into the job at 29 years old, I had experience under my belt, I'd won a few journalism awards, but yes, this was my first major story for *The Age*'s investigative unit. I couldn't walk into court with fluorescent nails.

I found a vial of pink nail polish and painted an extra coat on over the yellow, creating a much less offensive beige. As the colour of my nails dulled, so did my nerves. I was ready for court.

That morning, I walked through Hyde Park toward Macquarie Street. For the first time, I thought, *This is on you.*

You've started this and now it's time to face the music. I met Nine's executive counsel Kiah Officer, *60 Minutes'* executive producer Kirsty Thomson and Natalie Clancy at Beanbah, a cafe next to the court building. We made light-hearted conversation as we sipped on coffees in the perfect Sydney spring weather. As we were leaving, Natalie, ever the hawk-eyed producer, handed me a bottle of water. It would turn out to be a lifesaver.

We put our bags through security and got the lift to Level 18, which would become our home for the next six months. As we walked down the corridor to the courtroom, the first man I saw was an amputee wearing shorts. I smiled at him, and he smiled back. Then I looked up and saw a crowd waiting outside the courtroom. It took me a few seconds to work out what was going on. A few dozen of Dr Al Muderis's supporters had gathered, some standing, some using wheelchairs, others with walking sticks. Many were amputees wearing shorts with osseointegration implants poking out of bare stumps.

I asked Kiah where our meeting room was. Having seen the online abuse his supporters had hurled toward myself and my sources, I thought they might start heckling. I simply didn't have the energy. But before Kiah could answer, Dr Matt Collins KC arrived with two other robed lawyers, Declan Roche and Claire Roberts, barristers I didn't know at the time but would come to enormously respect.

Collins is a short man with a sharp gaze, a strong handshake and a near-photographic memory. He's completed a PhD on defamation, authored two books, one titled *Collins on Defamation,* and has won many accolades for his contributions to the law. It was the first time we'd met, and as I reached out to shake his hand, he leaned in and said: 'Whatever happens today, just know that I've gone through huge volumes of medical records and documents, much of which you have never seen. And what I can assure you is, everything you published stacks up.' There was an intensity in his eyes that made me believe him.

There was a last-minute problem with the technology used to stream hearings onto YouTube, so we were moved to a much smaller room. At last, we heard a loud *Knock! Knock! Knock!* 'All stand,' the court assistant crowed. 'The hearing of Munjed Al Muderis and Nine Network Australia is now in session.'

Justice Wendy Abraham entered and quickly made assurances that we would be moved into a larger room as soon as possible. 'Yes, thank you, your Honour,' Chrysanthou said. 'We have some people standing, which ordinarily wouldn't be a difficulty, but given many, many of the people in the courtroom are my client's current and former patients, it would be helpful if they had seats – if I can put that as politely as possible.'

The judge, nodding in what would become her trademark way of dealing with the feisty silk, shot back: 'Which is why we had a bigger courtroom. The courtroom was deliberately chosen for that purpose.'

At this point, I texted my editor, Mathew Dunckley, to ask if anyone from the newspapers was coming. The lawyers had requested senior editorial representation on the first day to show strength. But, as it turned out, there had been a communication breakdown – no-one was coming. I was the sole representative for the newspapers. *Great.*

It was 10.15 am when Chrysanthou officially started her opening. I haven't done much court reporting, or had exposure to trials before, so I really had no idea what this would entail, how long it would go for, or what the rules of engagement were. It quickly revealed itself to be a full-throated attack on me, my father, the patients I had interviewed and my company's journalism. At one point when Chrysanthou said 'that's *60 Minutes*', Dr Al Muderis's supporters shouted 'shame!' from the back.

'What your Honour will see over the next six weeks,' Chrysanthou declared, 'is evidence of a malignant, dishonest, and malicious campaign by at least one journalist, Charlotte

Grieve, and followed through by others who worked with her, Mr Steinfort and Ms Clancy ... that can only be described as single-minded in their pursuit to destroy my client.'

She used the word 'lie' several times over the course of the day, throwing her hands up in the air as she triumphantly revealed documents that proved, she claimed, without a doubt that we were 'despicably dishonest' and didn't know the meaning of the word truth. She denigrated our patient witnesses, accusing them of spinning tales fuelled by hate. She picked on some more than others, accusing 72-year-old Carol from Queensland of fraudulently presenting herself in a wheelchair when our photographer turned up to take her portrait, when in reality Carol was 'happily walking around'.

Chrysanthou resorted to name-calling for Brennan Smith, a war veteran she referred to as 'Mr Cuts-His-Own-Leg'. Chrysanthou said the reality was he 'happily' removed the tissue after he found it 'so easy he could just start doing it himself' rather than going to a GP. I couldn't believe what I was hearing. She used words like 'rubbish', 'character assassination' and 'hit job' to describe the stories, accusing me of doing a 'stellar sales job' to get patients on the record by falsely telling them my aim was to 'expose the truth'.

'Now, Ms Grieve and the other respondents don't appear to comprehend the meaning of truth, they don't appear to comprehend what an investigation entails, and they definitely have no concept of ethical practice as journalists or as human beings.'

She said the fact that we had more than 30 patients willing to testify meant nothing, because their affidavits were riddled with falsehoods. 'They have scrounged around from nearly 10,000 surgeries and they've found patients who have spoken to them about complaints.'

I was so taken aback by the personal, nasty and, at times, wildly untrue nature of the opening, my throat dried up and

I started coughing uncontrollably. Thank god – or Natalie – for that bottle of water. But as Chrysanthou went on, accusing our patients of subterfuge, picking up inconsistencies in their statements, revealing dates that were wrong, emails she described as the 'death knell of the defence', a kernel of fear entered my mind. *Had we got this wrong? Were we doomed to fail? What would that mean for the patients? For investigative journalism? For my career?*

These fears turned into a full-blown panic when Chrysanthou turned her attention to my father, who she described as 'one special patient'. Now, as my father and I were both witnesses in the case, I had not spoken to him about his affidavit, or anything the lawyers had discovered. So when Chrysanthou announced that out of all the patient affidavits, our side had only dropped one, this came as a surprise.

'The one patient who is not pressed, and whose affidavit has been withdrawn, remarkably, is the father of the journalist. So, Charlotte Grieve's father is of King's Counsel and has been an amputee for a very long time, and Ms Grieve revealed, a month after the publications, in an article, that he inspired the investigation.

'Ms Grieve finally told readers the conflict she had, and she says it came from a conversation with her father, and that he, as an amputee, had a consultation with Al Muderis years ago and was told, if he did not immediately have osseointegration surgery, he would soon be in a wheelchair, and then refers to my client using pressure. So she decided to have a closer look.

'He was told he was suitable. If he didn't undergo osseointegration, he would be wheelchair-bound within around five years, et cetera, et cetera. Now, that's not what happened.'

Next, she flashed up a letter on the courtroom screen sent from Dr Al Muderis's clinic to my father's GP. The letter read: 'Donald would be a very good candidate for osseointegration. However, he's functioning well enough that he can continue to perform well with a socket prosthesis. I have advised Donald to avoid osseointegration for the time being, until he goes downhill. Donald will consider his options, and he will see us if he needs to.'

Chrysanthou swung her body around to the judge. 'Well, if that is high-pressure sales tactics, then my client would be broke. This is her own father. And there's two options. She didn't even bother to ask for the document, to actually check, or she saw it and ignored it. One of the big allegations in this case is high-pressure sales tactics, and here we have, proving that false, Exhibit A, Donald Grieve KC, the father of the journalist.'

I was completely blindsided. I could feel the blood draining from my face. I maintained a poker face but my thoughts were racing: *How could that be the case? Had he misremembered? How could my entire family get that wrong?* A layer of sweat formed under my clothes. I felt physically ill.

In the lunch break, we walked back to Thomson Geer's office in Martin Place, where sandwiches were served in a large conference room that overlooked Sydney Harbour. Marlia Saunders, a partner and fierce advocate who had been working late nights to get the case into shape, told me it was disappointing the way Chrysanthou had opened. She'd been selective with evidence. Accusing witnesses of lying before they'd given evidence was almost unheard of, she told me. I wasn't sure if she was just saying this to make me feel better or if she really meant it. I was so shell-shocked, the only question I could ask was, 'Were there any surprises in there for you?' Marlia said no.

I can't remember what else we spoke about. There were so many moments in those first two hours that had shaken me to the point of almost complete silence. I felt drained and almost like my memory had been wiped. Just after 2 pm, we went back for the second instalment of Chrysanthou's opening. By this point, we were in a larger courtroom and Chrysanthou had brought props. She had a 3D-printed amputated limb, and attempted to demonstrate how osseointegration works. But she fumbled, and tried to make light of her errors through humour.

It wasn't clear what she was trying to demonstrate, beyond courtroom theatrics. She got key details wrong and was corrected by her junior when she stumbled over medical terms. I realised that I was much more across the details than she was. Slowly, the sting of her words began to dissipate. She said blatantly untrue things, a small example being that I should have read Dr Al Muderis's memoirs, when my affidavit clearly said that was one of the first things I had done. She had come straight from running another defamation trial against the ABC into this months-long juggernaut, stacked with complex issues, contested facts, dense medical reports and the application of the new public interest defence. How could she possibly have had time to wrap her head around the case?

Toward the end of the day, Chrysanthou asked for the parts of her opening that had not been streamed to YouTube to be broadcast again. The request was denied, but it was an early indication of her strategy of playing to the media. When that first day ended, I felt like I'd been hit by a truck. News reports had started to roll in, capturing the most damning parts of the day. 'Famed surgeon claims "terrible, terrible lie" in Nine broadcast', was *The Australian*'s headline. 'Surgeon's marathon defamation trial against *Herald*, *The Age* begins,' wrote *The Sydney Morning Herald*. When friends and colleagues texted to ask how it had gone, my replies ranged between 'one of the worst days of my life' and 'brutal'. I told myself the personal attacks were character building, and focused on staying positive. But a growing fear was niggling inside me. I'd been quarantined from large parts of the preparation for the truth defence, so I had no idea what Chrysanthou might have found in discovery, if there were any smoking guns that could destroy our case. People, including Collins, kept assuring me that tomorrow we would have our say.

That night, I went for a walk with my sister, Tess, in Centennial Park. As we walked along the dirt tracks and past the lakes, we devoured the details of the day – chewing over the gristly bits, analysing the strategy, the tone, the impact. 'This is their high point,' said Tess, a solicitor who quickly climbed the ladder at one of Sydney's top firms. 'He will pay $20 million for the articles today. It's all downhill from here.'

Before returning to the court for the second day, I paused for a moment in Hyde Park. Sitting on a park bench, I called Nick McKenzie, my colleague and friend. Nick is a true legend of our industry. His stories have triggered government inquiries and a royal commission, changed laws and moved share markets. I've worked alongside him on a handful of investigations, and it's clear he's in a league of his own.

When he answered, I explained that Chrysanthou's opening had been brutal, and I was worried about some of the details that it seemed we had got wrong. One example was that Carol Todd had told me she had been in hospital for five weeks after her initial surgery, and I had reported that in the story. But medical records subpoenaed for the case showed it was only two weeks. I had written the patient case study stories in the first person for this reason, understanding that memories falter. But Chrysanthou was citing this as proof the entire story was not to be believed.

'Did your court case turn up any errors? Did you feel like that was the end?' He said yes, in the Ben Roberts-Smith case, the records showed they got the date when a murder happened wrong. 'But that didn't change the fact that a murder happened,' he said. 'A trial is like a game of tennis. The points are flying both ways. There are going to be bumps in the road. Some days it'll feel like you're winning, others it'll feel like you're losing. But you've got to focus on the big picture – the substantial truth.'

There were significantly fewer of Dr Al Muderis's supporters in the courtroom for the second day. Bizarrely, each time Chrysanthou talked about how extreme it was for Brennan Smith to have taken a knife to his own skin, or made any reference to maggots, those that were there erupted with laughter. To this day, I still can't figure out how this could be funny but one thing was for certain: the judge hated it. Every time they interrupted with a cheer or jeer, she would bristle. It also seemed that the judge was already growing intolerant of Chrysanthou's performative style.

With extraordinary confidence, Chrysanthou continued to describe patients as 'perfectly happy'. She unearthed videos, and photos posted to social media capturing moments where they were smiling, walking or enjoying their lives. She presented this as evidence that these patients really were fine, and their complaints had either been exaggerated or entirely made up.

She ended her opening by begging our lawyers to narrow the defence, and present only evidence that demonstrated what she regarded as the key claims, rather than a scattergun approach of the various problems raised by dozens of his patients. She said running the trial in this way would be a waste of both her client's money and the court's time, describing the entire venture as a 'futile endeavour'.

'What about proving he falsely portrays himself as a devoted doctor?' she said. 'Which patients actually prove any of those things or even come anywhere near it?'

And with that, she was done. Our senior barrister Dr Matt Collins KC then stood up to open our case, his eyes slightly narrowed. His voice was much softer than Chrysanthou's, speaking as if each sentence was a rare delicacy. The aim was for our legal team to be the adults in the room. We would not stoop to name-calling, pleading and begging, over-the-top claims or wild conspiracy theories. Our strategy was to present a clear-headed, forensic and unemotive case, stringently guided by robust facts and the subtle art of persuasion. Part of me wanted more aggression, but at this point, I'd take anything.

First, Collins had to draw a line in the sand. He was appalled by what the court had endured so far.

'We are almost a day and a half now; rather than identifying the witnesses to be called and outlining the evidence it's expected they will give, our learned friend instead took the court to a selective subset of documents, made sweeping conclusionary statements that, in our submission, are not supported by the available material when it is considered as a whole, and repeatedly branded as liars persons who the respondents may call as part of their case. This was inappropriate. No evidence has yet been called in this case; much less been tested.

'Had this been a trial before a jury, we would have been obliged to ask your Honour to discharge the jury on the basis of what our learned friend opened on.'

Collins said we had reported the 'lived experiences of a significant number of Dr Al Muderis's former patients'.

'All of those patients are extremely vulnerable. In most cases, they are amputees as a result of a catastrophe in each of their lives who came to see Dr Al Muderis desperately seeking his help. They did not deserve to be disrespected, accused of lying before they have given evidence or had it tested under cover of the absolute privilege that counsel enjoys, the enormous privilege of addressing the court. Overwhelmingly, they have sworn affidavits in which they say that in one way or another their quality of life was diminished by reason of having been operated upon by Dr Al Muderis. Many will say that he ruined their lives …

We do not contend that Dr Al Muderis is some sort of monster. He is obviously not. To many, many of his patients, a large number of whom have been in the courtroom listening while his senior counsel denigrated patient after patient who had a different experience, we accept that for many of his patients he's a hero. He has enabled them to walk again. We would never seek to diminish how that has transformed the lives of those individuals. There was a public interest in reporting what happens when surgery of this kind fails, as it did in one way or another for all 30 of the patients the respondents will call. Before turning to the patients, though, we want to say something about Donald Grieve KC, the father of Charlotte Grieve, a journalist and the respondent to these proceedings.'

My father had sought to come to court the day before, but the room change-up meant he missed the opening. He assumed we'd had a last-minute settlement and went home. That night, I'd forwarded him the transcript. Incensed by being accused of making a false statement in his affidavit, a grave offence for anyone, let alone a senior barrister, he went digging through his records.

Unlike myself, my father is a meticulous record keeper. Like a magician pulling a rabbit from a hat, he unearthed the back-of-the-envelope sketch that Dr Al Muderis had drawn during their consultation five years earlier. The file was attached to his affidavit that had been filed with the court, but I didn't know this at the time. It had divergent lines drawn – one returning to his pre-accident state, another plunging off a cliff. Now *this* was a smoking gun. It precisely fit with his memory, what he had told me, and what I had written, and completely contradicted Dr Al Muderis's position.

Collins tackled the matter head-on.

'As is the case with so many of those reports, the written document is inconsistent with what the patients say Dr Al Muderis, in fact, said or did in consultations and with other contemporaneous records. The document our friend referred to is undated, it's unsigned, and it's not on a letterhead.'

Collins told the court my father had checked his emails overnight and found no sign of the letter. He then produced the hand-drawn graph, which he said was 'consistent with what Mr Grieve says happened in the consultation'.

Then he turned his attention to me, pointing to the transcript. He said Chrysanthou had presented only two options – either I had not bothered to look for the letter, or I had seen it and ignored it. In reality, he said, there was a third option: that my father never received it.

'Our learned friend sneeringly denigrated Charlotte Grieve, one of the respondents in this proceeding, a journalist, accused her of lying on the basis of a wrong assumption and a selective and misleading cherrypicking of the documents that suited the narrative by not telling the court about a critical document that showed Dr Al Muderis's account to be highly contestable.'

Collins spent the remainder of the day methodically going through each patient, revealing documents, facts and records that punched gaping holes in Chrysanthou's opening. He read out, word by word, one of Mark Urquhart's final letters to Dr Al Muderis's clinic, which detailed his most excruciating and extreme symptoms. 'I can deal with a lot of pain, but I'm done,' Mark wrote.

Collins went on to explain that 'Mark's complications were so serious that he will tell your Honour he has had the implants removed – both implants removed. The result is, because an amputation is performed, he has ended up with stumps that are so short that he can't use socket prostheses, which confines him now, for the rest of his life, to a wheelchair.

'But against that, our learned friend submitted to your Honour not ten minutes before I stood up that everything of significance in the matters complained of was false. It's a submission that just cannot be made by responsible counsel in a case of this kind.'

As Collins was calmly dismantling Chrysanthou's claims, and bringing the court back to reality, I could feel the tension in my chest release. My phone lit up. Mum: *News char?* I responded the day had been fantastic. Then, I texted my partner: *Time for a Matt Collins tattoo.*

In the privacy of the lifts with our lawyers, Collins turned to me. 'Feel a bit better?'

I couldn't say yes fast enough.

CHAPTER 9

Taking the Stand

Back in court for the afternoon, Collins read another letter sent to Dr Al Muderis, this one from Carol Todd, dated 3 November 2015.

> The reason I have not been calling you any more is because I find our conversations unsatisfactory and I find I get no response to my questions when I call you. The truth is I don't feel you are taking my problems seriously. I've been in constant pain since I had this procedure. Having this done was to prevent me from being in a wheelchair; it was to change my life. Well, it sure has, I now have no life at all ... Where does it all end? I'm not happy any more. I'm losing my temper out of frustration a lot of the time due to the pain and my inability to do the things I've always been able to do.

The letter went on to describe Carol's misery in heartbreaking detail, and ended on a particularly devastating note.

> I have a husband to worry about with Parkinson's and my grandson who requires special care. How can I give them

the care and attention they require if I'm continually trying to push through my pain? I'm a hard worker and a caring person who wants to help others, but how can I help them now when I am like this? I have to pretend I'm not in pain so I can help others and make their lives a little better ... It would be great if just one day I could sleep a whole night or wake up and have no pain. It has been two years of pain since the operation and I've been away from my family.
I cannot take it any more. I have had enough.

I felt a chill run down my spine. I had never seen this letter before. Carol had written it seven years before we first spoke. The letter went to Dr Al Muderis directly. How could he possibly say that we had got it wrong? He must have known she had long suffered, yet he sat back as his barrister accused Carol of being happy, of faking being in a wheelchair. It was disgraceful, unforgivable behaviour.

Collins took the court through the patients who would give evidence in the trial. Shane Mortimer, Dr Al Muderis's first osseointegration arm patient – a 'heartbreaking' case that went horribly wrong, leaving Shane without the use of his arm. He went through the Cambodian patients, fruit-stall owners and farmers with limited English who agreed to have the surgery after seeing videos of robotic limbs, only to be left with primitive prostheses, bleeding wounds and constant pain.

Collins completed his opening by taking the court through the records of just six of the 30 patients set to give evidence. He finished by repeating his initial comment. 'They do reveal strikingly similar experiences and will amply demonstrate the substantial truth of the respondent's publications.'

At the end of the day, Nick McKenzie texted me: *You going ok with the trial? Here to chat if you need any help. Keep your chin up.*

* * *

The next day in court started with some legal squabbling. Kiah explained to me that Chrysanthou's approach in the past has been to use technical legal arguments to strike out large chunks of the media company's evidence. This strategy can be lethal, because it leaves the media companies with little to nothing to prove the truth of the stories. Before this case got properly underway, Chrysanthou's team filed more than 3000 objections over details included in affidavits filed by our side. 'If we get to run our whole case, I feel really confident,' JP told me once. 'But if she gets half struck out, I feel really nervous about it.'

Justice Abraham said she didn't want to waste court time going through each objection one by one. In the end, she allowed the vast majority of the evidence in, and would make her own decisions about what weight to give each claim. An experienced prosecutor, barrister and now judge, Abraham knows the Evidence Act like the back of her hand, so could easily make calls on the strength of each claim or document on her own. It was an excellent result for our case, a decision that funnelled huge amounts of material into the court record.

To save more time, most witnesses went straight into cross-examination. This meant there was no 'evidence in chief', where soft-ball questions allow each person to tell their side of the story uninterrupted. The entire trial was, as a result, almost exclusively hostile, combative and exhausting to watch. Dr Al Muderis's witnesses went first, beginning with Dr Karar Doshi. He was an orthopaedic surgeon trained in India and had worked in Australia as a fellow with Dr Al Muderis for the past three and a half years. Collins asked a series of questions that teased out a description of Dr Al Muderis's workplace. The osseointegration clinics are held every second week, and were long, busy days, starting at 9 am and stretching through to 10 or 11 pm. On average, up to 40 patients would be seen in a single day, Doshi said. The consultation reports were often dictated by the fellow or the person in charge of the patient. Many such reports were labelled 'dictated not cited' meaning Dr Al Muderis hadn't re-read the document after it was typed.

Collins established the importance of accurate and detailed record-keeping for quality patient care, then explored Doshi's definition of informed consent. Doshi agreed that surgeons must tell patients about differing views of surgery, particularly regarding novel procedures where the risks and benefits aren't fully known, or there is a lack of long-term data. He agreed that for patients to provide informed consent, a surgeon must explain these benefits and risks free from medical jargon. They must also explain alternative treatments, which in the case of osseointegration include sockets, transitioning to a wheelchair or no surgery at all. Doshi agreed that informed consent includes providing patients with the opportunity to seek a second opinion, hiring an interpreter for non-English speakers and encouraging patients to reflect on decisions.

These general questions about Doshi's understanding of best practice went on and on. It felt like Collins was leading the surgeon into admission after admission that would later come back to hurt Dr Al Muderis, like there was some grand plan that no-one was privy to at this stage.

Collins then extracted Doshi's understanding of the role of a surgeon, particularly one that performs osseointegration. Doshi agreed that these surgeons have an obligation to follow up with patients several times while they are in hospital and rehabilitation. He agreed that the doctor–patient relationship is long-term, and that the surgeon has a responsibility to manage any complications that arise, whether months or years down the track. Doshi said osseointegration surgery itself isn't a complicated procedure, but treating the various complications that can arise is. He agreed that the surgery is elective, and that it would be 'quite wrong' to say the surgery is 'necessary', because there are always alternatives.

Then Collins turned his attention to maggots in the stoma.

'That's a recognised phenomenon among osseointegration patients?' Collins asked.

'Yes,' Doshi said. 'It's a known risk, yes.'

'So it's a serious complication?'

'Yes.'

'When it arises, it needs to be dealt with and dealt with immediately?'

'Yes.'

'And they shouldn't be left to deal with the problem by themselves?'

'No.'

'It wouldn't be acceptable, would it, for a patient to have maggots in their stoma and then have to wait for seven days to receive information about how to deal with the maggots?'

'That's ... they shouldn't be doing that.'

'It would be totally unacceptable?'

'Yes.'

'Now, the risk that patients may experience maggots in their stoma, even months or years after osseointegration surgery, is a material risk, isn't it, that needs to be disclosed to patients?'

'It's a risk, yes.'

'Yes, that needs to be disclosed to osteointegration patients as part of the process of enabling them to give their informed consent to surgery?'

'It's – you – you can mention it, but yes – yes. Yes ... yes.'

By the end of the cross-examination, Doshi had agreed that various hypotheticals were inappropriate, wrong, and a breach or 'gross dereliction' of a surgeon's duties. He admitted that the information about risks on Dr Al Muderis's website was incorrect and misleading.

After the day ended, JP called me to check in. He was thrilled about the way the objections seemed to be going. He wanted the judge to see as much of our case as possible, so she could truly get a sense of what we had discovered. Then, he switched to Collins' cross-examination.

'You'll be thinking, why are they saying all this? It'll come clear later,' he promised.

From the early days of the trial, JP was quietly assuring me that Collins had a master plan that would all click into place at the end. He always encouraged me to ask questions and share my thoughts and welcomed any criticism I had too. He assured me that no amount of messages, calls or emails was too much. But he also encouraged me to trust the process. In this phone call, he explained that the best cross-examination involved confined questions, and gave the analogy of a cricket pitch. Questions might start with 'this is a blade of grass, yes?' he explained. 'Then you zoom out, and zoom out, and you say this is a cricket pitch, yes? And then there's nowhere for them to hide. They can't lie because it's clearly a cricket pitch. They can't squirm out of it. We're getting them to admit the blades of grass now so Munjed can't deny stuff later.'

The next day, Dr Tim O'Carrigan was called. At the time, he was an orthopaedic surgeon and member of Dr Al Muderis's multidisciplinary team who advised on patients' suitability for osseointegration. Again, Collins began by asking about Dr O'Carrigan's usual practice, what he considered appropriate clinical decisions, then contrasted his answers to claims against Dr Al Muderis. When Collins asked whether it was unusual to perform amputation and osseointegration in one go, rather than giving the patient time to try sockets first, Chrysanthou jumped to her feet. 'I object!'

'I allowed it yesterday,' she said. 'With the fellow, because he's very junior and didn't really matter, frankly, but I think that if my friend wants to use answers from doctors as to general practices, in a field of this complex nature and that is so broad, he needs to be more precise.'

It was quite an extraordinary drive-by for Chrysanthou to make about her own witness, a surgeon who'd come to court to support her client. It was also an indication that she felt Doshi's evidence did not bode well for her case, so was trying to discredit him. The judge agreed the questions needed to be precise, then Collins accused Chrysanthou of 'trying to put answers into a witnesses' mouth' before changing topics.

In answering questions, Dr O'Carrigan agreed that the risk of pain and hyper-granulation should be explained, and patients should be given time to consider their choices. He accepted that oozing discharge is a common complication of osseointegration, and must be closely watched for signs of infection. He agreed that additional surgeries resulting in further loss of the limb are common and must be discussed. He also agreed that each outcome that is discussed should be recorded in consult notes. Collins took O'Carrigan back to the following statement on Dr Al Muderis's website: *Are there any disadvantages? There will be a small amount of discharge from the stoma.*

'It's not an accurate statement, is it?'

After some ducking and weaving, O'Carrigan finally conceded the point. Piece by piece, Collins seemed to be laying the groundwork to show that Dr Al Muderis either misrepresented risks, did not discuss them at all, or failed to record those discussions in the consultation reports. None of these options were good.

Next came the discussion of the risk that is central to the case – infection. In his affidavit, O'Carrigan stated that Dr Al Muderis regularly told patients 'there's a 100 per cent chance you will get an infection and infection is a matter of when not if'. This was a line that would crop up again and again. The problem was, it contradicted much of Dr Al Muderis's own research, and appeared to be merely an anecdotal, throwaway line. Worse, subpoenaed consultation reports showed that Dr Al Muderis actually told patient after patient they had a 'very low risk of infection'.

Collins tried to scrutinise these positions – which one was true? Was every patient destined to suffer infection, or were some patients really lower risk? And importantly, what were patients told?

'It's important, Dr O'Carrigan, when speaking to patients about the risks and complications of any surgery not to understate the risks?'

'Yes.'

'And it's equally important not to exaggerate the risk?'

'Yes.'

'The critical thing is to provide the patient with accurate information in all circumstances?'

'We strive to do that.'

'Well, it's very important, isn't it, because if the patient doesn't have accurate information, they can't properly assess the implications of the proposed course of action and therefore cannot provide informed consent?'

'It is important.'

The information asymmetry between doctors and patients in any setting is enormous. Add in a novel procedure and Dr Al Muderis's celebrity status, the scales are tipped even further toward the doctor holding all the cards. It was crucial that Dr Al Muderis provide rigorous research and dispassionate advice to ensure his patients could provide informed consent. Collins then flashed up a 2016 research paper that Dr Al Muderis had shown at amputee conferences. The paper divided infection among osseointegration patients into four risk categories, ranging from superficial, easy-to-treat skin infections to deeper infections that can require hospitalisation, antibiotic drips, and potentially implant removal and further amputation. The paper found that 65 per cent of osseointegration patients experienced no infection at all, 30 per cent had low-level infection and none had deep infections. Chrysanthou jumped up to object. She said it was unfair to ask about this research paper, because it was a point-in-time study based on a small subset of patients rather than general risks. Collins pushed back, saying this was research Dr Al Muderis used in his own expert report.

'Now, I understand the point my learned friend wants to make, which is this is a cohort. Of course, the point we want to make is the cohort is wildly unrepresentative of what Dr Al Muderis now says is the true position,' Collins said.

This point hit home. It was exactly what the confidential data scientist told me about the drawer bias. The research paper presented a skewed version of reality.

Next, Collins asked about maggots. Dr O'Carrigan said out of his nine patients, one had experienced maggots in their stoma. He agreed it was a recognised complication for osseointegration, and accepted that maggots are a serious matter, 'very dramatic' to discover.

'Now, it would be important, wouldn't it, to explain to patients considering osseointegration surgery the potential for maggots to propagate in the stoma months or years after the surgery?'

'Yes, it's … it is a risk and it's an unusual problem. And, you know, particularly in light of the current circumstances, it would be relevant to tell a patient that, yes. But …'

Collins cut in. 'Sorry, do you mean the current circumstances, the fact that my client has showed an example of a patient experiencing maggots in their stoma on *60 Minutes*?'

'Correct,' Dr O'Carrigan said.

'Yes. And so, sorry, is your evidence that, as a result of that having been revealed by my clients on the *60 Minutes* broadcast, there is now a heightened focus in telling patients about the risk of maggots in the stoma?'

'Yes.'

'That should have been being explained to patients before it was broadcast?'

'Well, it's a rare complication.'

'It's a complication you agree needs to be explained to every patient?'

'Yes, you need to discuss potential complications.'

At one point in the trial, my sister Tess sent me a link to the case of *Rogers v Whitaker*, which she described as the 'seminal case of duty to warn of risks'. Every doctor and lawyer learns about this case early on, as it changed the way the courts and hospitals view the duty to warn. In 1992, a woman named Maree Whitaker had near-blindness in one eye and was advised by Dr Christopher Rogers to undergo surgery to improve her vision. Dr Rogers failed to inform her that the procedure involved a small, but significant, risk that the surgery could cause inflammation resulting in blindness in her good eye. This small risk eventuated, and Whitaker ended up totally blind. Her case was that if she had known of the slightest chance of going blind in her good eye, she never would have gone ahead with the surgery. The courts agreed with her, and found that Rogers should have warned her about the risk, which it defined as a 'material risk'. Whether the risk would change a patient's mind has been the standard for the duty to warn ever since.

Tess texted: *The risk in that case had a 1 in 14,000 chance of eventuating and it was still required to be warned to patients who had specific concerns about the other eye going blind.*

The standard, she told me, was not tethered to the statistical probability of the outcome, but the significance the patient might attach to it.

I responded: *I would like to know if maggots were a potential outcome depending on the season ...*

Dr O'Carrigan launched into a lengthy explanation about which risks need to be explained. He agreed material risks, even if rare, such as death, need to be discussed. But he claimed that it's simply not feasible for every risk under the sun to be explained.

'The reality is that you cannot sit there and talk about every possible complication that could possibly occur in any possible circumstances for the foreseeable future in that patient's life as a result of that surgery. We do not have the time, it is not practical and patients' eyes glaze over ... You do not have hours and hours and hours to sit there and talk to a patient about every possible, you know, complication that could possibly occur in the history of the world. You just don't have that time.'

Collins responded: 'I'm not asking about every complication in the history of the world, Doctor. I'm asking about maggots. Maggots are a recognised complication; correct?'

'Correct.'

'And they were a recognised complication before *60 Minutes* highlighted it in their broadcast?'

'Yes.'

'And it was a matter that needed to be discussed with every osseointegration patient both before and after *60 Minutes*?'

'Yes.'

Collins finished with some questions about my father's consultation in 2018. Dr O'Carrigan was listed in the consultation report as being present. The team saw 30 to 40 patients per clinic day, and despite the fact this meeting was five years ago, he claimed to remember my father specifically saying that he had arrived 'wanting osseointegration'. O'Carrigan said the team had informed him the surgery wasn't necessary at the time because he was still quite mobile, but the surgery may help him at a later date.

'You recollect that patient?'

'I don't actually recollect his face, but I do recollect the consultation.'

As Collins started asking more questions, Dr O'Carrigan's memory became less precise. He said he would have to refer to the records. He couldn't remember the graph Dr Al Muderis had drawn about my father's predicament. Collins beamed it up onto the screen.

'Have you seen that before?'

'No.'

Collins took Dr O'Carrigan through the two sketched lines, one showing my father's mobility returning to his pre-accident level, the other declining rapidly. Dr O'Carrigan accepted this was logical, but he didn't recall the graph, or interaction.

'No. Is your evidence to her Honour that that didn't happen, or you just have no recollection of it?'

'My evidence is I have no recollection of it.'

'You don't dispute it could have happened?'

'It could have happened.'

With that, the first week was almost over.

The next witness was the one I was most worried about, the one who preoccupied that late-night brain space. When I was investigating Dr Al Muderis's patients in Iraq, I received an out-of-the-blue email from Dr Qutaiba Al-Maawi. He worked for the team that handled Dr Al Muderis's Iraqi patients and had heard I was working on a story. We found a time to speak, and I asked him about the patients, the complication rates, the broadening of criteria, and some of the claims my confidential source in Iraq had made.

Dr Al-Maawi was adamant that my source's criticisms were overblown, and provided me with exact figures of complication rates. He also provided documents that undermined some of the sources' claims, including that Dr Al Muderis used unregulated implants. He came across as somewhat defensive but was also helpful and seemed to have access to live data. Dr Al-Maawi offered to put me in touch with some patients who'd had positive experiences, and I took him up on the offer. I spoke with two of the patients he suggested, using a translator.

After the story was published, I received a panicked email from Dr Al-Maawi claiming I had misquoted him and demanding a correction. I carefully reviewed his email and discussed it with my editor. The complication numbers for the Iraqi patients I had reported were accurate, but he wanted clarifying details added in, and he didn't like my choice of words. For example, I wrote that 15 patients were on 'continuous pain medication' – the exact words he had used. Now he said this meant only Panadol, and I'd made it sound worse than it was. I agreed to add some descriptions to better explain the statistics, but his demands kept piling up. It was clear we weren't going to reach an agreement, so I stopped responding to his emails.

A few days after Dr Al Muderis had filed a statement of claim, a spray of complaints were lodged with the Australian Press Council, an industry-funded watchdog that investigates journalist misconduct. Dr Al-Maawi had filed one complaint, as had two other people I had interviewed. I was shocked to see one from Aitham, an Iraqi patient I'd spoken with months earlier. The complaint, written in English despite Aitham not speaking the language, said I was 'trying to find negative views' about Dr Al Muderis and the story was 'inaccurate and biased'. It said the reference to his experience in the story was 'completely false'.

'I am happy with my medical care I have no problems to contact my surgeon,' his complaint stated.

Luckily, I had recorded the interview with Aitham. I retrieved the tape and transcribed it word for word. What we had reported was entirely accurate. Aitham had said he was grateful for the surgery, and heaped praise on Dr Al Muderis, but said the job hadn't been finished, that he couldn't use his hand, and asked us to contact Dr Al Muderis on his behalf. 'I've tried calling and contacting him but unfortunately there's no answer. And when they do answer, they say he's too busy,' he said. 'Is there any chance the newspaper can help with maybe bringing me out to Australia so that I can finish or complete the surgery on the hand? So that I can finally use it?'

Seeing Dr Al-Maawi in court, I was certain that he was going to do all he could to portray me as an irresponsible journalist, and I feared that the changes I made to the story at his request could be used against me.

Barrister Declan Roche handled Dr Al-Maawi's cross-examination. Quickly, he addressed the complaints.

'That was in my emails to her, yes. I was specific about every line, what was published and why I'm not happy and what I have actually said,' Dr Al-Maawi told the court by video link from Baghdad.

But each time Roche tried to drill down into exactly what Dr Al-Maawi meant by this, his answers crumbled. He rambled. Some of his points seemed to suggest my reporting had actually presented a better version of patient outcomes than was accurate. His responses were inconsistent and, quite simply, did not make sense.

In less than half an hour, Roche established that the changes to the story were superficial and made in good faith swiftly after receipt of his email. This sideshow was gleefully reported by *The Australian* under the grotesque headline 'Witnesses amputate Nine's case'. The article cherrypicked the worst of Dr Al-Maawi's quotes, and mocked me for entering the story into the Walkley Awards. It became increasingly obvious that Dr Al Muderis's team was feeding information to News Corp journalists in an effort to make it seem as though our case was on the rocks. While I was initially concerned *The Australian*'s inaccurate reporting might spook our witnesses, over time, I came to view their coverage as utterly irrelevant.

CHAPTER 10

The Doctor is Called

The final witness before Dr Al Muderis himself was Claudia Roberts, the doctor's fourth wife. She joined Dr Al Muderis's clinic as a rehabilitation specialist in 2017, and within a few years, they were married, and had two children together. Roberts worked full-time at the clinic for three years before dropping down to part-time. Over the years, her role was expanded to clinic coordinator. She organised theatre lists, saw patients, planned medical itineraries, and more. She was often the point of contact between patients and Dr Al Muderis, relaying medical information through text messages or social media. Roberts filed an affidavit in the case defending her husband's practice, but even she noted he was 'blunt' and staff left because they couldn't handle 'the demands of the job'. She was an important witness in many ways, Dr Al Muderis's right hand in business and in life.

She arrived at court wearing a black fitted dress, with a Prada leather handbag, and neatly brushed blonde hair that swung just below her shoulders. Roberts wore an assortment of designer outfits while she attended almost every single day of the trial, often without her husband. She was his eyes and ears in the courtroom.

Roberts' evidence started with some introductory questions, then Chrysanthou quickly turned her attention to my father.

'Do you recall a patient called Donald Grieve?'

'Yes.'

'Do you recall when and on what occasion you met him?'

'I met him at his consultation.'

'Right. And do you remember about when that was?'

'It was at Hurstville Private Hospital and it was 25 October 2018 ... It was discussed to Mr Grieve that at that point in time, the risk for the surgery would outweigh the benefits, and we told him to avoid having the surgery for the time being.'

It was incredible that Roberts was able to so accurately recall a consultation from so long ago that, on their telling, had been uneventful and didn't result in surgery. When Collins started his cross-examination, Roberts' memory of that period faltered. He asked about a trip she took with Dr Al Muderis to America around the same time, and she couldn't remember the hotel they stayed in, the purpose of the trip, or key details about meetings with patients.

Dr Al Muderis's trips to America would become a focal point in the case. There are only so many amputees in Australia, even fewer who are suitable candidates for osseointegration. The US is a large market and, as court documents in the defamation case against Fred Hernandez revealed, Dr Al Muderis made $US75,000 profit on average for every American osseointegration patient.

To spread the word about the miracle procedure, Dr Al Muderis regularly attended amputee conferences in America. He booked hotel rooms nearby, where he held one-on-one meetings with patients. He offered discounts to people who signed up on the spot, and accepted payment in advance to secure bookings.

Under cross-examination, Roberts insisted these bookings were only ever 'provisional' and final approval for surgery required sign-off by Dr Al Muderis's multidisciplinary team in

Australia. But this position was undermined by evidence that at least one American patient, Billy Wynne, had put $38,000 on his credit card for the surgery, and sent messages saying, *I can't believe I'm just a month from getting surgery* before ever stepping foot in Australia.

As well as securing new patients, Dr Al Muderis also used hotel rooms to see existing patients about a variety of problems. When Collins started asking about these follow-ups, Roberts was quick to intervene. They were *meetings*, she said, not consultations.

'Why did you say not a consultation, though, Ms Roberts?' Collins asked.

'Well, I would like to explain that a consultation is when a patient comes to a clinic, they see a medical practitioner with the view of getting an assessment. The medical practitioner will make a judgment on their current situation and either seek advice or treatment – none of which Munjed did in America ... He did examine patients, meaning inquire into, to gather information, to give education, but it was only once Professor Al Muderis was back in Australia he would then make the, the assessment.'

'Yes. So you've given that answer, Ms Roberts, haven't you, because you know that it's a felony under American law for a person who is not a licensed practitioner to practise as a physician of the United States?' Collins said.

'I ...' Roberts paused. 'I'm ... still not familiar with what, what the laws are.'

'Yes. You know it was a grave offence, wasn't it, for a person who was not a licensed physician to provide medical services of any kind in the United States?'

'No, I ...'

Chrysanthou shot up from her seat. 'I object! Relevance, your Honour. I don't see the word "felony" or I don't see any references to legislation in my friend's defence.' Chrysanthou had been making objection after objection, trying to strike out evidence she said wasn't 'particularised' in our defence. It was an argument she had executed successfully in the past, but not here. Justice Abraham allowed the question. Collins repeated himself: 'You were aware, weren't you – you've been told it was a grave offence for an unlicensed physician to provide medical services in the US?'

'No, I was not told that.'

'Quite sure about that?'

'Yes.'

Collins then beamed an email from Dr Solon Rosenblatt, a former member of Dr Al Muderis's team, I'd obtained during the investigation onto the court screen.

Please do not call the gathering a clinic. Munjed will get into trouble for holding a medical clinic without a medical licence. This is a grave offence and could mean serious fines and also revoking of his visa.

'So does that refresh your memory?'

'I understand that's what Dr Rosenblatt says, but I – I still don't know myself.'

'I see. You think he might have been making that up, do you?'

'No, but I – I still don't know what their laws are myself.'

Collins changed tack. 'You understood, didn't you, that it was a very serious matter for Dr Al Muderis to provide medical services in the United States without a licence?'

'Yes,' Roberts said, voice lowered.

'Yes?' Collins clarified.

'Yes,' Roberts confirmed.

Over the course of the day, Collins showed Roberts endless emails and text messages she'd sent in which she used the terms 'consultation' and 'clinic' to describe these 'meetings'. At first, she claimed her choice of words was an 'error'. But eventually, it became impossible to deny.

'You see you've used the word "consultation" again?'

'Yes.'

'And that's because that's what was occurring?'

'Yes.'

Roberts was in the witness box for two days. Collins methodically took her through correspondence and records from patients who said they had been ignored, showing text messages that had gone unanswered, pleas for help ignored. Time and again, Roberts tried to writhe out, saying she 'may have' or 'could have' responded to these messages by call, or 'would have' responded some other way – only to be shown further evidence that there had, in fact, been no response. Eventually, she admitted her responses were inadequate. She also agreed she was not qualified to give medical advice about hyper-granulation, infection, or anything medical – she was a physiotherapist after all – but admitted to doing so on multiple occasions. She claimed her usual practice was only to relay information from Dr Al Muderis, but was shown example after example where this could not have been possible.

'So you responded that silver nitrate was the only product that could be used to treat hyper-granulation?' asked Collins, while displaying text messages.

'Yes I did.'

'But you don't have any medical training to give that advice?'

'That's correct.'

It was during Roberts' cross-examination that Rowena Mattiske's case was mentioned in public for the first time. I first spoke to Rowena midway through the media investigation. On our first call, it took more than three hours, without me asking many questions, for Rowena to explain her medical history. Hers is a long, complicated and harrowing story that started with a day like any other day. She was working as a teacher at a school in 2004 when a child tried to escape. She chased after him, and tripped on an uneven pavement. This single wrong step would be the start of years of unsuccessful medical interventions that ultimately led to her foot being amputated. She had a 'foot party' before the operation and was so excited for the amputation to provide relief from her troublesome foot. But using sockets caused her enormous amounts of more pain, and she ended up in a wheelchair. She first heard about osseointegration in 2015, and discussed it with her local orthopaedic surgeon. 'The science is not yet tested,' the surgeon warned her. 'I've seen too many people with infections. Ro, do not even go there.'

But Rowena had young children and desperately wanted to play cricket, go hiking and body surfing like she used to. She found herself constantly being left behind as her family went off on an adventure, leaving her quietly weeping.

In her first consultation with Dr Al Muderis, he was confident the surgery would be successful if they combined osseointegration with a total knee replacement. The consultation report said Rowena understood the risks of the surgery, 'however we regard Rowena as a relatively low risk … Her procedure would be very standard.'

Dr Al Muderis's clinic coordinator, Belinda Bosley, did not agree. Osseointegration for below-knee amputees had proven to be less successful, and combining this with a total knee replacement only pushed the proposition further up the risk curve. 'Munjed, we can't do this,' Belinda shouted, during an argument that played out in front of Rowena and her son. 'Yes we can and we will,' he responded.

Despite all the red flags, by that point, Rowena had tunnel vision. She saw the surgery as a ticket back to her old life, and wanted it badly. In 2016, she underwent osseointegration over two operations, and the following year, she was able to walk, unaided, and returned to her normal, bubbly self. She travelled to Europe with her family, and strode confidently along cobblestone roads and in nature for long distances, enjoying life to the fullest. Not long after, however, things took a turn for the worse. Rowena suffered infections and unbearable pain. She had multiple surgeries to fix the problem, but each time, her situation got worse. She experienced pain so severe it was like being hooked up to an electric fence. Her leg turned purple at one point and swelled so large she said it looked like an elephant's leg. As Dr Al Muderis dismissed her she started noticing other patients in bad ways – one man crawling on all fours because he was so scared to walk on his new leg, crying as he told Rowena: 'I hate this thing. I wish I never did it.'

Dr Al Muderis eventually decided in August 2020 the only way forward was to cut off the knee and amputate her again, turning Rowena into an above-knee amputee. When I first spoke with her, she was bedbound on a cocktail of antibiotics to control the infection that was back with a vengeance. She didn't know what was next for her.

Rowena has an almost pathologically positive attitude. She wants badly to see the best in people, and situations. She deeply appreciated Dr Al Muderis's work, and used words like 'genius' to describe him, but deep down, she knew her care wasn't good enough. Dr Al Muderis had never warned her about what could happen, she said, and never explained medical information to her in plain English. When things did go wrong, he became rude, dismissive and flippant about her struggles.

When she didn't get better, she sensed he was frustrated. She had to beg for answers and assistance, and never felt satisfied with either. In the pursuit of mobility, Rowena had been robbed of her life, her soul, her sanity. She needed heavy pain medications to get through the day, and a wheelchair to get around. The hardest part for Rowena was the impact on her family. They shrouded her in love, but she felt like a burden.

The pain grew so heavy, she contemplated suicide. Rowena had been dismissed by Dr Al Muderis so often that she started to blame herself for what had gone wrong. But as I listened to Rowena, over several phone calls, she resolved that she wanted to tell her story, on her terms. She wanted others to know they deserved better too.

I drafted a summary of her story, and read it out to her over the phone. 'It's perfect,' she said. But as we were nearing the print deadline, Rowena called to say she couldn't go on the record. Her family was too scared. Her story was never published.

When the trial came around, I gave the lawyers Rowena's contact details. She wanted to be a witness, and they drafted an affidavit, but when it came time to sign the document into a sworn statement, she was in hospital battling yet another infection. At the eleventh hour, a junior lawyer rushed to Rowena's bedside so she could sign. Finally, Rowena had the chance to tell her story, under oath, in court.

I was conscious that not all of Rowena's pain and problems led back to Dr Al Muderis, but she was his patient for many years and had observed his practice up close. She had come to believe that mobility was not the only marker of a good life, as Dr Al Muderis preaches, and wished she never went ahead with the surgery. Her story was nuanced, but deeply moving. Having her on board as a witness was a gamechanger.

Now in court, Collins displayed messages from Rowena to Roberts asking for help, saying her knee was still 'swollen and extremely painful to walk on with two crutches', 'very warm to touch' and she had 'pain so sharp at times that it takes my breath away and am resorting to a wheelchair'. Rowena wrote that she spent 90 per cent of her time in bed resting. *Just checking this level of pain is normal ... I'm not complaining just being honest with you and real. I appreciate your input very much.*

Despite Rowena's persistence and politeness, she was fobbed off. There was no record of Roberts responding, over and over again. More messages flashed onto the courtroom screen, where Rowena described the pain as 'beserk', 'crazy', 'constantly zinging like an electric shock that won't turn off'. Six hours later, another text: *So sorry to text again. I really need some direction about this leg. Something is definitely wrong.* Time and time again, Collins asked if Rowena was entitled to a quick response and Roberts agreed that she was.

In other parts of Roberts' evidence, she admitted to denigrating surgeons seen by Dr Al Muderis's patients once they became dissatisfied with his care, based solely on information her husband had told her. She eventually admitted that much of the evidence she claimed to remember was in actual fact a reconstruction of what had happened, based on documents she had read in preparation for court.

Toward the end, Collins returned to the topic of my father. He tested Roberts' memory of the day, which she had earlier been so quick to recall. 'Well, then, who was present?'

She rattled off a list of names, including Kevin Tetsworth, who was not listed in the consultation report as attending.

'You maintain that?'

'To my recollection, he was,' she responded.

'So is your evidence that the consultation report is inaccurate to that extent?'

'No, it must have been my recall.'

'Your recall is defective?'

'For ... for that instance, yes,' Roberts said.

Roberts then admitted that she couldn't remember the graph drawn by Dr Al Muderis, and thus accepted her memory must be incomplete. It was a significant departure from her earlier claim of a precise recollection.

With that, Roberts' evidence was over.

* * *

Next up was Dr Al Muderis. I was intrigued to see how he would respond to some of the questions now that we were in a court setting. The evidence against him had only grown since our last interrogation with the cameras rolling. I knew Dr Al Muderis could be polarising – able to charm some into believing he was a genius, while others quickly saw though his false assurances.

Before Collins got started, there was legal argy-bargy about Dr Al Muderis's so-called independent expert reports. Medical negligence cases are essentially a battle of experts. The patient says they've been harmed, and opposing experts assess the treatment and argue over whether it met or fell below a reasonable standard. The judge then decides which set of experts she prefers – a key part of determining negligence. The independence of these experts is essential. They must carefully weigh the available medical evidence against their own knowledge, free from any bias that might sway them one way or another.

This lawsuit was essentially 30 medical negligence cases dressed up as a defamation case, and Dr Al Muderis wanted to be his own independent expert. This was virtually unheard of. He argued that osseointegration is a niche field, particularly for patients using his patented implant system. There was simply no-one else with the necessary experience or knowledge to provide expertise on the matter. Our lawyers allowed Dr Al Muderis to submit these so-called independent expert reports, where he made findings on his own treatment of his own patients, but had one objection. The judge found the whole situation perplexing.

'So he's …' Justice Abraham said, pausing. 'Sorry, you've referred to it as independent. Do you accept it's independent?'

Roche said we considered Dr Al Muderis's reports 'purportedly' independent, but our main concern was how his reports had gone beyond delivering assessments of treatment into denigrating our experts. Dr Al Muderis had taken it upon himself to review the academic papers each of our experts had published, and tally their appearances at amputee conferences based on his own observations, before concluding that none were truly experts. Roche said this crossed a line – it was the judge's job to assess expertise and the weight of each report. Chrysanthou tried to soften the edges, saying it was 'his opinion' rather than a statement of fact, that our experts weren't really experts.

'That's not an expression of opinion,' the judge said, askance, eyebrow cocked.

'I think it's implied that his opinion is none of these four gentlemen are experts,' Chrysanthou said.

'I do draw the line at the witness, who is a party to the proceeding, saying he has concluded that they're not experts. So that's not being read,' Justice Abraham ruled.

Finally, it was time. Chrysanthou stood. 'Your Honour, I call Professor Munjed Al Muderis.'

I was back in Melbourne by this point, watching the hearings on YouTube from my desk in *The Age* newsroom, hastily typing notes. The stream showed several camera angles – the judge, the witness and the cross-examiner. The footage was grainy and glitchy, but I hung on every word. *Wearing a blue tie. Pin of Australia on his jacket. Looks nervous.*

Unlike most other witnesses, Dr Al Muderis was permitted to give some evidence in chief. Chrysanthou asked open-ended questions about his qualifications, his humanitarian missions, the Cambodia trip, allowing him to give long responses about how 'disgusted' he was that his 'honourable' work has been misrepresented by 'dishonest' journalists. Then, Dr Al Muderis began talking about Lisa Calan. In many ways, Lisa *was* the perfect candidate for osseointegration. The majority of bilateral above-knee amputees end up in a wheelchair, Dr Al Muderis explained, because the hard sockets bash against each other, making it near-impossible to walk. Studies have shown that above-knee amputees using sockets require up to 60 per cent more energy to walk than a full-bodied person. 'For a person who is in her 20s to resign to being wheelchair-bound for the rest of her life, that's unfair,' Dr Al Muderis said. He was right.

He explained that Lisa had suffered post-traumatic stress disorder, panic attacks, significant pain and an opioid dependency. 'That's not inconsistent with the majority of patients who have major limb loss.' He went through what he described as the 'routine' process, where she was seen multiple times pre- and post-surgery. Chrysanthou asked whether Dr Al Muderis followed her progress, and how she had fared.

He said Lisa has 'done extremely well' and 'was highly functional'. The doctor conceded she suffered pain, falls and granulation but said she was travelling the world and, by that calculation, she was fine. 'She walks unaided,' he said.

Chrysanthou clicked a button, and an article flashed onto the screen. It had been published by *The Age* and *Sydney Morning Herald* in 2017 and described the 'cutting-edge' surgery as Lisa's 'last chance'. At this, Dr Al Muderis took a deep breath and tears welled in his eyes. 'Do you remember seeing that article at about the time it was published?' Chrysanthou asked.

Through a broken voice, and short breaths, he said: 'I do.'

'You're getting upset, is that because you're recognising the photos?'

'I'm sorry.'

He gave a long answer about how unfair it was to use the same photograph in my article years later that captured Lisa sitting in a wheelchair, her freshly osseointegrated stumps and raw flesh around the implants pointing toward the camera.

'They presented in that particular article indicating that that's her status currently, which is not true. It's very misleading and it's very dishonest,' he said, crying still.

My brow furrowed. I checked the article again. The caption clearly states the photograph was taken in 2017. There was also a second photograph from the same shoot embedded further down that showed Lisa walking on prosthetic limbs using crutches, and the article clearly explained she had given interviews years earlier where she had celebrated the surgery.

My colleague Ben Schneiders was sitting next to me. We looked at each other, shocked by this broken man in the witness box. From our vantage point, it looked like the pain he felt was real. But when asked why he was upset, his answer had nothing to do with the suffering described by his patient. His pain was for himself, at the unfair treatment he claims to have endured. One of the solicitors later told me the tears went down like a lead balloon in the courtroom. The judge did not look impressed. This all came before the true highlight of the day.

After Lisa had got in contact with me, we had sent questions to Dr Al Muderis for response. He was in Ukraine at the time, performing osseointegration on victims of war. He was angry we kept publishing stories about him when he had more important things to be doing. He wanted it to stop, but his lawyer told him this wasn't possible. When Chrysanthou asked what impact this had on him, Dr Al Muderis delivered the killer line. 'And for the first time ever, I felt that democracy may not be the answer, and freedom of speech is not a good thing sometimes,' he said, pausing before adding, 'If it's abused that way.'

* * *

Collins' cross-examination of Dr Al Muderis started on 21 September 2023, almost exactly one year after the first story was published. Collins had been meticulously preparing for weeks, and almost appeared to be looking forward to it.

'I'm sure you appreciate this might take some time,' Collins said. 'There are quite a number of matters I need to put to you.'

Starting with Lisa Calan, Collins asked about a health questionnaire she filled out prior to surgery. Dr Al Muderis was immediately defensive.

'You were aware, weren't you, that she had current issues with neuromas and pain at the time you first saw her?'

'She had pain.'

'Yes. I'm suggesting that she disclosed, at the time, well prior to your first meeting with her, that she had current issues with neuromas?'

'She had pain.'

'Yes. No, I'm asking about neuromas?'

'She had pain.'

It appeared the only concession Dr Al Muderis was prepared to make was her pain, which he stressed was pre-existing and not his domain. He resisted the suggestion her post-operative pain was 'excruciating', despite her being hospitalised and put on a ketamine drip. He denied knowing about her infection, despite records of antibiotics prescriptions and explicit references to 'stump infection'. He accepted that, despite knowing Lisa could not read or speak English, at no point was a registered interpreter hired to explain the procedure. He admitted she was given reports about osseointegration risks entirely in English.

Lisa was promised her care would be monitored in Türkiye and given a list of doctors to contact for help. Dr Al Muderis had previously said, when being questioned by Chrysanthou, the world was a 'small village' and technology meant he could easily connect with Lisa, and her clinicians, from afar. He described their communication as 'robust and continuous'. However, under cross-examination, Dr Al Muderis admitted he did not know any surgeons in Türkiye, let alone any who understood osseointegration. Collins then showed the court message after message from Lisa that had been ignored.

I'm worried about the treatment, so I need your help. I don't want anything beyond your control. Please do not leave me here alone.

'Do you have a recollection of doing anything in response to that message?'

'I did respond to her.'

'Yes. What did you do?'

'I either responded by phone or by message …'

Collins smelt the lie and went for blood. 'You've just said that in the witness box because it's a convenient answer to the question I've put to you?' Dr Al Muderis stood firm and repeated how Lisa had his mobile number. But like Roberts before him, this position did not hold up. Collins showed more messages.

Dr Munjed, why do you not communicate with me? Is there a specific reason for this?

'You remember receiving that?'

'Yes.'

'Yes. You understood by this time, didn't you, that Ms Calan was dissatisfied with the level of follow-up from you?'

'I understand that she's putting an assertion that I'm not communicating which is false.'

Dr Al Muderis said Lisa contacted him at inconvenient times. But then, another message: *I am very sad. Dear Munjed, please come back to me at a time that suits you. What time are you free? Amy or I can call whenever is convenient for you.*

And, later: *Do you think I can come to Australia for treatment? My pain has become intolerable and I'm unable to have any semblance of a normal life.*

'Remember reading that?'

'I don't recall.'

'You don't doubt that that's an honest expression of how she felt at this time?'

'Yes.'

Collins seized on this rare admission, throwing Dr Al Muderis's legal strategy back in his face.

'Because you come to this court, Doctor, relying on photographs of this patient walking on her osseointegrated legs as if to say she has got nothing to complain about?'

'I don't understand the question.'

Collins asked the question twice more, worded slightly differently each time. Chrysanthou interjected. 'I do the arguing, not my client,' she protested, distancing Dr Al Muderis from the backbone of her case theory – that patients who post happy photos on social media are clearly lying about their complaints.

The judge said that nobody was suggesting anyone other than the lawyers were arguing. 'But it's the applicant's case. His evidence yesterday, as he has just conceded, that she's—'

'Mobile,' Chrysanthou cut in.

'Well, a bit more than mobile,' the judge replied.

Collins asked about another message, in which Lisa wrote that her situation was worse than before the surgery. Dr Al Muderis said it was a subjective message, he doesn't understand the words, and in any event, he never promises anyone a 'normal life'.

'My job was to provide her with osseointegration surgery, which I did to the best of my knowledge and ability, and she walked. That's what I promised her. That's what I delivered.'

'Thank you,' Collins said.

A photo of a bleeding leg flashed onto the screen. *Very, very pain. Please help me.*

'Do you see that?'

'All I can see is that her stoma looks perfect.'

'Yes. Well, she's just saying, "Very, very pain. Please help me." You see that as being a cry for help, don't you?

'I disagree with the statement … I disagree with she's crying for help, because she knows I'm not the pain specialist.'

'So she's asking the wrong person for help, is she?'

'Well, I don't understand the question. I'm sorry.'

'Doctor, the proper human response on receiving a message like that is to respond to it in a sensitive and timely manner. Do you agree?'

'I disagree with the statement.'

'You disagree. Thank you.'

Hours passed and Dr Al Muderis insisted he'd done nothing wrong. He's not qualified to respond to her pain. It's not his job. He fulfilled his promise. She's walking. He can't manage chronic pain. He can't manage psychological issues.

'I'm just a carpenter,' he said at one point. He won't fall into the 'guilt trip' of accepting responsibility for her pain. He gives his mobile number to all his patients, all 27,000 of them, he told the court. No other surgeon does that. He goes above and beyond. If there's an emergency, that's what emergency departments are for.

But, Collins reminded him, Lisa was asking whether this pain, related to osseointegration, his unique surgery, that not many people understood, was normal or not. And Dr Al Muderis did not respond. He did not tell her that she needed to go elsewhere. Dr Al Muderis fortified his position by sidestepping the nub of each question. Collins grew frustrated.

'Doctor, please. Did you understand that she was asking you for a response to the question, "Are my levels of pain normal or not?"'

Dr Al Muderis wouldn't budge. He 'clearly' explained to her on several occasions that he's not a pain specialist. Collins asked whether this was ever put in writing.

'I don't recall putting it in writing. I may have. I'm not sure.'

Then, Collins asked whether the doctor, at least, agreed Lisa's messages accurately conveyed how she felt. The answers swung between 'I don't understand', 'That is a false statement', 'I may have', 'I don't recall'. As Lisa's cries for help were stacked on top of each other, the doctor's lack of response became darker, more disturbing, more deliberate.

Another message: *I'm very saddened by this situation. I've spoken to my other friends who've undergone the surgery, and they said they had no problems in communicating with Dr Munjed. So I wonder why, in my case, you are not staying in contact.*

Dr Al Muderis cut in. This time he agreed with what Lisa had said, partially: 'Well, it's a true statement that I have not had any problems communicating with my patients. That is [a] very true statement because I don't have any problems with communicating with my patients.'

Another message: *I'm not asking for too much. I only want, as a patient, to receive information and recommendations from my doctor.*

Dr Al Muderis returned to vigorously defending his actions. He invited Lisa to Jordan, then Iraq. Collins asked about Lisa's fear of Iraq, given she is an ISIS terrorist attack survivor and Kurdish rights activist.

Dr Al Muderis snapped. 'Iraq is the only country that recognise the Kurdish flag!' he protested.

Collins reminded him this was his patient who felt unsafe, reading now from Lisa's affidavit: *Being an activist, Baghdad would not have been a safe place for me. I believe Dr Al Muderis should have known this. For these reasons I did not take this invitation seriously.*

Dr Al Muderis's rage only grew: 'The president of Iraq is Kurdish! Iraq recognise the rights of Kurds, Iraq respects Kurdish people and protects them. Iraq is the safest place for Kurdish people at this point in time and since 2003, so that was false.'

'So Ms Calan is lying, is she, when she says that?'

'The statement is false! Iraq is not unsafe place for Kurdish people! Iraq is the safest place for Kurdish people on this planet as we speak.'

'Did you tell Ms Calan that that was your view?'

'I didn't need to tell Mr Calan – Ms Calan that – that because that's a well-known fact!'

More messages: *As you know, I've been in Türkiye for over three months. From the minute I left Australia, I have caught an infection two times and have been undergoing treatment at the hospital, often having to stay as an inpatient for a long time.*

With this, Dr Al Muderis delivered what became one of his trademark answers: 'There are facts, there are feelings. That, that's a reflection of her feelings; that doesn't necessitate to be a factual ... I will not take the blame for not answering a message about "my pain is increased". That is not necessarily related to an orthopaedic problem. This is not my job, Dr Collins … I am sorry if she has pain. I did not cause her that pain. She had intolerable pain because the bastards that blew her leg off. I tried to help her and I try to help every patient I deal with. It's unfair that I get accused of causing the pain that I never did.'

The doctor was clearly agitated. Collins offered him a break.

'No. Thank you. No. I do apologise for being emotional, but I am very passionate about what I do. I'm very passionate about this technology. And Channel Nine has took it back 20, 30 years at least. This is the future for amputees. And this is what should be the future for amputees. People deserve to have better treatment than a socket prosthesis that is 600 years old. People deserve to have better mobility. And what Channel Nine has done has destroyed that dream for hundreds and hundreds of thousands of people. All around the world people knows now that this misconception about pain and misconception of false accusation that osseointegration create all these horrible things is not true.'

The judge intervened, and ordered a ten-minute break. 'Just bear in mind that you're here now to answer questions. We are going to go much more quickly if you listen to the question and answer the question. This isn't an opportunity to make speeches, with respect.'

Dr Al Muderis apologised, and the court adjourned.

After the break, Collins asked Dr Al Muderis about the draft passage in his memoir that Lisa had been asked to approve, which described her operation as a 'complete success'. This time, his answers were shorter. A series of 'I don't recalls' were dispatched so quickly he interrupted Collins' questions. 'Talking over the questioner doesn't help,' said the judge. 'Listen to the question.'

I know this is a mass message, but I wanted to write it anyway. Dozens of messages, calls and communications went unanswered. I've been struggling alone for five years. I will never forgive your approach to me.

Dr Al Muderis batted away a question about the accuracy of the email, saying he couldn't comment on feelings. Someone else might have written the message, he suggested.

From the bar table, Chrysanthou said softly, 'Considering she doesn't speak English.' Dr Al Muderis repeated this line, word for word. 'Considering she doesn't speak English,' he said.

Our lawyers erupted into a quiet flurry, shooting glances and whispering loudly at each other.

Collins shot his opponent a death stare before returning to the witness. 'Did you just hear Ms Chrysanthou say that at the bar table, Doctor?'

'I can't hear. My hearing is really not ...' Dr Al Muderis said.

'Okay. Well, I heard it, and I would ask my learned friend not to mutter at the bar table words which I then hear coming out of the mouth of the witness.'

'I'm sorry. I didn't hear anything,' Dr Al Muderis said.

After showing more messages chronicling Lisa's despair and hopelessness over many years, Collins asked one final question on the topic: 'Do you accept, Doctor, that the story published by my client on 30 December 2022, about Ms Calan, recounted her experiences in terms that were consistent with the communications I've taken you to, that were sent to you, in 2017, 2018 and 2019?'

'I do not accept.'

I was watching all this from Melbourne. My parents were travelling in Europe but had woken in the middle of the night to tune in to what they were now calling 'The Char Show'. My mother called me in the lunch break and we discussed, almost with disbelief, how damaging the day had been for him. She couldn't believe what she was watching. Neither could I. While I knew in my bones the stories were true, this day in court turned that feeling from a quiet assuredness into an angry fire within me. Each time I saw Lisa's messages flash up on the screen – *Very, very pain. Please help me.* – and then listened to Dr Al Muderis shirk responsibility, I thought to myself: *This is wrong.*

CHAPTER 11

Facts not Feelings

On the second day of Dr Al Muderis's cross-examination, Collins turned his focus to Mark Urquhart. Dr Al Muderis had refused to answer questions about Mark during our television interview, so I had never heard him explain how he treated Mark. I was intrigued to see how he could justify the decision to embark on such drastic surgery for such a vulnerable patient. 'He's one of our heroes,' Dr Al Muderis told the court.

Again, Dr Al Muderis was defensive. He was quick to correct Collins' questions, such as the pronunciation of certain medicines or where Mark lives. He dismissed concerns raised by other specialists as being beyond their qualifications. When Collins asked if Mark was more complex than other patients, Dr Al Muderis pushed back. 'Not necessarily,' he said, 'you cannot scale complexity.'

Dr Al Muderis became increasingly skilled at saying what he *couldn't* do, and what he *wasn't*. Over his ten days giving evidence, Dr Al Muderis was at pains to explain what stood outside of his job description. I'm not a pain specialist. I'm not a lawyer. I'm not a radiologist. I'm not a psychologist. I'm not a physician. I'm not a statistician. It was a continuation of his response to many of Tom's questions in the *60 Minutes* interview: I'm not the true pioneer. I'm not an engineer. I'm not in the business of promotion. And finally: 'Look, I'm not perfect.'

He gave a similar answer when asked if Mark was ambitious, or prone to look at the upside, rather than the downside, of surgery. 'I can't assess personalities, I'm sorry.' Mark wanted to climb Mount Everest, to run competitively at elite levels, to walk his daughter down the aisle. Collins asked Dr Al Muderis whether Mark's expectations exceeded what was possible. After first saying he did not understand the question, the doctor reluctantly accepted it was 'reasonable' Mark's expectations needed to be assessed.

Collins suggested that one key goal of Mark's was to run at the Invictus Games, the sporting competition started by Prince Harry for injured soldiers and veterans. Dr Al Muderis said he couldn't remember discussions about running, and in any event, it was out of the question for bilateral, above-knee amputees with osseointegration. 'I would remember such a thing, definitely ... It's not physically possible.' Dr Al Muderis said it was 'unknown whether he would be able to walk', let alone run, competitively. With that, Collins then displayed a consultation report.

Mark has expressed his ambition is to run in the Invictus Games.

Without flinching, Dr Al Muderis accepted the report was accurate. His memory must be faulty. The consultation report summarised two options. The first was a through-knee amputation, to trial sockets first. *The problem with this is this would make him rather tall, therefore decreasing his centre of gravity and this would reduce his control in running.*

The second option, which ultimately went ahead, was the double above-knee amputation and osseointegration, which would give Mark a *'lower centre of gravity, more control and opportunity, possibly to run with suitably made prosthesis'.*

'You see that?' Collins asked.

'It could give him the opportunity. That's right,' Dr Al Muderis responded, seemingly ignoring his previous answer that it was not physically possible for someone like Mark to run, ever, full stop.

Over the next few questions, Dr Al Muderis hedged his answers, using 'may' and 'possibly' – giving himself leeway to change his answer if another document was unearthed that undermined what he'd said.

'Did you tell Mr Urquhart there is a risk of infection in association with osseointegration which may result in the loss of his femur, but it's a very low risk?'

'I may have.'

'Did you say to Mr Urquhart any infections would clear up with antibiotics?'

'I may have said that infections would possibly clear up with antibiotics.'

When the questions turned to whether Dr Al Muderis warned Mark of the complications he did suffer – the maggots, the horrible smell, the constant pus and weeping, the bone poking out of his leg, the answers were more resolute. 'I don't recall saying that,' Dr Al Muderis said repeatedly.

The video of maggots eating the flesh of Mark's amputated limbs was burnt into the consciousness of anyone who'd watched *60 Minutes* that night, or read the stories online. Dr O'Carrigan said all patients are now warned of this risk. Dr Al Muderis's other colleagues accepted this was a serious, and not uncommon, side effect of osseointegration – one that patients should be warned about. However, in this lawsuit, Dr Al Muderis argued that publishing the maggot video was defamatory. It was, he claimed, a sensational effort to attract viewers, rather than an accurate reflection of a patient experience.

Dr Al Muderis maintained that yes, maggots are distressing, but in reality, they're harmless. He explained that maggots are used in clinical settings, but ultimately conceded that the controlled use in a sterile environment is different to a surprise discovery at home. Osseointegration patients finding maggots in stomas was so common, a 'maggot protocol' was prepared, to instruct patients on how to remove the small white worms from their bodies. This was given only to patients who reported maggots, rather than pre-emptively. Mark didn't receive these instructions until a week after he asked Dr Al Muderis for help. It was one of the many times he felt abandoned in a time of need.

Silence descended over the court as the maggot video was played. Dr Al Muderis remembered receiving it, but couldn't recall the date. He had received a few videos like that, he said, and accepted it was a distressing situation for Mark. Collins asked whether maggots in the stoma required an urgent response. The doctor wobbled.

'It ... Well ... I am sorry, as in the matter required urgent response, or the distress required urgent response?' *Facts not feelings.*

'Well, the distress in the first place?'

'The distress, yes, definitely.'

'You know, don't you, Doctor, that Mr Urquhart didn't see the maggot protocol until he came to see you in your rooms seven days after he had complained?'

'That may be the case.'

'Yes. You accept that's just not acceptable, don't you, as a matter of follow-up?'

Dr Al Muderis said he 'may have spoken to him over the phone' and told him to go to the chemist for the maggot-busting ingredients. 'But I don't recall ... I can't recall.'

With that, Collins snapped. 'Doctor, you've made up that phone call because you accept that it was not acceptable to wait a week before providing guidance to Mr Urquhart?'

'I'm sorry, I'm not making up anything. I'm just saying I may have called him. I don't recall.'

Later, Collins turned to the Febreze incident – the cruel joke made by Dr Kevin Tetsworth about the putrid smell coming from Mark's legs. Mark's face still crumpled when he thought back to that smell, so pervasive he could taste it. 'He complained from foul odour constantly,' Dr Al Muderis said, frustration in his voice.

'Well, he was entitled to make that complaint, wasn't he?' Collins asked.

'Sorry?' Dr Al Muderis responded.

'He was entitled to complain of that?'

'Absolutely,' Dr Al Muderis said.

Collins took Dr Al Muderis through several letters Mark sent him during the cross-examination, detailing his complaints and feelings of abandonment. Dr Al Muderis agreed with parts of what he had written, at first. Mark *had* suffered repeated problems after his surgery. Mark *was* entitled to hold these views. But these rare concessions came to a brutal end as the doctor's impatience flared up again.

Continual recoveries are difficult to get over, but I've never complained to you about anything ever. I suck it up and do my best.

'He didn't suck it up,' Dr Al Muderis said. 'He was very communicative … So he did not just stay away and mind his own business.'

Dr Al Muderis accepted Mark deserved an apology, but with tight guardrails. He was sorry for his colleague's comment, but nothing further. The exposed bone, the foul odour, the maggots – did not warrant an apology. These are complications from surgery. 'It's not anyone's fault,' Dr Al Muderis said.

In another email, Mark referred to his legs as a 'disgrace'. He had sent videos and photos to his doctor of the cauliflower-like flesh gathered around his implants, and different coloured bodily fluids that poured out. When asked whether Mark considered his legs a disgrace, Dr Al Muderis said Mark had never used that word before. 'That was the first time to come to my knowledge from this particular email.'

It was clear the doctor was looking for a loophole to escape reality. He denied the specific word 'disgrace' to dodge the substance of the question. Collins wrestled to pin him down.

'Okay,' Collins said, voice rising now. Back to basics.

'He had repeated hyper-granulation?'

'Yes, he did.'

'Repeatedly reported a foul odour emerging from the stoma?'

'On a few occasions, yes.'

'Repeatedly about maggots?'

'No, that's not true ... It was twice.'

'Repeatedly complained about the exposed bone?'

'On a few occasions.'

'Repeatedly complained about intensity of pain?'

'Not to my recollection, no.'

As Collins went through each of the problems set out in his letter, Dr Al Muderis persisted in nit-picking the question. He downplayed Mark's problems, or said they weren't true. Collins wanted him to explain his position. Is Mark lying when he said he went through 'nine months of hell'?

'Well I had several correspondence with Mr Urquhart and he was performing well before that particular email.'

My legs continually bleed and are hypersensitive.

'You knew that to be true?'

'No.'

'Do you reject that?'

'Well, I don't recall he has mentioned hypersensitivity before.'

'What about continual bleeding?'

'That's, again, I don't recall him complaining about bleeding.'

The doctor would not accept a single sentence. 'I don't know if that's true,' he said. 'I'm not sure.'

In the same letter, Mark told his doctor how he sat on the toilet and blood spurted all over the floor one day.

'That would be a matter of concern to you?' Collins asked.

Dr Al Muderis ignored the question. Instead, he said he was concerned that Mark was considering seeing new doctors.

I just want to be comfortable, that's all.

'That's not an unrealistic expectation, is it, in a patient of yours?'

'Well I don't know how to qualify that, because the whole purpose of the surgery was to give him mobility.'

More messages. This time after Mark left the Facebook support group. *I leave it in absolute disbelief. I have to do this, but you have left me no choice. Not just disbelief, but upset. You haven't fixed the exposed femur.*

'That was all true?' Collins asked.

'No, that's not true.'

Collins pressed again. Mark was wrong about the piece of bone coming from his own legs?

'Well, I don't recall, but my understanding was the exposed bone was resolved.'

You brush it off like it's nothing.

'That's true, isn't it?' Collins asked.

'I didn't brush it off as nothing. But an exposed bone with osseointegration is not a serious problem. It's not uncommon to have it.'

Collins tried to encourage the doctor to see the situation from the patient's perspective – this was a serious problem for Mark, one that he had repeatedly raised.

'Well, from a medical perspective, it was not a serious problem.'

'You understood it was bothering him, didn't you?'

'Well, he is mentioning it.'

Collins continued reading the message: *I had such high hopes but I rolled away with a sad heart and a very painful pair of stumps.*

'You understood he considered the surgery to be a failure?'

Dr Al Muderis disagreed. He didn't understand what 'pair of stumps' meant, he said. 'It doesn't make sense to me.'

Collins could barely contain his disbelief. 'Is that a serious answer, Doctor? You're an osseointegration surgeon.' Dr Al Muderis repeated the same answer.

One last note, I will not be singing your praises from the rooftops anymore. I honestly do not think I could, nor will I recommend you, which saddens me.

Collins tried again. 'You accept at face value that he considers his surgery to have been a failure?'

'I don't accept that. Mr Urquhart was doing very well with walking. He was very happy with walking.'

'Until he wasn't, Doctor,' Collins said.

The room was now heavy with the dawning realisation that this was a man who cannot handle, or is in abject denial, about reality. 'Until he ceased his relationship with you because of the repeated problems that you've conceded he experienced?'

Dr Al Muderis repeated that Mark walked. The maggots were unrelated. 'Doctor, is your evidence to her Honour that Mr Urquhart achieved the goals he sought out?'

'With walking, yes.'

Collins continued reading the letter. Dr Al Muderis denied each line was true.

I just feel totally ignored by you. I've repeatedly asked for the right stoma and exposed bone to be attended to, simply because of the wretched smell I smell all day, every day. It's my own dying flesh I'm smelling, and it was the dead flesh the maggots were munching on.

'You don't consider that you owe him an apology?'

'No.'

'The article and broadcasts you sue my clients over in this proceeding include parts in which Mr Urquhart tells his story?'

'Well, they were false allegations.'

'You accept, don't you Doctor, that that's nonsense and that Channel Nine reported faithfully what Mr Urquhart told Channel Nine?'

Chrysanthou objected, bringing the line of questioning to an end. But the point had been made. The doctor was denying the bleeding obvious.

* * *

The days were dense. Collins took Dr Al Muderis through patient after patient, asking him to respond to each claim in painstaking detail. When the focus turned to Carol Todd, I sat forward. This was another patient whose treatment I was particularly keen to hear Dr Al Muderis explain. In many ways, Carol's experience as an amputee before osseointegration most closely resembled my father's. Both had been independent for many decades using sockets. Neither were suitable for osseointegration, yet only my father escaped.

Dr Al Muderis confirmed he knew Carol's husband suffered from Parkinson's disease and the main reason she wanted the surgery was to care for him. He reluctantly accepted that Carol experienced pain and discharge from her legs, but when asked about infection, Dr Al Muderis became guarded. He dodged and weaved, avoiding question after question. Collins took the doctor through records that showed Carol's hospitalisations, antibiotics hooked into her neck, tests that showed worsening infection. It was a drawn-out struggle, until finally Dr Al Muderis was boxed in and agreed that in 2014, Carol showed signs of sepsis.

The concessions did not last long. After being shown messages from Carol with photos of her red and pus-filled stump, to which he responded, *Please call me back. There is an infection.* Dr Al Muderis insisted this was not necessarily a diagnosis. Only when Collins presented evidence that Dr Al Muderis prescribed antibiotics did he accept the presence of infection. In what had become a pattern, the doctor downplayed Carol's pain. When asked if she reported 'significant pain', all he could say back was, 'She had pain.' When shown messages from a concerned prosthetist, Dr Al Muderis snapped: 'He's not a doctor.'

Collins then showed Carol's letter, which explained why she hadn't been calling. *I find our conversations unsatisfactory,* she wrote. *The truth is I don't feel you are taking my problems seriously.* Dr Al Muderis denied this meant Carol wasn't getting adequate responses from him. Collins continued reading.

The surgery was to change my life. Well, it sure has. I now have no life at all.

'You accept, don't you, that that's her expression of her perception of the outcome of the surgery performed on her?'

'I accept that this is what it's stating. I don't know about her perception.'

At that point, Collins brought it all together, returning to the evidence of Lisa Calan and Mark Urquhart.

'I showed you messages from other patients of yours that also expressed their disappointment at being your patient. Do you recollect receiving messages from Ms Calan saying how disappointed she was? You reject her complaints, don't you? Because you say that you delivered what you promised to her? And she has got, in your mind, no legitimate basis to have any grievance with you?'

Dr Al Muderis squirmed, flailed and thrashed as he failed to answer squarely. But the line of questioning alone was powerful. Collins was reminding the court: this was not one sour grape. These were rolling complaints sent directly to the doctor from many, unconnected patients, years before I started making inquiries. His patients had complained to him, in writing, of pain, neglect, sadness over long periods with no solutions. These complaints had nothing to do with me, or the publications, or the investigation. This was about the people he had failed.

'And Mr Urquhart? We went through messages that he sent you when he terminated his relationship with you on the basis that his life was worse than it had been before the surgery? He has no proper basis for being dissatisfied? And Ms Todd, has she got any legitimate basis for being upset with you?'

Dr Al Muderis repeated that Lisa, Mark and Carol had suffered complications, but their operations were successful. On any objective measure, Dr Al Muderis said, Carol was doing well.

'You told her Honour that you considered the surgery to have been a success?'

'To my understanding, she had a successful osseointegration surgery … The patient underwent a procedure that was performed by inserting the implant in her leg, and she managed to walk with that, to my knowledge, to this day. So from the functional point of view, which is what this surgery is designed to provide, that was successful.'

It was a remarkable answer. Even accepting his limited notion of success being defined by mobility alone, for Carol, it had failed. She was in a wheelchair, unable to walk. He had broken her bones when he first performed the surgery and she'd had nothing but trouble since. He had told her she was at a low risk of infection, but she had been hospitalised more times than she could remember, treated aggressively to avoid sepsis. That he still maintained this was a successful surgery was unbelievable. *Unethical at best, dangerous at worst.*

* * *

I watched the entirety of Dr Al Muderis's cross-examination that stretched past two weeks, either sitting in the courtroom or tuned in to the YouTube stream. Shocking is the only word that encapsulates what transpired. There were a series of mind-bending moments when logic and reason seemed to completely collapse. Like when Dr Al Muderis claimed he did not understand the definition or meaning of the word 'clinic', despite using the word repeatedly to describe his meetings with patients in US hotel rooms. And his response to questions about reports he'd written stating that osseointegration was 'acceptable worldwide' when in fact it was still illegal in the US.

'America is not the world,' Dr Al Muderis retorted. 'The world is much bigger than America and it has been acceptable in many parts of the world.'

It was an incredible answer. To argue that the term 'worldwide' can exclude the largest economy in the world, the most powerful democracy in the world, the country with the largest military, was fanciful. It was another small reminder of the surgeon's willingness to lie, his failure to make concessions, eroding his credibility one papercut at a time.

I had a similar reaction when a video was played of Dr Al Muderis changing a piece of metal protruding from an amputee's stump in a US hotel room, with bare hands and tools strewn across the bed. As the video played, one of the courtroom workers held her hand to her face. Another had his mouth wide open. The judge watched intensely. Dr Al Muderis batted away questions. He denied ever treating patients in America. *Nothing to see here.*

Chrysanthou tried desperately to kill lines of questioning, strike out evidence, protect her client. One particularly telling exchange came when Collins was trying to test whether Dr Al Muderis had an animus toward another surgeon, Phil Huang, after a judge sided with Dr Huang over Dr Al Muderis in deciding that Kerry Ford was not suitable for osseointegration. Dr Al Muderis had made a habit of belittling Dr Huang's qualifications to patients who sought his advice, as did his wife. But when Collins suggested Dr Al Muderis might be embittered by losing to Huang in the Ford case, Chrysanthou jumped to her feet.

'Your Honour, that is absurd,' she declared.

'Everything can't be absurd,' the judge replied.

'Well, it is, your Honour.'

'Well, can I just pause there. It doesn't help that every submission is "absurd". I would prefer substance.'

It seemed clear that the judge was not being swayed by Chrysanthou's performative bravado. The wild-haired barrister exuded 'main character energy' and had developed a reputation for fighting every single point like her life depended on it. Her dramatic courtroom appearances made for entertaining viewing, but the judge wanted the opposite. She reminded Chrysanthou over and over of the need for clarity, precision and facts.

Collins' job was to give Dr Al Muderis the opportunity to respond to every single allegation against him. This covered patient complaints, but also allegations of financial conflicts of interest, false advertising, sexual relations with staff, fudging of medical research, international trips built on false promises, and whether he properly enabled patients to give informed consent, fulfilled his duty of care and duty to warn.

He was asked about allegations he bullied staff. He denied telling Shona 'any monkey off the street would know that' when she asked a question about infection. He denied saying, 'I'm sick of these stupid questions' after Shona refused to write a consultation report for a patient she hadn't seen (we had the email). He described his relationship with Shona as a 'very short encounter' that started before she worked for him. He denied telling Shona 'not even your mother wanted you' or calling her 'dumb-dumb'. He denied frequently humiliating Shona in front of patients, reducing staff to tears, or screaming at them, and denied some nurses refused to work with him. These allegations were made by several, unconnected eye-witnesses. Each denial became harder to believe.

Then, he was asked about a food-fight he had with Belinda Bosley on an Emirates flight. This time there was no denial. 'We used to banter, we used to have heated discussions. She used to shout at me. I shout at her back. It's not dissimilar to what happens on the side of the bar table. We are passionate about what we do … We have heated discussions. That's not belittling.'

There were some moments where Dr Al Muderis did have a firmer grasp on medical details, but his pig-headedness on accepting basic points cast a cloud over everything he said.

As the days rolled by, and the evidence stacked up, I became more and more perplexed as to why he had brought this case in the first place. Surely, he must realise everyone else couldn't be lying. In his pursuit of protecting his reputation, he was willing the court to make findings that could shatter the illusion of the devoted miracle doctor, the carefully crafted myth, under the full glare of the nation's media. Why would he put himself in this position?

The case put a spotlight on complaints from new patients who had never told their story publicly. None had complained to a regulator or sued for medical negligence, but they all knew there was something not quite right with their treatment. Fay Young, an 80-year-old woman, had been given a hip replacement by Dr Al Muderis. The procedure left her with a cracked pelvis and chronic pain, confined to a wheelchair at home. Fay's last message to Dr Al Muderis was left with his receptionist, saying she no longer trusted him and was upset with 'what he has done to me'.

Megan McIntyre, a below-knee amputee from South Australia, came forward after reading the stories to share how she too felt pressured by Dr Al Muderis into signing up for the expensive surgery. He had no recollection of her, he said, under cross-examination.

Anna Rochford, who lost her leg from an aggressive bone cancer and used her superannuation to pay for nerve surgery that went so horribly wrong she was diagnosed with PTSD. She described the unforeseen pain she endured after the surgery as like lightning rods striking her legs – agony that she never fully recovered from. None of these details had ever been made public before.

One of the most shocking cases to be propelled into the public domain was that of Patient X. This patient was first mentioned to me by a confidential source during the depths of my investigation. Dr Al Muderis's actions had haunted this particular surgeon for years, and he had never spoken to a journalist before, but was compelled to speak up.

Patient X suffered from anorexia nervosa and lost both her legs due to complications from the disease. A symptom of her anorexia was compulsive exercise, particularly running, and non-compliance with medical guidance. When both of her legs were amputated, she became worried she would have to stop running. Eventually, she ended up in the care of Dr Al Muderis, who agreed to perform osseointegration on both of her legs. More than one health professional objected. They didn't think the patient was healthy enough for such an invasive procedure, and worried she wouldn't comply with the arduous post-operative rehabilitation. The confidential source said the treatment was particularly worrying because the patient's primary aim was to 'continue her pathological addiction to exercise'. He thought this was a gross dereliction of a surgeon's duty to care for the whole patient.

My source refused to provide me with the woman's name or details due to patient confidentiality, but I couldn't let it go. I dug and dug and dug through online and real-world channels, and eventually ended up on the phone with Patient X. She said she was thrilled with the osseointegration and wouldn't hear a bad word about Dr Al Muderis. This was another patient who caused me to reflect on the duty of the surgeon to say no. Documents later subpoenaed as part of our trial would reveal that Patient X did have doubts just before she went into the operating theatre, recorded in an email.

'Please don't think I'm being ungrateful, as I understand how valuable Munjed's time is. But I did honestly feel that the decision to do osseointegration on both legs at the same time was rushed.'

Regardless, the surgery went ahead. The first story we published only made a single-line reference to Patient X's case, but now, the court was hashing out all the painful facts in excruciating detail. Through medical records presented in court, I learned that Patient X's anorexia began when she was 15 years old. By the time she saw Dr Al Muderis, she was 34, and records stated she had 'primary amenorrhea'. I had to google the term. It meant she had never menstruated. My heart sank, but that was only the beginning. She had osteoporosis and arthritis, and had suffered multiple fractures in various limbs. She had a non-healing ulcer on her right foot, and had suffered infections so severe she became septic. Her face was scarred from the impacts of the infection.

She was malnourished, depressed and experienced feelings of worthlessness and guilty rumination. She was regularly hit by waves of despair. Her condition was so severe that at some point she had been placed under a community treatment order. When she first met Dr Al Muderis, she needed a wheelchair. The psychology report provided to Dr Al Muderis recorded that her BMI was extremely low, and that she continued to exercise a minimum of three hours per day. Dr Al Muderis said he couldn't understand this, given she was in a wheelchair. Growing up, I knew teenage girls who suffered anorexia. They can exercise in any circumstances. They find a way. To me, that Dr Al Muderis didn't know this, or didn't bother to find out, was an indictment.

Under questioning, Dr Al Muderis could not accept that he was embarking on a surgical course that no other doctor was prepared to take. 'Her problem was treatable,' Dr Al Muderis said. 'She didn't have a seriously complex problem ... I was prepared to help her regain mobility.'

The doctor couldn't bring himself to acknowledge that Patient X was high-risk, and denied she was rushed into surgery – despite the email written by Patient X using these exact words. After the operation, records showed that her legs were red, warm to touch and smelt. She took the prosthetic foot home, breaking rules designed to stop her exercising. 'I'm sorry,' Dr Al Muderis said. 'It's her foot. She decided to take it home. It's her choice.'

That he had been warned about Patient X's non-compliance was seemingly irrelevant. 'Patients, ultimately, are in charge of their own decision, Dr Collins,' he said. 'We're not here to dictate to patients what to do.'

Finally, he returned to his narrow definition of success. 'This patient, when she came to me, she was wheelchair-bound. She was completely crippled. She is now fully active and engaged in her life. That is factual. That's what happened.'

On the second-last full day of questioning, Collins turned his attention to my father. The hand-drawn graph was beamed onto the screen. Collins asked Dr Al Muderis if he had prepared this during the consultation.

'I didn't prepare that, I just drew it at the back of the envelope. I wasn't preparing it.'

'Something you drew in Mr Grieve's presence in order to explain to him the information you're providing to him?'

'Correct.'

Slowly, but surely, Dr Al Muderis agreed that the parting lines depicted various outcomes for my father's mobility. One line jolting upward reflected his ability to return almost to his pre-accident level of mobility if he had osseointegration.

'And then you had identified two other scenarios and one was a very quick drop off in mobility down to nothing. In other words, being wheelchair-bound?'

'Correct,' Dr Al Muderis said.

I breathed a short sigh of relief, before returning to confusion. What were we arguing about then? How could Dr Al Muderis in one moment say my father and I were telling hideous lies, and the next accept what I had written was true?

After more than two weeks of what often felt like a relentless grind, the final question arrived. Collins asked again whether Dr Al Muderis had called his nurses 'dumb-dumb'.

'I don't recall.'

'You don't recall. There are no further questions, your Honour.'

It was then Chrysanthou's turn for re-examination. What was initially estimated to take the morning ended up stretching into the afternoon. Chrysanthou asked the doctor how he felt about the fact that we had maintained Mark Urquhart had been abandoned, in the face of one email where he heaped praise on the doctor. There was legal argy-bargy over whether the email had been cherrypicked, given Mark's position later changed, and whether Chrysanthou needed to read out the contents in its entirety. The judge grew impatient. But eventually, Chrysanthou got the answer she wanted.

'It saddens me to see that one of our national heroes would end up in a wheelchair,' Dr Al Muderis said.

'So I'm very disappointed, that the way, sadly, an amateur journalist [has] used vulnerable patients in this way,' the doctor stated.

'No further questions, your Honour.'

At 3.27 pm on 6 October, after spending over ten court days in cross-examination – a new record for Collins – Dr Al Muderis left the witness box for the last time.

CHAPTER 12

Kindred Spirits

Over the next week, the court heard the remainder of Dr Al Muderis's witnesses. These were the people he put forward to support his reputation and claim his medical practice was squeaky clean. Among these were the 'independent' experts that Dr Al Muderis had asked to analyse the medical records of patients who had complained.

As previously explained, the independence of these witnesses is critical. My sister once told me that in preparation for a trial, she had to strike out an expert witness after they discovered the person had, many years ago, had a fleeting personal connection with one of the key parties. My sister was certain this affiliation would have no bearing on the person's expert conclusions but, as she explained, it's all about perception. Good law firms will spend significant time scouring through an expert's past in search of any scrap of information that might be used to undermine their independence. They will grill experts to uproot any potential biases that might come out under cross-examination – anything that could erode the judge's trust in their opinion. The reliability and strength of this expert evidence can make or break a case.

These age-old norms and practices seemed to have flown out the window in this case. Expert after expert admitted to having joint shareholdings or close personal relationships with Dr Al Muderis that hadn't been disclosed. The junior barrister from our side, Declan Roche, cross-examined some of these witnesses.

First up was Dr Razvan Stoita, a middle-aged man with big eyebrows. The trial had started to feel like a slog, but Roche's new style of questioning had everyone back on the edges of their seats. With a sharp jaw, bright blue eyes and light stubble, Roche wasted no time in establishing that both Dr Stoita and Dr Al Muderis were colleagues, directors and shareholders of the Limb Reconstruction Centre.

'That's correct,' Dr Stoita said. 'We're partners in that.'

'So you have a direct financial interest in the success of the Limb Reconstruction Centre, don't you?'

'Yes, I do.'

'And you're good friends with Dr Al Muderis?'

'I think I am. We are friends, yes.'

'And you regard yourself as a supporter of his?'

'I am, yes. I am a colleague and supporter, yes.'

Dr Stoita had provided six expert reports in the proceedings. He accepted that he had already formed a view that Dr Al Muderis was a good surgeon before writing these reports. He wouldn't go as far as saying he was an advocate for Dr Al Muderis, but admitted that he offered to support him right after the *60 Minutes* program was broadcast. Within seconds, the exact text message was beamed onto the screen.

You have got scores of patients publicly showing their support and you've got all of us ready to go into bat for you. Just let us know.

Dr Stoita admitted he had followed my reporting since the story broke. About a month after the investigation was first published, *The Age*'s newsletter team had asked me to write a first-person piece about how the story came about. Up until that point, I had kept my father's relationship with Dr Al Muderis close to my chest. But, by then, Al Muderis's lawyers had already sent a letter, cryptically accusing me of having a conflict of interest through my father, so I felt it was only a matter of time before it became public.

Before I started to write the piece, I called my father to ask how he felt about me telling his story. He encouraged me to write the truth without a moment's hesitation. My mother was somewhat more cautious, and we spoke about it at length. I said the decision was entirely theirs. I didn't want to involve them if they weren't one hundred per cent on board. She agreed and I wrote the story titled 'Behind the scenes: Exposing the downside of a celebrity surgeon's practice'.

'There are plenty of places that news stories come from. A tip-off, a source, a leak. But sometimes, a story simply comes from conversations with people you know. In this case, the investigation into surgeon Munjed Al Muderis came from a conversation with my father,' I wrote.

The court was shown a text message Dr Stoita sent to Dr Al Muderis about this article: *You should sue her personally for defamation. Lying through her teeth.*

Then came Dr Al Muderis's response: *We need to be solid on this.*

'You've come here because you want to support Dr Al Muderis as your colleague, friend and business partner, don't you?' Roche asked.

'No, I've come here because I've been asked to provide an expert report and my duty here is to the court and to the patients,' Dr Stoita said.

While swatting suggestions he was not impartial, Dr Stoita said the Limb Reconstruction Centre wasn't the only financial link they shared – they were also both shareholders in the new short-stay hospital owned by Medibank and Macquarie University Hospital and jointly owned medical equipment. He accepted these points should have been disclosed in his reports, but said he simply hadn't been asked to do so.

'I have nothing to hide,' he said.

Dr Stoita said he hadn't specifically discussed evidence with Dr Al Muderis during the trial, but admitted to speaking with him often, to check in, to see how he was coping.

'You've obviously done more than that,' Roche said. 'You encouraged Dr Al Muderis to bring these proceedings. You expressed the view that the journalist was lying through her teeth. So you've obviously done more than offer general expressions of support? I'm asking you what other discussions you've had with Dr Al Muderis about this case?'

Dr Stoita said it was difficult to pinpoint, as they speak all the time. 'This morning, I called him and asked, "Should I wear a tie at court today?" because I normally don't wear a tie at work. So then yes, he said he was up all night trying to prepare his case.'

I was watching this part remotely, which was fortunate because at this point, my poker face was in pieces. I couldn't believe what I was hearing and my mouth was wide open. How could a claim of independence be maintained when they were literally discussing what to wear to court that day? Dr Al Muderis's message, *We need to be solid on this*, did not have the air of someone with nothing to hide.

Roche continued to press Dr Stoita for details of their conversations in recent weeks. When Dr Stoita said he couldn't quite recall, Roche asked for all text messages between the pair since the beginning of the trial to be handed over. Chrysanthou said they couldn't provide the text messages at this very moment. What Roche did next was utterly astounding.

'Well, he can,' Roche said, pointing to Dr Stoita. 'He has got his phone on him.'

'Of course,' Stoita said as he dutifully reached into his pocket. Roche then physically purloined Stoita's mobile phone from him. I didn't even know that was possible. I was watching on, in shock, at this change of pace and tone. Roche was taking no prisoners. With Dr Stoita's phone in his hand, Roche asked how they mostly communicated – WhatsApp, text, regular phone calls to and from work. They had discussed the case, Dr Stoita confirmed, and some of the patients involved in the trial. The text messages on Dr Stoita's phone didn't resurface again, but the point had been made. Any suggestion that Dr Stoita could possibly be considered independent was eviscerated.

Dr Kevin Tetsworth was another so-called independent expert to take the stand. This was the man who told Mark Urquhart to spray Febreze on his legs to conceal the putrid smell. He'd treated a number of patients I'd spoken to. He was also the surgeon who insisted that Kerry Ford's remaining medical options were osseointegration or euthanasia, when voluntary assisted dying wasn't even something the patient had considered. Straight out of the blocks, Dr Tetsworth admitted he was a co-director with Dr Al Muderis of at least two companies, and joint shareholder in a third.

'You don't disclose those directorships anywhere, do you?' Collins asked, back in control of the cross-examination.

'Not specifically,' Dr Tetsworth said, before insisting it was 'common knowledge'. 'I think that the courts would be aware of the fact that we have a relationship that goes on for many years.'

'I didn't ask you that,' Collins shot back. 'I asked, did you disclose it in your affidavits or expert reports?'

'Not specifically,' Dr Tetsworth repeated.

'Not at all, Doctor,' Collins snapped. He was frustrated.

Dr Tetsworth tried to insist that these business dealings were of 'such limited consequence and importance to the proceedings' that they didn't need to be disclosed. Problem was, that wasn't his decision to make, and the answer only made him look more arrogant.

'You're a longstanding friend of Dr Al Muderis?'

'Yes.'

'He considers you to be a mentor to him?'

'Well, that's news to me but pleased to hear that.'

Collins beamed text messages onto the screen.

You are my mentor, Kevin. You may not feel that but you are.

Dr Tetsworth had responded: *Kindred spirits, that's how I see it. You've been a great mentor for me as well.*

More messages showed Dr Tetsworth had offered to 'testify in support' of Dr Al Muderis if he ended up in court. He accepted this meant he was supportive, 'as anyone would be of a friend'.

Collins said this meant Dr Tetsworth was not independent. He did not agree. More text messages were beamed onto the court screen, this time from Dr Al Muderis: *I will need your support. Thank you.*

Dr Tetsworth replied: *Always got your back. Just let me know. I'm sure you would do the same for me.*

'You were conveying you will do whatever it takes?' Collins said.

'Sure. I'm there to support him if he needs a shoulder to cry on or a hug or just to go out and share a drink or spend some time and take his mind off things.'

Next, Collins pointed out the doctor's use of 'dark humour' in a message where Dr Tetsworth said he hoped Brennan Smith didn't bring a knife to their consultation. Dr Tetsworth said this was a legitimate concern, not a joke 'in poor taste'. Later, Collins asked him about the now-notorious Febreze comment. 'He stormed out of the room, didn't he?' Collins asked.

'It's hard for him to storm out of the room,' Dr Tetsworth said, his lip curling slightly. 'He's a, you know, double amputee who was, at the time, struggling to mobilise well.'

My stomach turned. The judge's face was deadpan, but as the words exited his mouth, her head jolted away from the witness.

'Is that a joke, Doctor?' Collins said. He denied it.

At the end of the day, JP called. He was giddy, but still guarded. There was a growing sense of optimism within our camp, but JP desperately tried to rein it in. There is nothing worse than complacency, and that was not the type of ship he was sailing. 'You want every win,' he said. 'Nothing is taken for granted.'

Still, JP allowed himself to indulge in some glee. He was amazed by the evidence from both Dr Stoita and Dr Tetsworth. 'They're properly compromised,' he said. 'They're not independent. Another all-time great day in court. To torpedo his witnesses like that is just amazing.'

* * *

Like a monk observing a strict regime, on Day 23 of the trial, I woke up and returned to Bondi Beach for a swim and run before getting ready for another day in court. I took an Uber into the city that day, and as the car wound through Woolloomooloo and up toward Macquarie Street, the driver said: 'Going to court? Big day? The Federal Court isn't for lost wallets.' I smiled and tried to change the subject. 'Yes. But it's a beautiful day. 30 degrees, I hear.' He sidestepped my weather chat. 'Well, it'll be much better for you when it's over. When the hammer goes, "Bang".' He wasn't wrong.

This day, however, marked a turning point in the case. It was time for the first of our witnesses to be called – Dr Dimitri Papadimitriou, or Dr Papa, as he is known by his patients. Dr Papadimitriou was the surgeon who operated on Leah Mooney's crooked leg, and they had stayed in touch since. He gave evidence in her medical negligence case against Dr Al Muderis, and continued to treat her as a patient.

I had tried several times to reach Dr Papadimitriou when reporting the story about Leah, but he never returned my calls. He was the type of surgeon who just wanted to get on with his job – which did not include talking to journalists.

When Dr Papadimitriou got in the box, the energy in the courtroom shifted. His demeanour was light, friendly, approachable, confident, transparent. He was a busy orthopaedic surgeon who specialised in traumatic injuries, and had experience working in some of New South Wales' busiest hospitals. He was one of the few surgeons who was prepared to speak publicly about his concerns regarding Dr Al Muderis.

The questions began with the first time he met Leah Mooney. Dr Papadimitriou recalled the evening when he was called to the hospital by an infectious disease specialist and found a very sick woman. The pus from the wounds on her leg had crusted over and her knee was virtually frozen stiff. Leah told him about the two operations Dr Al Muderis had performed and his reluctance to diagnose the infection. Dr Papadimitriou ordered scans, which showed the joint was destroyed. 'It was completely eroded,' he said. 'There was a broken drill bit in the tibia, as well.'

The tests confirmed what was obvious: Leah had osteomyelitis, septic arthritis in her knee, and major erosions of the bone in her femur, kneecap, patella and tibia. 'Any prospect of joint salvage, we had missed the boat for,' Dr Papadimitriou said. 'The joint was already destroyed.'

Dr Papadimitriou moved quickly to prevent Leah's predicament from getting any worse. He prescribed antibiotics and performed another operation on her leg, which confirmed the worst of his suspicions. The infection was 'very extensive' and he said it was rare to see 'septic arthritis' reach that stage, because normally it would have been treated much earlier. He explained that Dr Al Muderis performed the surgery in the 'exact opposite' way to how it should have been done, noting that it was 'striking' that Al Muderis had blamed the plate manufacturer.

'The plate itself was fine. It was the application of the plate that was the problem,' he said. 'The bone had been put in with the screws holding it crooked, basically.'

Then came the killer question: 'Doctor, in the circles in which you move, what is Dr Al Muderis's reputation as a surgeon?' Collins asked.

Chrysanthou rocketed to her feet. 'I object! There is no plea of bad reputation. It's not in the outline.'

Chrysanthou was spitting out legal arguments as quickly as she could. It didn't help. The judge allowed the question, on the basis they could argue about admissibility later. Collins carefully repeated the question.

'Amongst my colleagues, the orthopaedic surgeons, he has a poor reputation. He is considered to lack judgment, empathy, and on several occasions, felt to have made poor decisions. It's felt that, through his conduct, many people believe it's an unethical or unprofessional conduct …'

I could hear soft snorts of laughter from the back of the courtroom. Chrysanthou's junior started whispering loudly to her. She shot up again. 'Your Honour, I object. He's now going into conduct … And going beyond reputation.'

This time, the judge agreed and Collins changed topics. But for the first time, the court had an insight into the types of conversations I had been having with dozens of surgeons all around the country. Dr Al Muderis did not have a good reputation. In fact, his bad behaviour was an open secret. 'Everybody had a story about him,' as one surgeon had told me. And Dr Papadimitriou was a surgeon I'd never even spoken to. *Unethical at best, dangerous at worst.*

During cross-examination, Chrysanthou suggested patients aren't the 'best historians' and that Dr Papadimitriou should have asked Dr Al Muderis for information about Leah's care, rather than relying on what she told him. This line of questioning did not serve her client well. Dr Papadimitriou retorted that whether he asks treating surgeons for advice depends on whether it would 'enhance or detract' from his knowledge. This seemed to enrage Chrysanthou.

'What do you mean detract? How can more information detract from your knowledge?'

Again, the answers only dug Dr Al Muderis's reputation into a darker, deeper pit. Dr Papadimitriou said it was obvious that when a patient has been told a certain story 'in attempt to dismiss her concerns' or 'cover up a complication, you don't expect to ring that person and then get the truth from them'.

'You expect them to be evasive. You expect them to put you on the wrong track,' he said.

Chrysanthou rebutted that he had only just met Leah Mooney. 'Are you saying seriously that you took her word as so truthful that you formed the view that speaking to my client to get more information would detract from the care you had given?'

Dr Papadimitriou said he had already formed a view on 'your client', so was 'factoring that in'.

'Right,' Chrysanthou said. 'So you were factoring in your personal bias against my client and you let it interfere with the care you gave to this patient?'

'Not personal bias,' Dr Papadimitriou replied. 'You have an understanding of patients that you've seen before, circumstances they've found themselves in, things you've seen and heard about people, and that's exactly how you form a character judgment.'

Dr Papadimitriou's evidence was damning. He clearly explained the mistakes Dr Al Muderis had made, and their devastating impact on Leah. His dispassionate assessment of Dr Al Muderis as a liar who lacks judgment went to the heart of the case.

The day finished late, adjourning at 4.48 pm. Less than 20 minutes later, *Sydney Morning Herald* court reporter Michaela Whitbourn's story for the day was published. 'Al Muderis has "poor reputation" among surgeons, court told,' was the headline, describing an 'explosive day of evidence'.

The article sent Dr Al Muderis's team into a frenzy. Chrysanthou was with Dr Al Muderis when he read it and said he was 'nearly as upset' as when the first stories came out. His lawyers sent an email to the newspaper to complain.

The next day, Leah and Tim Mooney were scheduled to give evidence – the first patients.

As I walked toward the courtroom, I saw them in the corridor and asked how they were feeling. Tim said he'd been up since 2 am. We entered separately. They took a seat in the back row. I glanced back and saw Leah's leg jolting to one side, locked stiff, as she clasped her walking sticks.

Her mouth was upturned and she looked around anxiously. I smiled at her, and she smiled back. My hands were shaking as we waited for the judge to arrive. It was an important day. I felt nervous, but also angry. Angry that Dr Al Muderis wanted to subject this woman to what would no doubt be aggressive questioning. Leah's case against Dr Al Muderis had already been settled, with a court finding in her favour. He didn't need to relitigate it here again, all these years later.

The court assistant declared the hearing in session, and everyone stood as the judge entered, her diminutive frame swallowed by the heavy judicial robes.

Chrysanthou launched into damage control as everyone took their seats. Not wanting to repeat the poison words from the day before, she directed the judge to the transcript line numbers where Dr Papadimitriou had eviscerated her client's reputation. She reminded the judge about the agreement to allow the question and argue about admissibility later. Chrysanthou explained that she was under the impression this meant his answer was 'off the record', whatever that meant. She was now making a formal application to 'have the evidence struck from the record' and said she would use the ordeal to calculate damages later.

The judge agreed, but asked why this was important now.

'Yes, and I wish to show your Honour why it's urgent now. Could I tender articles published shortly after we returned from court?'

Chrysanthou produced printed copies of the online article, which was circulating across Melbourne and Sydney.

Chrysanthou said this was not the first time she'd been concerned about the media's reporting of the trial. The judge looked perplexed, and slightly irritated, before Collins stood up. He said there was no restriction on the publication of evidence given in open court. Chrysanthou responded with a lengthy explanation of all the people who said her client had a good reputation, interspersed with legal arguments and quotes from affidavits. She was pounding the room with evidence of Dr Al Muderis's glistening reputation, and crying foul of the highest order. All this time, Leah was fidgeting in her seat, looking worried. I debated whether to text one of the lawyers and ask them to take Leah and Tim outside, but thought between Tim's hearing and Leah's mobility issues, it might be more trouble than it was worth. I stayed silent – a decision I would later regret. The sideshow finished with the judge slapping a temporary non-publication order over Dr Papadimitriou's assessment of Dr Al Muderis's reputation.

Then, the court's attention turned to Leah. Before she could get in the box, junior barrister Nick Olson had some objections about her affidavit. The first was important. It opened a window into Dr Al Muderis's approach to infection. Leah had said her leg was red, weeping fluid and very painful, and that she was diagnosed with an infection and given 12 days of antibiotics. Olson tried to argue that this was hearsay – she didn't actually know she had an infection, she was just told that by some doctor.

'What about the fact she took drugs for 12 days?' the judge asked. 'She obviously knows because she took drugs.'

Olson continued with technical legal arguments, and the judge ultimately ruled that the evidence would be limited to Leah's state of mind. Why was Dr Al Muderis so reluctant to accept the presence of infection? It didn't make sense.

At last, Leah was called to the stand. She walked up to the witness box, slowly limping. She took the affirmation, sat down and then sipped some water, using both hands to cradle the glass. She looked worried. The court assistants smiled at her as she settled into her seat.

Chrysanthou began with a series of rapid-fire questions establishing the sequence of events: the skiing accident in Canada, the return to Australia, the X-rays revealing she had a very serious fracture that required urgent surgery.

'And he told you that your leg might never fully repair?'

'I don't recall that,' Leah said.

Leah was asked about conversations from more than 13 years ago, when she had just been rushed back from Canada on heavy painkillers for emergency surgery. Leah said her memory was hazy, she couldn't remember some details. But there were certain things she did remember. Like when she came out of the operating theatre, and her leg pointed sharply to one side. Chrysanthou tried to suggest this simply wasn't true, and in any event, it wouldn't have been possible for her to notice a crooked leg because it was so swollen.

'It was,' Leah said firmly. 'My son was with me, and he noticed it as well.'

Chrysanthou's questions often relied on intonation. She would say 'You did X', with her voice raised slightly at the end to indicate it was a question. Sometimes this created confusion because it sounded like she was stating a fact, and the witnesses would nod, or accept, even if it didn't sound right.

'You need to be very careful with your questions,' the judge said during the questioning of Leah. Another time, she cut into one of Chrysanthou's rambling questions. 'There's three propositions in that question,' Justice Abraham said sternly.

Despite the confusing questions, Leah's story remained the same. Her leg was swollen, painful, pus-filled, and she asked Dr Al Muderis time and again to take it seriously, to no avail. 'He didn't think that I had an infection.'

After an hour, Leah seemed to be running out of puff. She was staring downward, her answers taking longer each time.

There was a sadness brewing inside of her that looked like it was about to spill over. Chrysanthou noticed, and paused. 'Ms Mooney, do you need a break or are you okay?'

Leah said the earlier tirade about how unfair the media reporting was had gotten her down. 'I was listening to all you guys,' she said. 'It did, you know, take a lot out of me ... I wanted to go out of the room.'

I knew I should have asked she be taken out. Leah took a deep breath, looked at Tim and soldiered on. When Chrysanthou suggested the reason they sued Dr Al Muderis was money, she made it clear that the opposite was true. 'We wanted justice,' Leah said.

Leah became more and more confused and exhausted the longer the day dragged on. The judge noticed. She took time to explain things to Leah and asked how much longer it would take. 'The witness has been in the witness box a long time,' the judge noted.

Most of the time, the judge was cool, detached, impenetrable. But at moments like this, I contemplated how her life and career might have shaped her. A woman of Lebanese heritage, Wendy Abraham did not fit the preconceived view of what a judge could be in this country. She was appointed silk in 1998, and went on to prosecute some of Australia's toughest criminal trials, including the Snowtown murders, and later the Bowraville murders – the unsolved deaths of three Indigenous children. She was appointed judge in 2019 and at her swearing in ceremony, Arthur Moses SC singled out her 'courageous advocacy' in the Bowraville trial 'on behalf of the voiceless in our community'.

As Justice Abraham checked in on Leah, and gently untangled the court's mysterious processes, I remembered these comments, her commitment to victims, and ability to 'break down and explain the law' in 'gruelling circumstances'.

Chrysanthou's questions had stretched into the lunch break, but she promised she could wrap it up in ten minutes.

'Are you seriously going to be ten minutes?' the judge asked. 'I will sit on if you are actually going to finish in ten minutes. Your estimates to date have been way out.'

That wasn't fair, Chrysanthou responded, but she agreed to keep it tight. Returning to Leah, she suggested her pain after the fall was mostly in her hip, not leg.

'I'm not sure about that,' Leah said. 'But I think my leg would have been uncomfortable … Which it always is, yes.'

On the final question, Chrysanthou turned her attention to me. My story about Leah mentioned that she decided to speak out after reading the article about Temperance Gollan, whose mother had died following a botched operation by Dr Al Muderis. I still clearly remember Leah standing in her kitchen, surrounded by her boys, as tears rolled down her cheeks. Leah regretted not taking her case all the way to trial, and still carries guilt for believing she could have done more to stop Dr Al Muderis early in his career. Thinking back to that moment still makes my heart wrench. Leah was wrong about all this, Chrysanthou argued, because she had actually emailed me before the story about Temperance was published.

'I'm not sure,' Leah responded. 'But I remember that my main reason for contacting Charlotte was I was very distressed because that was a long time …' she trailed off.

She explained again her court case and how the Medical Council of NSW didn't follow up her complaint.

'If they had, none of us would be here today,' she said. 'I was very, very sad that they lost their mother, because I lost my own mother when I was young, and it's really distressing. And when I brought that back up I remember having arguments with my family because they didn't want us to go through it again, but I felt that I had to do that because I think that was just so sad, you know.'

Chrysanthou cut her off. 'And Ms Grieve came to speak to you at your house on 6 October?'

Leah finished her previous answer. She said she had seen the little box in my article asking anyone with information to come forward. 'And that's what I did.'

'Right. And she interviewed you and your husband on 6 October at your home?'

'Yes. And our sons were there too, all of our family, yes,' Leah said.

'And did she encourage you to reagitate your HCCC [NSW healthcare regulator] complaint that you made in 2012?'

'No.'

'Because a week after you were interviewed by her you agitated that complaint?'

'I would have done that myself because that was the whole thing. None of us would be here if – if they had acted on that, and it wouldn't have happened to that – the lady that died, and – and the girls wouldn't be distressed.'

'I have no further questions, your Honour.'

'Can I talk to my husband?'

'Yes,' Chrysanthou said.

The lunch break was called, and I smiled at Leah as warmly as I could without saying anything. I was still restricted from speaking to her, or Tim, so I kept my distance, but tried to convey through my eyes how thankful I was. She had done so well, under incredible pressure, but it wasn't over yet.

After lunch, Tim took the stand. Justice Abraham reminded him there was fresh water if he needed it. Leah was sitting next to me and started digging into her bag. 'He can't drink like that,' she whispered. The aggressive treatment to stop Tim's cancer had resulted in a facial reconstruction that meant he was missing one eye and large parts of his face, and skin grafts reached the edge of his lip. After some rustling, Leah pulled out a little box neatly packed with straws. I motioned to one of the solicitors, who quietly crept up to the witness box and handed one to Tim. *They're a unit*, I thought to myself.

Once again, Chrysanthou started with the chronology: the accident in Canada, the prognosis. Tim, like his wife before him, did not remember anyone telling them her leg might never fully recover.

'Now, do you remember, were you with your wife when Dr Al Muderis visited her on 3 February, two days after the surgery?'

'I was always with my wife, yes.'

Chrysanthou suggested that no-one said anything about Leah's leg being crooked. 'No, we all said it pointed out, looked crooked. It's not straight. We were quite concerned about it. The whole family.'

Chrysanthou kept trying to cut in, but Tim was determined to finish his sentence. He was speaking loudly, his words charged with emotion. He was protective of his wife, lashing out in a way a bear might swipe at a predator. He had watched his wife be wounded in the witness box, accused of lying about the most painful part of their lives, and was now setting the record straight. Beside me, Leah could see the feelings stirring up in him. As she watched her husband, alone up there, tears welled in her eyes. 'I hate it when he gets upset,' she said, mostly to herself.

When Chrysanthou returned to Leah's leg and suggested the family noticing the crookedness 'didn't happen', Tim's anger only grew. This was a traumatic experience they had all gone through, and this person had the temerity to say he was wrong, had misremembered, or worse, was lying.

'She couldn't stand up for months,' he said loudly. 'It was pretty obvious that something was done incorrectly.'

Chrysanthou tried to pinpoint exactly when they noticed Leah's leg was crooked. Tim couldn't remember the exact date, but said 'it was very, very obvious'. He spoke about how devastated they were that Leah needed a second surgery, and how Dr Al Muderis repeatedly brushed off their concerns. 'He was a very dismissive sort of fellow,' he said.

Tim spoke to Dr Al Muderis on the phone in the weeks after the surgery about what had happened. 'He said, "It has to be fixed, I cannot leave it like that." He said, "My reputation depends on it."'

Chrysanthou swiped back, denying those words ever left her client's mouth. 'Well I would suggest to you that I was there and I heard it. And that is definite.' Tim was only becoming more certain in his answers. He erupted with laughter at some of Chrysanthou's suggestions he considered fanciful. But any comic relief swiftly ended when the barrister suggested the family sued the doctor after Tim told Dr Al Muderis: 'I just need to look after her welfare after I die.'

Tim was insulted now. He was being portrayed as a money-hungry false-claimer who wanted an insurance payout. As Leah had said before him, it was only ever about justice.

'That is really, you know,' he said, breathing loudly. 'I'm a successful tiler, businessman. I can look after my wife. Leah and I are a unit. We're blessed with four wonderful children, and that's our wealth. But we are also quite comfortable. And I'm not worried about Leah in the future. She's taken care of, you know what I mean? Now, I would not have said that to him. And I did not say that to him.'

Finally, as she had with Leah, Chrysanthou ended her questions on me.

'Do you remember last year approaching journalist Charlotte Grieve?'

'Yes.'

'And did she suggest to you that you should reagitate the HCCC complaint, given the articles that have been published?'

'We may have suggested it to her but she may have suggested to us but we may have suggested to her.' His answer went around in a circle, suggesting he didn't remember.

'No further questions, your Honour.'

My chest released. I followed Tim and Leah out of the courtroom, and we walked together down to the street. I thanked them for everything and said how well they had both done. They are softly spoken people, but looks can be deceiving. There is a fiery determination within them both. They were on a mission, and wouldn't be stopped, no matter how painful.

They told me that they were still in touch with their local member of parliament, independent Dr Sophie Scamps, and were again waiting for the HCCC to process their complaint. How could Dr Al Muderis get Leah's treatment so catastrophically wrong yet there be no record on his profile? These were questions we would discuss over and over, as we lamented how the system turned a blind eye to powerful doctors and cashed-up institutions in the wrong.

That night, I went out with the legal team for a fancy dinner in the city. Collins told me that in any normal trial, at this point, the respondents should feel deflated, defeated, downtrodden. The applicant's case should have revealed major weaknesses in our defences, shown all their trump cards and left us bloodied and bruised. This case didn't feel that way. It seemed that Dr Al Muderis's legal team had underestimated our witnesses and overestimated their client. The wheels were already starting to fall off Dr Al Muderis's case.

I bumped into Nick McKenzie that night, who was coincidentally at the same restaurant. As everyone ate tapas and drank champagne, a big, perplexed grin crossed Nick's face. 'You look like a team that's already won?'

CHAPTER 13

The Battle for Confidentiality

The trial was so long it had to be separated into several chunks, with months-long gaps in between. Part one ended with Leah and Tim's evidence in October 2023 and the trial would resume in March the next year. In the lull between hearings, I tried to return to something of a normal life. I spent the weekend in Sydney, where I saw Camp Cope's final performance at the Opera House with my partner and celebrated an old friend's upcoming wedding. But my efforts were short-lived. That Sunday, two days after the first tranche of hearings concluded, I received an email at 7.14 am from News Corp journalist Jenna Clarke. She was 'touching base' regarding an item to be published the next day about Dr Al Muderis and 'understood' we had submitted the investigation into the Walkley Awards. 'Were you aware of any petitions made to the Walkley Board on behalf of Professor Munjed Al Muderis regarding your work?' she asked.

I forwarded the email to my editor. Three weeks earlier, we'd had a strange run-in regarding the Walkleys that revealed just how far Dr Al Muderis's lawyers were willing to go in the name of protecting his reputation. I wanted to engage with the journalist and let her know what happened, but was advised to stay silent.

Journalism is one of the most overly awarded professions. Few industries have as many rolling ceremonies held to hand out pieces of plastic to people for simply doing their job. Still, there is no denying these awards are an important part of our industry. Journalists who receive awards are given greater freedoms to pursue the stories they think are important, and the recognition drives investment in public interest topics. The most prestigious among these awards are the Walkley Awards and, in late August 2023, I entered the Dr Al Muderis series into the investigative journalism category. I was proud of our work and believed, and still do, that the story was good journalism.

About a month later, *The Age*'s editor, Patrick Elligett, received a phone call from a senior figure at the Walkley Foundation, wanting an update on the defamation case. I didn't think much of it at the time, but Patrick had an uneasy feeling he wasn't getting the full story. He said they were vague about why they were asking, and they eventually disclosed that the Walkley Foundation had received legal letters from Dr Al Muderis's team. They would not provide us a copy of the letter or disclose exactly what it contained.

Larina Alick, our in-house lawyer, was furious. Larina had recently sat on a steering committee for the Walkley Foundation to devise a policy for how the awards should deal with entries that attract lawsuits. In short, the policy stated that defamation litigation should not influence the views or decisions made by the Walkley judges. The journalists must disclose any claims or complaints, but nothing further. This was particularly important because journalism that is critical of powerful people often attracts legal threats. Media companies routinely settle cases for commercial reasons, agreeing to retract or issue a clarification to avoid costly lawsuits, despite the strength of the journalism. Stories can be legitimate, truthful and in the public interest but still unable to be proven in court. Well-resourced individuals use defamation to kill important stories all the time, and the quality of a story should not be shaken by the eagerness of its subjects to destroy it.

I later learned that Dr Al Muderis's lawyers sent a 'letter of complaint' to individual directors of the Walkley Foundation. It was a fully-fledged attack on our journalism, executed behind closed doors, and we weren't given a fair opportunity to respond. The first time we got a peek into what that letter contained was when *The Australian* published the story the same evening Clarke had emailed me.

The article suggested that Dr Al Muderis was not just preparing evidence for court. He was also apparently instructing his lawyers to attempt to influence the judges of the Walkley Foundation, and then apparently tried to interest a News Corp journalist in furthering the attack. Clarke's email to me made no mention of the specific claims her story would include about both myself and my father, which I felt robbed me of the ability to address those issues directly. It was a small example of the tactics that some litigants use to try to control the narrative, playing the media in tandem with the court to advance their position.

Despite all this, I had to stay focused on the task at hand. With 24 trial days behind us, there was now a new battle – the fight to protect the identities of my confidential sources. After climbing one mountain, another would appear. This time, the entire case was on the line. If we lost the confidential source battle, we would have to drop the public interest defence and rely exclusively on truth. There was also a small but real risk that I could face prison if the court ordered me to identify my sources and I refused. On the other hand, if we won, we would strengthen the journalist privilege and have a chance to create history by running the first successful public interest defence. It would also mean myself, Tom and Natalie would be subject to further cross-examination. But first, we had to have the fight.

During the investigation, I spoke with 23 confidential sources. These people had only agreed to speak if their names would never see the light of day. They included patients, surgeons, doctors, physiotherapists, data scientists, nurses, and prosthetists. There were many reasons these people did not want to speak publicly about Dr Al Muderis.

The patients, in particular, had already spent large sums of money, often their life savings or superannuation, on the surgery. One man I spoke with had no money left, couldn't work due to pain, and relied on government welfare. He was disabled, broke and exhausted. He knew what happened to him was wrong but there was no way he was willing to risk speaking out against Dr Al Muderis, a man known to be litigious. Other patients were afraid Dr Al Muderis would refuse to treat them if they spoke out about their mistreatment. Many thought he was the only person who could perform this surgery, and they needed him for the rest of their lives.

The healthcare professionals, mostly surgeons, had different concerns. By and large, they were worried that Dr Al Muderis would launch professional warfare against them. One surgeon feared Dr Al Muderis would lodge complaints through the regulators, tying him up in an investigation that could stretch years. Some were prevented by workplace policies from speaking to the media. Others were bound by patient confidentiality. One thought he could have a greater impact by pushing for regulatory action behind the scenes. And like the patients, almost every surgeon was worried that Dr Al Muderis would sue them personally for defamation. He had a track record of doing exactly that.

In a small conference room, Collins laid the stage for the battle ahead. Dr Al Muderis had made an application to reveal the identities of 13 of our 23 confidential sources. Collins separated these sources into three distinct categories – sources who corroborated claims for people who went on record, sources who gave me 'scurrilous' information about the doctor's personal life, most of which was not published and, finally, sources who gave me new information to follow up and contact details for people who later went on the record.

Using this metric, it became obvious that most of the claims made by the confidential sources were either corroborated by people on the record or not published at all. The judge would need to carefully weigh Dr Al Muderis's right to a fair trial against the public interest in upholding the journalist privilege and the adverse consequences for the sources if they were identified. If we could show that the information provided by the confidential sources wasn't material to the outcome of the story, or the trial, we would have a much better chance of victory.

Collins gave the example of another confidential source battle he had been involved in, when Nick McKenzie had described a Victorian businessman as the 'head of the Melbourne mafia' in an investigation for *The Age*. The man sued for defamation and wanted to know who Nick had spoken to, so made a similar application to have the identities of Nick's confidential sources revealed. In that dispute, Nick's lawyers argued the only people who could testify that Madafferi really was the head of the Melbourne mafia were underworld figures who would be murdered for saying so. That story relied heavily on anonymous sources, and if the court compelled Nick to reveal their identities, they would be killed.

Nick won his battle to protect his sources in a judgment that set an important precedent for upholding the journalist privilege, but it also set the bar incredibly high – the courts would protect journalists' sources in matters of life or death. This case, Collins explained, was vastly different. These sources faced consequences far less severe than murder, but on the flipside, the credibility of the investigation did not live or die on the information they provided.

After walking through the steps of what we'd need to prove, Collins cocked his eyebrow and looked me directly in the eyes. 'This is an important test case,' he said. 'If we can't win in a case like this, provisions for source protection are not worth the paper they're written on. And if we do win, it will set an important precedent for strengthening the laws for protecting sources.'

Collins said an appearance like this can make a journalist's career. Barrister Declan Roche said it'd go down in the textbooks, 'The Grieve Case.' He smiled. 'But no pressure.'

I understood the challenge ahead, and got to work. I cleared a day from my reporting work to start calling the confidential sources. The aim was to first see if they would voluntarily waive the confidentiality and, if not, get them to explain why not. This wasn't going to be an easy task. We were in the thick of a massive defamation trial that was splashed across mainstream media and I was asking them to go public with information they had shared in confidence more than a year earlier. I set up a Google Doc and hit the phones.

The first person I spoke to was an orthopaedic surgeon, known as Confidential Source 2 (CS-2). Back in the first weeks of my investigation, I reached out to this person through LinkedIn and he called me from a private number. He was nervous and only relaxed when I guaranteed the conversation was strictly off-record. CS-2 was unsettled that Dr Al Muderis owned the patent for the osseointegration implant he used. He said this was not illegal but unusual and created a 'very strong financial motivation' that he believed was 'driving indications for surgery' rather than the patients' needs. 'He's making a lot of money putting the devices in.'

This source was also concerned by the feverish supporter base Dr Al Muderis had cultivated. He knew the doctor's waiting room was stacked with enthusiastic supporters who spoke to prospective patients only about the benefits. 'That's coercion,' he said, frustrated.

CS-2 was the first person who told me about allegations that Dr Al Muderis had sexual relationships with his staff and said complaints had been made to Macquarie University Hospital and AHPRA that went nowhere. He said the way Dr Al Muderis treated staff was 'blatantly misogynistic' and would not be tolerated in the public system. Private hospitals turned a blind eye because he brought in work, he said, and money.

In that first conversation, I asked CS-2 whether osseointegration would alleviate phantom pain. My father remembered Dr Al Muderis being absolute – 'you betcha' – when asked about this. CS-2 said the implant itself makes no difference. He said there was some evidence that combining osseointegration with a nerve surgery called TMR could help, but that the results varied wildly. CS-2 was particularly concerned about Dr Al Muderis performing TMR, because he said nerve surgery required specialist training, which Dr Al Muderis did not have. He said this was a pattern for the doctor, who often strayed outside of his training. CS-2 said many doctors had similar concerns, but everyone was afraid to speak out. I ended that phone call feeling confident we were on the right track, but also with more questions than answers.

Almost a year after that first conversation, I was now calling CS-2 to ask if he would agree to unveil his identity. I started by explaining the situation – that I had listed him as a confidential source in my affidavit, and had handed over my notes, with redactions to protect his identity. Now, Dr Al Muderis had lodged an application to have his identity revealed.

The legal definition of confidential source requires there to be a 'promise of confidentiality'. Dr Al Muderis argued that because my notes did not include any specific reference to this promise, it didn't exist. He claimed that I was calling these people confidential sources to avoid scrutiny of what really was said. Nothing could be further from the truth. I wrote my notes only for my own purposes, and had never imagined they would be subpoenaed. I could easily remember who was on the record because there were so few surgeons prepared to be named.

Despite Dr Al Muderis's theories, I actually wanted my confidential sources to go on the record because it would only strengthen our case. It would have been immensely helpful to have a conga-line of surgeons from all around the country expressing deep and longstanding concerns about Dr Al Muderis. But his legal team had another view, so my first step was testing each confidential source's perspective on the 'promise'. I asked CS-2 to explain his understanding of the terms of our conversation.

'I remember you telling me I would remain confidential,' he said. 'That my name wouldn't be released. You very clearly said that to me about not revealing my name.'

I agreed and said I would protect his identity no matter the consequences, if he wished, before outlining the case for him to go on the record. He was hesitant and asked to see a copy of my redacted notes. I emailed the document after hanging up, and he responded the same evening.

'Thanks Charlotte,' he wrote. 'I don't want to waive confidentiality. I would not be happy with those comments coming out on public record and certainly not being made available to Dr Al Muderis legal team.'

This was the beginning of a long slog of similar conversations. Some sources became agitated or freaked out at the mere suggestion of waiving confidentiality. Others were clear-headed but still stressed. If Dr Al Muderis was willing to go after Nine, they figured, he was even more likely to come after them.

'You said my name wouldn't be mentioned anywhere,' another surgeon told me. 'From what you told me, it was your reputation and your career that would be on the line if you disclosed confidential sources because that's not what journalists do.'

I had worked many casual jobs during university that involved approaching strangers on the street or phone. Most people either ignore you or tell you to go away. I trained myself to let each rejection wash over me, moving on to the next person with a blank memory and a fresh approach. These skills became critical in my journalism career – the persistence to keep asking the same question, keep picking the phone up, keep making the pitch, no matter how many times people said no. For every thousand doors that are slammed in your face, one will open. But at that point, no doors were opening.

Another source said he'd think about it, but a few days later sent a text message with his answer. *It is my view that Al Muderis' interest in getting names is not to test the veracity of your claims, but to seek revenge on those you spoke to. I hope your legal team can convince the judge of that.*

Deep down, I strongly suspected he was right. I took a screenshot of the message and sent it to the lawyers.

After I made my way through the list of confidential sources, I had to write a new affidavit summarising these conversations, recording the 'promise of confidentiality' and 'adverse consequences' for each source. This document also showed, in painstaking detail, how every piece of information from every source was supported by on-record sources, putting meat on the bones of Collins' case theory. This took hours upon hours of digging back through old notes. Solicitor Issy Gwinner meticulously prepared individual references for every point. Towards the end of the document, I outlined the implications on my future work, and on journalism more broadly, should these sources be identified, and the reasons I believed these stories were in the public interest. Issy and I worked around the clock, and finally, the 137-page document was ready.

'When hospitals, regulators and the courts fail to address the conduct of doctors, journalism is the last resort for an aggrieved patient to have their story heard and to possibly bring about change. I am concerned if I am forced to reveal my sources in this case, well-intentioned doctors will be dissuaded from speaking to journalists, and that this will ultimately have a detrimental effect on patients in the long run.'

The affidavit was filed and a hearing date set. This would be my first time in the witness box, a taste of what was to come before the main event. My stories might have damaged Dr Al Muderis's reputation; now the focus of Dr Al Muderis's legal team would be to destroy mine. I had a few preparation sessions and quickly discovered it would be a minefield. Unlike normal cross-examination, where you listen to the question and answer truthfully, for this I had to know when and how to use the journalist privilege. This meant I could refuse to answer questions if my response would identify my confidential sources in any way. All I needed to say was 'ethically, I cannot answer that'. But I also had to be on high alert for questions about doctors who were *not* confidential sources. If I started making admissions about who was, and who wasn't, a source, this could allow Dr Al Muderis to determine their identities through a process of elimination.

To make matters even more complicated, we had already informed the other side that none of the healthcare practitioners we called as witnesses were confidential sources, so I could answer questions about them. For each question, I had to navigate a multi-step calculation and refuse to answer only when strictly necessary. The privilege is just that – a privilege – and cannot be misused.

The night before, I had a Zoom meeting with a handful of barristers to run through some potential questions. I had my camera turned on and noticed how tired my face looked. The meeting lasted three hours as we hacked away at thorny topics. 'They will try tricky ways to trip you up,' I was advised. 'Be careful. Don't get defensive. Listen to the question, answer the question. If the answer is I don't know, that's the answer. Remember, it's not personal. She's going to put to you that you're lying, that you're no good at your job. That you deliberately made this up to bring down an Australian hero. If you need a break, take one. She needs to find a weak link in this case. You're an easy target. You have a very calm, professional manner. That will help you.'

My head was spinning by the end of that meeting. One wrong foot and the public interest defence could blow up. After the meeting, I called JP and war-gamed a scenario I was worried might unfold. I was deep in the weeds and panicking. Calmly, he said they would probably object to what I described. But then he did what he does best. He zoomed out of the small developments and encouraged me to focus on the bigger picture.

'Look, at the end of the day, you've just got to back yourself. You've done nothing wrong. Your memory has been so sharp throughout this process. Back yourself. Be confident. Don't give in to her bullying,' JP said.

After the call, I left the house. I'd been cooped up in my bedroom for too long and was feeling the stress. I walked down to the Five Ways, bought a strawberry donut and began wandering the hilly streets of Paddington. I called my partner and pretended to be the cross-examiner.

'What does off the record mean to you?'

He laughed, before giving a serious answer. It was obvious, he said, everyone knows what it means and I surely do too. He was right: I was over-thinking things. After a few more mock questions, I hung up the phone and continued walking to Rushcutters Bay. The salty breeze cooled my face. I told myself once more: *Zoom out. Back yourself. The truth will prevail.*

The application needed to be heard by a separate judge because a finding had to be made on my credit. If the judge decided I was a liar, this could bias the rest of the trial. Justice Robert Bromwich stepped in – a white-haired man who joined the bench in 2016 after serving as the Commonwealth Director of Public Prosecutions. Like Justice Abraham, a large part of his life had been dedicated to representing victims and working with police. I prayed this might help us.

PART THREE

CHAPTER 14

Abuse of Process

On 10 November 2023, I went for a run, got dressed and walked into the Thomson Geer offices for one last briefing before court. After some small chat, they left me alone to look over my affidavits one last time. I took a photograph on my iPhone at 9.04 am which captured the moment. Two chunky plastic folders sat side by side emblazoned with *AFFIDAVITS OF CHARLOTTE GRIEVE* next to a takeaway coffee cup at the end of a long conference table, totally empty. At 9.25 am, Patrick Elligett texted me: *Best of luck again today Charlotte. We're all behind you.*

In court, I sat behind the bar table, waiting to be called. My heart was pounding so hard my chest rattled with every beat. As I looked at the clock, I thought of a woman named Jane Orford. Jane described herself as one of Dr Al Muderis's worst patients, after he failed to diagnose an infection in her leg that cost her 20 centimetres of bone. 'It's devastating,' she told me once. 'I was able-bodied, now I'm disabled.' The worst part for Jane was how Dr Al Muderis made her doubt herself. He dismissed her concerns so many times that she started to question her core instincts. I spoke with Jane often, and she told me about her life and the depths of her despair. She, too, had become suicidal after the miracle surgery went wrong. Jane was amazed we had exposed the doctor and sent almost constant messages of support. 'You are gutsy and inspirational,' she emailed once. 'Never forget or lose sight of that.'

Reading my stories, Jane said she realised for the first time that she wasn't alone. To her, that meant everything. She was barracking for me, always, and her encouragement kept me focused on why this all mattered. One Friday night, I was at the pub with friends when my phone buzzed with a text from Jane's husband. *Hi Charlotte, Just wanted to let you know that Jane had a heart attack yesterday and was placed on life support, unfortunately we had to make the hard decision to turn it off.* A baseball bat straight to the heart. I cried. The next Monday, I arrived at work and there was another package from Jane, with a letter thanking me for my work and a little stuffed bear reminding me to take care of myself.

As I sat before Justice Bromwich, I thought of Jane and all the other patients who weren't believed.

Each side had to deliver short opening statements. Chrysanthou rehashed her arguments that the public should not be misled about medical matters and said that unmasking these sources was essential to understanding the entire investigation. She claimed these people were not genuinely confidential sources. 'The only people that she's trying to keep them confidential from are the court and the applicant and his lawyers,' she declared.

Barrister Renee Enbom KC was representing me in this application. Renee is an experienced barrister who has been at the centre of many of Victoria's historic moments, from royal commissions to the inside of the AFL's tribunal. With long blonde hair, Renee has a glamorous, fast-paced approach to life – quickly getting across details of complex matters, one after the next. When it was her time to speak, Renee picked up an earlier comparison Justice Bromwich had made about the importance of protections given to police informants. She knew his history in public prosecutions and spoke his language. 'Journalists, like police members, *know* when they have promised a source that they will not disclose the source's identity,' she said.

'Journalists *know* that if they breach their promise, they're destroying a relationship with a source. They *know* that they will be damaging their own career and reputation as a journalist. And they *know* that if they breach their promise, they will be risking the ability of all other journalists to obtain information from sources pursuant to a relationship of trust and confidence.'

Chrysanthou's juniors then tried to strike out parts of my affidavit that said identifying these sources would have a detrimental impact on my career. Denied. Then, they tried to knock out evidence about the deficiencies in healthcare regulation, saying I was no expert. Unfortunately for them, the judge already knew how broken the system was.

'I think they have had a very patchy history, going right back to Chelmsford,' the judge said.

Justice Bromwich was referencing the 'deep sleep therapy' scandal of the 1990s, where experimental treatments were given to mentally ill patients to devastating effects. People struggling with drug addiction and depression were plied with massive doses of barbiturates and kept unconscious for days or weeks. Laying naked on beds, they were fed through tubes and sometimes given electric shock therapy without consent. Vulnerable people emerged skeletal, zombie-like and permanently scarred. Twenty-three people died. The regulators were warned but did nothing. Objection denied.

It was 12.30 pm when I got into the witness box. My hands were shaking and my face was hot. *Shitting myself*, as Nick McKenzie had said so many times during the Ben Roberts-Smith trial.

'Ms Grieve, you say that you consider the protection of anonymous sources to be at the heart of what journalists do, is that right?' Chrysanthou said, staring at me intensely.

'Yes.'

'And you understand that a confidential source is a person who would not have agreed to speak to you unless confidentiality was agreed?'

'Yes.'

She drilled into the various terms – 'off the record' and 'on background' – which I agreed were ambiguous. She then turned to my conversations with anaesthetist Ajay Kumar, who worked with Dr Al Muderis many years ago. When I first spoke with Kumar, he requested that the conversation be 'off the record', and so I later listed him as a confidential source in my first affidavit. However, when I went back to clarify his understanding of the conversation, Kumar became evasive. He refused to answer and swung between 'it was off the record' and 'there was no confidentiality agreement', then filed an affidavit with Dr Al Muderis's lawyers detailing our conversation, effectively 'outing' himself as a source. That was fine by me, but Chrysanthou seized on the backflip as crucial evidence that I had invented, or misunderstood, the nature of these relationships. If I could be so hideously wrong about Dr Kumar, were the remaining 13 confidential sources *really* bona-fide confidential sources? Did these flimsy conversations more than a year ago really achieve the legal threshold to be afforded the journalist privilege?

Given the ambiguity around these terms, Chrysanthou asked, shouldn't I have recorded the agreement in my notes? I said it wasn't necessary because I could rely on my memory. 'Very few people were prepared to go on the record,' I said.

Chrysanthou claimed only 23 out of 70 sources were confidential. That didn't sound right but I couldn't remember the exact figures. I agreed to review my affidavit and answer the question again after the break. The questions went on. She asked whether journalists must assess motivations of people who request confidentiality, and whether information they share must be treated with greater caution. I agreed to both. Then she started zeroing in on the people I'd spoken with, asking questions about their backgrounds and whether I had any pre-existing dealings with them. A warning light flashed. This veered close to details that might be used to identify a source. I deployed the shield.

'Ethically, I can't answer that because I don't want to rule anyone in or out as a potential confidential source,' I replied.

'Sorry. So you're saying you did have pre-existing contact with some of these sources?'

'Ethically, I can't answer that.'

It was like a red rag to a bull. Chrysanthou doubled down. 'Well, I think you can, Ms Grieve,' she said loudly. 'Did you or did you not, prior to your investigation into my client, have prior contact with any of these sources listed in your affidavit?'

I deployed the shield for the third time.

JP's advice was ringing in my mind: *If you're in doubt, take the privilege. It's yours to use. You've done nothing wrong.* Chrysanthou didn't like it. We locked horns – she wouldn't let it go.

'I'm not trying to be evasive, I just don't want to do anything that violates my ethical codes of conduct. If this helps, in broad terms, one of the confidential sources I was aware of before I started my investigation. Aware of their existence, hadn't spoken to them, but I was aware that they were alive.'

'Right,' Chrysanthou shot back. 'And why is it the case that you think that telling us which confidential source that is would disclose that person's identity?'

'It just,' I stumbled. 'It just may. I mean, there's … It's … It's a small industry.'

'Well, "may" is not sufficient,' Chrysanthou said, fiery-eyed. 'Which confidential source were you aware of before you commenced the investigation?'

Renee jumped to her feet. 'Your Honour, I object.'

The judge immediately recognised that my answers were in the 'territory of not confirm or deny' and said 'as soon as you go down that route' the source was at risk of being identified. The line of questioning ended.

Next, Chrysanthou turned to what she considered was the silver bullet that would expose me as a dirty, filthy liar: I had deleted correspondence with two of my sources, and only disclosed this the night before the hearing.

As well as handing over every scrap of related material in my possession during the exhaustive discovery process, I was also asked to write a list of things that were no longer in my possession – LinkedIn messages I no longer had access to, notes scribbled on pieces of paper since discarded, anything I might have deleted. There is no issue with journalists deleting things before they are sued, as long as they disclose that they have done so.

The list alone that set out all my documents was more than 100 pages, and I'd handed over several thousand pages in discovery. I'd also handed over my phone to the forensic IT person to download all my texts. Discovery is a constant process – you hand over more documents that arise as the case progresses. It was only the night before the hearing when a question from one of the solicitors about communicating with Fred Hernandez and Mitch Grant jogged my memory about Facebook messages I had deleted. I had communicated with both Hernandez and Grant through other means, so I thought I'd handed everything over. Chrysanthou saw it differently. She accused me of deliberately withholding the deleted Facebook messages for malicious reasons, and did everything in her power to get me to make that admission.

'Why did you delete them?'

'It was after the TV interview with Dr Al Muderis and on the sidelines of that interview, he had mentioned those two specifically as some theory that he thought they were responsible for the stories … And so it was, sort of, a knee-jerk reaction after that. I thought, to protect them, I'll just quickly delete these messages. I didn't think I was doing anything wrong, but, in hindsight, I wish I hadn't deleted them because I have nothing to hide.'

She didn't buy it. She accused me of being dishonest, and deliberately concealing messages. I denied each question, and eventually the judge ordered a 45-minute lunch adjournment.

Like all witnesses, I wasn't allowed to speak with anyone in the break. I sat alone at a cafe on Macquarie Street and did my homework. I pulled out my two chunky affidavit folders and calculated the percentage of sources who were confidential on a notepad. In this moment, it felt like I was frozen in an alternate reality where my every movement was up for scrutiny. It was an uneasy feeling, one that grew more pronounced as the trial went on. I felt like I was being surveilled, that every step, every conversation, every thought I had could be torn apart by lawyers, used to portray me as a liar, a manipulator, an all-round bad person and a lousy journalist. While I mostly managed the stress of the case quite well, there was no denying this feeling crept closer to paranoia the longer the threat of cross-examination hung over my head.

I pushed the feeling aside and focused on the task at hand – counting the sources. It was windy and the pages blew wildly in the gusts, but eventually I wrestled with the binders and wrote out the lists. By 1.45 pm, I was back in court, lingering at the back of the room and clinging to the now-crumpled piece of paper with tallies scribbled down.

'If you would return to the witness box, Ms Grieve?'

'Sorry, I was just wondering if I could bring some notes up that I made in the homework,' I said, my words coming out garbled.

'The homework,' the judge repeated, smiling. 'Just dutifully doing what you were asked to do.'

The next line of questioning related to the various codes of conduct. One of the key points in this case was that I could not reveal the identities of my sources because it would breach codes of conduct. Again, to me this felt like trying to squeeze the unpredictable and unwieldy profession of journalism into the tight confines of a document. Like when we *know* a source is confidential, we *know* the ethics of our profession. It's something you build an innate understanding of, through a process of trial and error, and gut feel, rather than checking your every move against a list of dot points prepared by human resources.

Chrysanthou took me point by point through the Nine Network's code of conduct, saying I hadn't adhered to it, accusing me of not pushing people hard enough to go on the record, or not checking their motivations. I knocked back these suggestions, thinking of the times I'd pleaded with surgeons to go on the record. Still, Chrysanthou persisted.

'And I want to suggest to you at no point is it indicated in your affidavit or notes that you ever paused to consider the sources' motives?'

'I think you,' I paused and corrected myself. 'That question, I feel like I've answered. I did consider quite carefully the motivations of everyone I spoke to, and I appealed to them directly at multiple stages to waive their confidentiality and go on the record. I would much prefer to be in a situation where all of my confidential sources were named, because they're people of integrity and it would assist this case. The only reason I'm sitting here is because they haven't waived that confidentiality despite my requests.'

'But you're sitting there, actually,' Chrysanthou paused, as if the word 'actually' declared this was the real situation, 'because you agreed to listen to their information and use it, confidentially you say, when you didn't have to agree. That's why you're sitting there, isn't it?'

'I did have to agree. They wouldn't have spoken to me unless I promised them confidentiality.'

Chrysanthou couldn't understand how or why anyone would request confidentiality at the start of the conversation. In her mind, every conversation began with me offering up confidentiality in order to dig up dirt. She turned her attention to my conversation with Confidential Source 1, the man who sent me a list of patients who had been harmed.

'For him to express any concerns about talking about my clients, doesn't that mean that you must have said to him, "I want you to tell me terrible things about Dr Al Muderis"?'

'No.'

She asked the same question again and again, worded slightly differently each time. I explained how the conversations began with general questions about osseointegration, which often quickly turned into a conversation about concerns about Dr Al Muderis's practice. She asked if I was surprised by the speed at which concerns came up. Finally, I agreed with one part of her question. 'It *was* surprising to me that, quite quickly, that turned into a conversation about long-held concerns about Dr Al Muderis's practice that this particular source had. I *was* surprised that he was so forthcoming with his concerns.'

'But you weren't just investigating osseointegration. That's a lie, isn't it?'

'I was investigating osseointegration and Dr Al Muderis, but I didn't want to really disclose that early on, because I didn't know if there was a story. So I was just having general conversations with people, saying, "What's your thought on this?", you know, "What do you think about this?" And then if they brought up Dr Al Muderis, then I would ask questions about that.

'That's just not true.'

'That ... That is true,' I said.

It went round and round, Chrysanthou accusing me of lying, giving 'absurd' answers or making 'no sense at all'. By the early afternoon, my stress had evaporated and I was entirely relaxed. Chrysanthou's entire case was based on a wrong premise – that

I was lying – so answering the questions became easier. I was telling the truth. She was barking up the wrong tree, and the more she spoke, the clearer it became.

She spent what felt like an eternity focusing on why I didn't specifically write out the 'promise of confidentiality' in my notes, coming back to it again and again. In her mind, if it wasn't written down, it didn't exist. But in reality, this was a legal concept I'd only learned about through the process of litigation and I had no need to write down things I could easily remember.

'The solemn promise that you're here to protect in the witness box was an irrelevant thing to write down?'

'At that time, no I didn't,' I said. 'I had no idea that I would be in this situation right now.'

Toward the end, Chrysanthou triumphantly revealed printouts with photos of surgeons she declared were my confidential sources. Renee tried to object on relevance. The judge couldn't see how the printouts were relevant either, but said: 'We will give her a bit of latitude.' As Chrysanthou shoved papers in front of me, I maintained a deadpan face. I refused to answer her questions. She moved on.

As the afternoon stretched into early evening, it started to feel like Chrysanthou was asking me questions out of curiosity. None of the topics felt sensitive, or went to proving I had done anything wrong. I felt like my answers were now helping the court reach whatever conclusion it needed to reach, rather than being boxed into a corner with nowhere to go. Chrysanthou's questions ranged over a web of confidential sources, conversations, notes and documents.

'Well, what I've noticed, Ms Grieve, is nowhere in your notes do you record the questions you were asking?' The accusatory tone had softened into a sincere query.

'Sometimes I do,' I responded. 'For example, on page 491 where it's in capitals and it's: ADVERTISING OF SURGERIES? That would have been a question.'

'A question that you asked?'

'Yes.'

I had nothing to hide, so assumed the role of helpful courtroom assistant. I took her to documents to explain my answers, decoding my at-times convoluted note-taking practices. As I relaxed even more, I also felt emboldened to push back more firmly at questions I found absurd. Slowly, but surely, I felt like I had the upper hand. I was more across the details of the case. I knew the material better. I didn't feel that her cross-examination landed any blows.

'Ms Chrysanthou, we're coming up to 5 o'clock,' the judge said eventually. Court usually finishes at 4.15 pm.

'I know,' she said. 'We're not going to finish, your Honour.'

Renee got to her feet. 'Your Honour, this is not okay. The estimate on Tuesday was two hours. The estimate this morning was half a day. We've now gone beyond half a day.'

Chrysanthou said she would take another hour and she could finish tonight if everyone was prepared to sit late. 'I'm not sure I'm going to allow a full hour,' Justice Bromwich responded. 'You're going to have to trim your cloth.'

Chrysanthou spent the overtime going through each confidential source one last time. She said the Iraqi prosthetist 'spilled his guts' to me for 30 pages before requesting confidentiality, meaning he wasn't a confidential source. 'Disagree.'

Then she turned to broad, sweeping questions. 'What you say about your conversations with these confidential sources and adverse impact on them is wholly unreliable, isn't it, Ms Grieve?'

'That's incorrect.'

'And this second affidavit, in particular, is self-serving and misleading?'

'I reject that.'

'You're not a very accurate recorder, are you, of what people tell you?'

'I disagree.'

'And you have selectively sought to speak to people you think would be adverse to my client so you could tip a bucket on him. Isn't that the point of your investigation?'

'No.'

Finally, the questions came to an end. In re-examination, Renee cleared up one error in Chrysanthou's questions with a document, and then it was over.

'All right, Ms Grieve. You have concluded your evidence. You can step down and you are free to go, which I am sure you won't need much persuading of,' Justice Bromwich said.

'Thank you. Sorry,' I said.

I left the building feeling physically lighter. As I walked through Hyde Park, I put my AirPods in and started playing an album that had become a fixture of my post-hearing routine – Kanye's *College Dropout*. There was a line in one track that stood out on this day more than any other – that money can be used to get out of prison, but it can't buy freedom.

I had no idea how the judge would rule, but I felt I'd answered the questions honestly, and there'd been no major surprises, no trump cards, no smoking guns. Still, there was one point Chrysanthou had got right – these doctors weren't facing life-or-death consequences if identified. The courts had rarely ruled in the name of journalism, so I didn't hold high hopes. But I knew I had done my part as best as I could. Kanye's lyrics got me thinking about the futility of throwing money at deeply ingrained problems. Dr Al Muderis was investing everything in this case, but the more he fought, the more shocking details about him spilled into the public domain. Three days after that day in court, Fred Hernandez was shackled and put into prison in Nevada, USA, for an indefinite period. Dr Al Muderis had filed another lawsuit against him, and he was found in contempt of court. *Litigious.* Those confidential sources weren't lying.

Six long weeks after my stint in the witness box, on 19 December 2023, the judgment finally arrived. JP texted at 9.10 am: *We won.*

I responded immediately: *No way!!!!!! The whole thing?*

Yep, he responded with a shocked face emoji.

All the sources could remain confidential. Dr Al Muderis was ordered to pay costs. I was in Melbourne as the lawyers piled into the Sydney courtroom to hear the judge's decision. They sent me a photograph of the page that detailed Justice Bromwich's findings on my credit. I read it on my phone as I walked to a hot yoga class in Collingwood and could not wipe the smile off my face.

> I consider Ms Grieve to be shown, not just by what she said and how she said it, but by the description of what she did and the application of logic, reason and context, to be an earnest, intelligent and conscientious person, relatively new to investigative journalism, but anxiously doing her best, both as a journalist and as a witness. I formed the strong impression of her doing her best to tell the truth, extending to the whole truth to the extent that maintenance of the claim of journalist privilege permitted it, and that her evidence was not inherently incredible, implausible or unreliable. She is undoubtedly worried about being forced to disclose the identity of sources whom she genuinely regards as requiring her not to do so. Her evidence was not flawless; but in my experience few witnesses are flawless when giving evidence of detail and complexity, especially when recalling dealings with numerous other people. She struck me as somewhat taken aback by the process and by the vigour of the cross-examination, but not as being overwhelmed by it. Overall, I consider she withstood the cross-examination well; indeed better than many seasoned witnesses I have

observed over many years. She made many appropriate concessions and did not argue with counsel, but rather politely disagreed or otherwise held her ground. That was so despite numerous questions being asked to which objection properly could have successfully been taken, but was not. She was largely left to fend for herself in what was obviously a very unfamiliar situation. Ms Grieve coped well with all of this, never once showing anger or irritation, but rather concern to do her best to answer, without failing to protect the identity of the confidential sources. If anything, she was unduly apologetic about some of the answers she clearly felt she had to give. Most of the weaknesses in her evidence were there to be seen independently of cross-examination and this was not substantially affected by what was put to her. She was at times rattled,rather than shaken. I am amply satisfied that Ms Grieve was a credible and generally reliable witness of truth whose testimony can, with minor qualifications, be safely accepted and relied upon.

Justice Bromwich rejected claims my evidence was self-serving, implausible, nonsensical. He found the law does not require the promise to be made at the beginning of the conversation, nor does it need to be documented in writing. He accepted that the fears expressed by surgeons – of being targeted with litigation, bullying, complaints, even stress and loss of sleep – were legitimate adverse consequences, even if the risk of some of these eventuating were low. That these fears were genuinely held was enough.

His Honour eviscerated the conduct of Dr Al Muderis's lawyers in excruciating detail. Each paragraph was more damning than the last. His lawyers had submitted my evidence was 'fantastical on any view, and to put it more mildly, illogical bordering on absurd'. But Justice Bromwich said: 'To be blunt, that characterisation better applies to the submission than the evidence.' In the end, he was not satisfied the arguments made by Dr Al Muderis had 'come close' to outweighing the public interest in maintaining the sources' confidentiality.

He wrote about the importance of confidentiality in allowing information to flow to journalists, and identified the 'chilling effect' if these arrangements were broken.

'The greater the power, wealth or influence, or perceived power, wealth or influence of a person against whom disclosures are made, the greater the risk, or perceived risk, of adverse consequences if the identity of the source becomes known to that person, and the greater the likelihood that such information will not be forthcoming.'

Justice Bromwich summarised the public interest matters in this case, and finished by saying, 'The conclusion I reach ... is that there was and is a substantial public interest in the identities of the confidential sources not being disclosed contrary to the promise given by Ms Grieve that this would not take place.'

It was a searing judgment from beginning to end, entirely in our favour. I received an email a few days later from veteran defamation lawyer Peter Bartlett, saying he'd never seen a judge rule so strongly in support of the duty of a reporter to protect their sources, nor come out so strongly in recognition of a reporter's integrity. 'I have been around a while,' he wrote. 'This decision is huge not only for you but for all media. Congratulations.'

My colleague Sarah Danckert, a dogged investigative journalist with a wicked sense of humour, texted: *I'd get a tatt of 'earnest, intelligent and conscientious' ... Talk about a slam dunk.* My family and I recited our favourite paragraphs, taking delight in the total annihilation of the strategies mounted by Dr Al Muderis. This victory unlocked what was needed for the public interest defence. It meant more cross-examination down the track, which would mean more work, more scrutiny, more insults. But, at that point, I couldn't be more thrilled.

The judgment, however, did not stop Dr Al Muderis from trying to figure out who my sources were. He issued a whole bunch of subpoenas to Mitch Grant – his former patient – seeking to manoeuvre around Justice Bromwich's ruling by working out who spoke with who. Dealing with these subpoenas involved another lengthy, and expensive, round of hearings and arguments, only for Justice Wendy Abraham to knock them back again.

I was in Darwin on another reporting trip when the latest judgment landed in my inbox. The sun was setting over Fannie Bay and I'd finished work for the day. I ordered a cool beer and submerged myself in the shallow end of the pool so I could read the 37-page ruling on my phone. It was dense with legal jargon, precedents and long passages. But when I reached the end, I found what mattered: the conclusion.

'[Al Muderis's] submissions demonstrate that these subpoenas are squarely directed to revealing the identity of certain confidential sources,' Justice Abraham said.

'Given the circumstances in this case, the issue of these subpoenas is an abuse of the court's process. There is no other way to protect the interests of justice but to strike out the subpoenas issued and to refuse to grant leave to the remaining subpoenas.'

I was walking through the newsroom the following week when a colleague stopped me in the corridor. 'Charlotte two. Al Muderis zero.'

CHAPTER 15

Truth Begins

The victory in the confidential source battle gave us new confidence going into the second tranche of the trial, starting 4 March 2024. For the next eight weeks, the court heard evidence from patient after patient who described their experience with Dr Al Muderis. These were our witnesses – people who either appeared in the initial investigation or came forward in the aftermath. These were people with their own histories, lives, hopes and dreams – people from all over the world, from different cultures, languages, ages, backgrounds. While each patient was distinct, there were many similarities – vulnerability, hope, fear, determination. Many were connected by the promise Dr Al Muderis had made – you will walk.

There had been a change of leadership at the newspaper while I had been preparing for the trial. Luke McIlveen had just started in the role of national editor for *The Age* and *Sydney Morning Herald*. On the first day of this tranche of hearings, he wanted to come along for a day in court. I was intrigued to see how he would respond to this drawn-out, expensive legal battle.

Carol Todd was first to give evidence that day. I had spent hours on the phone with Carol but I had never met her in person. As she was escorted through the court hallways by solicitors,

I walked over and introduced myself, knowing I couldn't say much more. Her face lit up, and we embraced briefly before she was whisked away again. It was obvious that Carol was under a lot of stress and that pit in my stomach returned, the responsibility I felt for putting her there.

Everyone filed into the courtroom, with Luke and I sitting side by side in the back row. Carol's friend pushed her wheelchair up to the witness box. Carol's red shawl was perched on her shoulders and her white hair was neatly brushed, but there was a wariness across her face. JP had warned each and every witness that it would not be easy. Chrysanthou's modus operandi was to overload the patients with details and dates to confuse them into doubting their stories. He had one piece of advice he gave to everyone, including Carol: 'Back yourself in. Don't let her wear you down.'

Chrysanthou tried to thread the needle of the concoction theory by asking Carol a series of questions that fell flat, before turning her attention to me.

'Do you remember receiving a call from Charlotte Grieve in early June?'

'Yes. I remember she rang me. Yes. And she spoke about it all. And she wanted to know whether I wanted to help. And at the time I said, "No I don't want to get involved in anything like this." And then I had a thought about it, and I thought, Well I've got nothing to lose because I tell the truth. So I went ahead with it. But I didn't want to go on *60 Minutes*. I didn't want to have nothing to do with that. I don't want my face up there. But I did get ... I put my ... in the paper with me in the wheelchair, which wasn't lying because ... I've got an electric one at home. And I'm in it full-time now.'

Carol was clearly aware of the declaration that Chrysanthou had made in her opening that she faked being in a wheelchair.

'Do you remember any person calling you and trying to persuade you or talk to you about going on the record?'

'Not persuading me, no. Because I had said I didn't want to do it. I was asked did I want to go on it. No-one persuaded me to do it.'

Chrysanthou jumped from topic to topic so quickly Carol became flustered. 'I'm not used to this,' she said at one point. The questions switched to the first time Carol heard Dr Al Muderis speak about osseointegration.

'He explained there were risks and complications?'

'Yes.'

'And that they didn't know anything about it – everything about it, sorry, because it was still a relatively new surgery?'

'I don't remember him saying it was a new surgery or anything like that … He virtually sold it to you that he—'

Chrysanthou cut her off, but Carol kept going. 'I'm sorry, but he did. He came over to me and my husband and it was like a new life.'

The questions went on, as Chrysanthou slowly went through the chronology, asking about Carol's pain, and all that happened, transporting Carol back to each moment. She stopped answering the questions, and instead said how she felt.

'I don't have time to sit down and work out what my pain is doing because I've got to look after my kids. I've got to look after my husband. I've got to look after family, you know? This is why I don't understand what everybody is trying to do to me, because I'm not the one to whinge and carry on. I just get on with my life, whether I'm in pain or not. I just keep going.'

Carol was crying now. The room was tense as she wept. I was furious that this case was even happening. That Dr Al Muderis's own patients were being subjected to intrusive and prolonged cross-examination. Vulnerable, hard-working people who he had failed.

'All right, you are all right, Mrs Todd?' Chrysanthou said.

'No, may I have a drink of water, please?'

The judge swooped in. 'Would you like a short break?'

'No. I'm fine,' she said, holding the cup and steadying herself.

Carol forged on, explaining how everyone in the waiting room had said the surgery was wonderful, that Dr Al Muderis said she may experience infection but that it was no big deal. She talked about her broken bone during surgery, the stabbing pain and how Dr Al Muderis kept saying he 'reckons everything is okay'. The questions kept coming, about major surgery she'd had ten years ago. Carol was overwhelmed.

'It's just too many dates and times and I'm trying to do my best,' she said, eyes darting around the room.

Carol cried twice more in the witness box. In a short break, I saw Carol's friend waiting outside the bathroom and walked over to check on her. I could hear Carol dry-retching in the toilet. So overwhelmed, she was now physically ill. My blood boiled again at what this doctor was doing to his patients.

Back in court, Chrysanthou kept peppering Carol with specific dates from a long time ago. She suggested Carol had misremembered or lied. Carol stood firm. She knew what had happened, and she was there to prove it. She had nothing to gain, nothing to lose. It went on and on. Carol said she was never warned of all the terrible things that had gone wrong. Dr Al Muderis didn't listen, she said. Eventually, the questions ended abruptly.

'No further questions, your Honour,' Chrysanthou said.

Afterward, Luke McIlveen turned to me and said, 'She's incredible, isn't she?' I was so pleased he could see that too. That same week, Luke called an all-staff meeting in the *Sydney Morning Herald* office, where he praised Carol's courage and reaffirmed his commitment to investigative journalism. It was a great outcome, both for the case, and for the newspaper's investment in high-stakes reporting. It's the type of expensive and time-consuming work that only mainstream media can do.

Carol gathered her belongings and her friend helped her out of the witness box. As she was wheeled out of the courtroom, I quietly stood up and followed. I grabbed both of Carol's hands and thanked her for everything. She looked overwhelmed and exhausted. An hour later, I sent her a text message. *Hi Carol, thank you again for today. You should feel proud, you did so well. Let's hope the truth will prevail. Have a safe flight home and now that your evidence is over, we are free to speak so keep in touch.*

Carol responded that night. *Thank you so much for everything you have done. I will keep in touch with you. I don't know what I would have done without all of you.*

This would become a common response from patients who'd been reduced to tears in the witness box, subjected to vigorous and intrusive questioning, insulted, shaken, only to come out the other side proud to have been able to tell their story, and defend it. Dr Al Muderis had made patients doubt themselves by dismissing their suffering, or saying it was their fault, and now they were telling their stories on their terms. It was powerful.

Any brewing feeling of assuredness came to an abrupt end when the next patient got in the box. Anthony Marlborough contacted me after the initial investigation was published. I had a brief conversation with him, but didn't pursue the story further. There were so many people coming forward at that time. I was looking for people whose experiences explored broader, systemic problems, like regulatory failure or the at-times hopeless pursuit of justice through the courts. Tony Marlborough's story struck me as just another allegation of medical negligence. It sounded bad, but my editor Bach's words were ringing in my head, *There's only so many patient horror stories we can publish.* After our initial conversation, Tony largely slipped out of my mind.

Until I was watching him in the witness box. He was a big man, a self-described 'fitness fanatic' and retired 74-year-old veteran. He'd served in Vietnam for six months, where he came under artillery fire and returned with malaria and Hodgkin's disease. Doctors said he had six months to live. After chemotherapy and 'training like you wouldn't believe', Tony went into remission and lived an active life until 2012, when a pain in his leg started to slow him down. His GP referred him to Dr Al Muderis, who recommended a knee replacement. Tony went ahead with the procedure, but after three weeks of rehabilitation, his foot was pointing sharply to one side. He went back to see Dr Al Muderis, who then recommended a hip replacement. With that, things went from bad to worse. Tony was sitting in the cafe of the rehabilitation centre with his wife when suddenly something in his body changed. He was frozen. 'I think I've got a problem,' he said. 'I can't move. I can't get out of the chair. I think my hip is out.'

His wife told him not to be silly, but he knew his body. He called the nurses, who rushed over with a wheelchair. When they pulled him up, he let out a huge roar. The pain was unbearable. He was rushed to hospital and given morphine until Dr Al Muderis arrived and operated, but almost immediately afterward, the hip popped out again. Tony said Dr Al Muderis acknowledged he had done the initial surgery wrong, and offered to fix it again, but by that point, all trust had gone. 'I don't want you to bloody touch me,' Tony told the doctor.

From that day on, Tony said his quality of life had been terrible. He couldn't walk, could barely limp. His foot still pointed sideways, and he almost always felt unbalanced. He had fallen multiple times since the surgery, and could no longer push his granddaughter on a ride, or garden. Like many of Dr Al Muderis's patients, Tony never complained to the regulator or contemplated litigation, but one day he saw the episode of *Anh's Brush With Fame* that highlighted Dr Al Muderis as a humanitarian hero and thought to himself, *That's not the person I knew.* He called the ABC, but never heard back. So, when he saw the *60 Minutes* investigation, he reached out again.

Tony is a strong-willed man who does not suffer fools, traits that would soon become exceedingly apparent. Chrysanthou's cross-examination quickly turned into an explosive unravelling.

Dr Al Muderis's insistence the trial be brought on quickly meant that most patients wrote affidavits from memory before they had access to the subpoenaed medical records. This exposed them to Chrysanthou's scrutiny; she was determined to portray any lapse in memory as a deliberate, nasty lie. From the beginning, Tony said his affidavit was mostly written from 'guesswork' and agreed that dates and times might be wrong. But he corrected Chrysanthou when she suggested things he couldn't remember, like steroid injections she said Dr Al Muderis administered to his knees.

'I don't know where this has come up,' Tony said. 'And quite frankly, I wouldn't believe anything he said … I think I would know if I had steroid injections in both knees.'

This was a theme that would continue and intensify, as Chrysanthou accused Tony of being wrong about almost every aspect of his experience with Dr Al Muderis. Tony accused Chrysanthou of asking 'the same stupid question', and roared at suggestions his memory was wrong. 'Are you saying I'm a liar?' he screeched. The judge tried to keep him on track, and pulled some of Chrysanthou's questions back too, but any effort to maintain order was hopeless.

By 4.15 pm, Collins said it was clear Tony wanted to leave. He was bucking like a wild bull.

'I'm not coming back,' Tony yelled. 'I'm not! This is stupid! I'm not coming back to put up with all of this! I can listen to questions but she's asking me the same thing. I should know what happened to my body. I know when it happened, and she's just asking me stupid things.'

The more Chrysanthou said Tony was wrong, the angrier he became.

'This bloke makes stories up! I think he is making stories up for this case. I think that's the sort of bloke we're dealing with.'

'Come on. It's on the X-ray. Go to the place and look at the X-ray! Your Honour, do we have to go on with this?'

'Yes, you do,' the judge said.

'She's just telling lies!'

'She is asking you questions. You can disagree with the questions. You can say she's wrong,' the judge said.

'Why is she calling me a liar? I'm not a liar. I have never lied in my life.'

'That's not true, is it?' Chrysanthou said.

'You be careful,' he said, menacingly. 'Are you calling me a liar?'

Chrysanthou ignored him and kept asking about appointments he couldn't remember. It was a tornado. It went on and on, until Tony finally snapped. 'Can I just say she's right about everything and can I go?'

'Well, that's not going to help you either,' the judge responded.

'It's not helping me. I'm not doing this for me!'

'Well, Mr Marlborough, you swore to tell the truth,' the judge said.

'I am!' he screeched back, yelling at the judge now. 'Are *you* calling me a liar, now?'

Chrysanthou was trying to bring it home, saying line after line was false. 'No, I didn't, but are we finished now? Suggest what you like. Yes. It's all made up!'

'Mr Marlborough, it's not in your interests to be flippant,' the judge reminded him again.

'It's not in my interests? What can you do to me? I'm not doing anything,' he yelled. 'He lies through his teeth. He's getting away with murder. Let him do it, and if he hurts other people, it's not my fault. I tried to help.'

The lawyers agreed to end the questions.

'Thank you, Mr Marlborough,' Chrysanthou said.

'No, don't thank me. I will never, ever go witness for anybody again, after that,' he screamed.

* * *

The truth defence was off to a dramatic start but the next day was pivotal: Mark Urquhart was giving evidence. He was the most prominent patient in both the print and television stories. It was the video of his legs covered in writhing maggots that viewers would never forget. This was the footage that made Dr Al Muderis's team properly explain this risk to patients. Mark was now defending himself, and my reporting, but also all the other patients whose truths were on the line. The stakes felt like they couldn't be higher.

I texted Mark in the morning to say I'd be in court and looked forward to seeing him. He texted back a photo of the sunrise, saying it was his 'dragon slaying day'. He was feeling good, so I was feeling good. His battle was my battle.

I arrived at the court half an hour early so I could catch Mark on the way in. He arrived wearing all black – a crisp pressed shirt and pants pinned under his thighs. 'You've got this,' I told him.

Straight out of the blocks, Chrysanthou asked questions that seemed designed to confuse him, like 'Who wrote this affidavit?' Her tone was accusatory. Everything felt like a trap. Almost immediately, he looked backed into a corner, and the whole room felt it. Over the course of the day, Chrysanthou scraped over every painful detail of his life – the paratrooping accident, his opioid addiction, the double amputation of his legs, the pain he felt, the smell from his wounds, his failure to achieve his goals. She prodded and probed, testing every aspect of his evidence. At one point he paused, struggling to collect his thoughts, she smacked him down again. 'We're going to be here all day if you can't answer the question,' she barked.

Chrysanthou was raking over his trauma, accusing him of lying, telling him he was confused, wrong, malicious, and then scolding him for taking time to consider his answers. Her need to vigorously test his evidence clearly overrode any obligation she could have had to take heed of his PTSD diagnosis, which made remembering details difficult and revisiting events stressful. She seemed indifferent to the hardships life had delivered him, from a tough childhood to severe disability, and all the complex trauma that had created. She put propositions to him as if they were fact, without basis. He politely disagreed, quietly saying 'No ma'am, that's not right' or 'I'm telling the truth, ma'am'. I felt sick in my stomach as I watched him deal with the onslaught. In the first break, my jaw clenched, I asked Matt Collins why he wasn't objecting more.

'Is there nothing in the rules that offers protection for vulnerable people? Can't we object? This feels unfair,' I protested.

'Don't be angry at Chrysanthou,' Collins told me. 'Be angry at Dr Al Muderis.'

The back-and-forth continued into the afternoon. Mark said over and over that he wasn't good with dates, that he couldn't remember certain conversations but remained polite and calm throughout. While he was hazy on details, when it mattered, he knew exactly what had happened.

'You wanted the operation so you could walk your daughter down the aisle?'

'That has always been a conversation right from the get-go with Munjed, ma'am.'

'And you told Ms Grieve that?'

'Again, ma'am, maybe. I don't remember the exact conversation.'

'And you told Ms Grieve that Dr Al Muderis had achieved that for you?'

'Again, ma'am, I may have. And that's actually true. He did. But there's a whole other bunch of facts, too.'

Chrysanthou asked questions with double negatives, spinning Mark around and around. He said he didn't know how to answer the questions, 'ma'am'.

'Well, it would be untrue to say that your osseointegration did not work out because Munjed did not act quickly enough when you complained?'

'I'm not a doctor, ma'am.'

'So you wouldn't know if that was true or untrue?'

'Ma'am, I only know my own body.'

Even when Mark said he didn't remember a conversation, Chrysanthou kept asking about the same conversation. It was exhausting to watch. She jumped back and forth in the timeline and dove headfirst into the worst moments of his life.

'Now, I just want to ask you a bit about your background, going back quite a number of years now. You suffered severe injuries from accidents in 1992 and 1993. You had 29 confirmed injuries and PTSD?'

'There is that on my record, ma'am, yes.'

'As a result, you became addicted to painkillers?'

'I have openly discussed that, ma'am.'

'Before you had the surgery, you were in a lot of pain?'

'Yes, ma'am.'

'Sometimes burning pain?'

'Yes, ma'am.'

'And stabbing pain?'

'That's part of nerve pain, ma'am.'

'And you had that before you had the osseointegration surgery?'

'I was a T7 incomplete paraplegic, ma'am.'

'You were keen, weren't you, as at 2015, to have a double amputation?'

'Ma'am, with all due respect, no-one is ever "keen" to cut their legs off. No-one is ever "keen" to have a parachute accident that causes them to the extent of pain that that happens, so that they have to go and seek help. Nobody is … Nobody. No. I did not. Nobody seeks that out, ma'am.'

This answer hit home. It was a reminder of the reality of the suffering experienced by patients who had come to see Dr Al Muderis.

Next, she suggested it was Mark who 'convinced' Dr Al Muderis to perform osseointegration surgery on him.

'Ma'am, I don't convince anyone of anything.'

'And it took you a long time to convince him?'

'Ma'am, again, I can't convince a doctor to do that kind of surgery on me.'

'And he told you he doubted you would be able to walk again?'

'No.'

'You knew there were no guarantees?'

'Again, ma'am. If the surgery was done correctly and I had the chance, I believe that I could have made it to the top of the world, but that chance was taken away from me.'

'No-one told you that even if the surgery went perfectly, you would still be walking?'

'What I'm saying is Munjed actually had the convincing of me that he was such a good doctor that his ability to do what he does, I would have the ability to do what I wanted to do.'

'That is not true?' Chrysanthou said, yelling again now.

'Come on, ma'am,' Mark responded.

'That's not true?' she protested, louder still.

'What is the truth then, ma'am?'

'He never promised you?'

'I didn't say he promised.'

Chrysanthou was arguing with Mark about words he never said. She was speaking over him, cutting off his answers. 'Well, let the witness finish,' the judge said at one point.

As the questions jumped back and forth, Mark started to look exhausted.

'You were told it would be a long, hard road? And you were prepared and happy to accept it all?'

'Again, because I believed in Munjed so much, because he believed in himself so much, I thought he was going to do just the most fantastic surgery, and it was going to be all bells and whistles and run off into the sunset.'

'You believed in yourself?'

'I believed in both of us, ma'am, is what I'm saying.'

'You understood it was a lifelong journey?'

'Again, ma'am, yes. You're having both legs cut off, so it's a lifelong thing. You don't get out of it.'

'I'm suggesting to you that the decision that you refer to that my client had made was that you weren't a suitable candidate for osseointegration at the time he saw you?'

'But here we are.'

'Well, can you answer my question, Mr Urquhart,' Chrysanthou said in an angry voice. 'Because otherwise we're going to be here for a very long time?'

'That's all right, ma'am. I'm just getting confused here with my reading and everything. Bear with me, please. I'm just trying to work out – can I have a pen to write these dates down in my head, please, ma'am.'

I texted JP again: *This line of questioning feels wrong. But he's handling it well.*

So well, JP responded.

As the hours passed with Chrysanthou shooting dates and figures at him, Mark began to crack. 'Ma'am, I'm getting stressed now. Could I take half an hour? Can I have lunch?'

'Just bear with me a moment,' the judge said.

Collins stood. 'So from our perspective, your Honour, we are very concerned, obviously, about the mental health of all of the patients who are being cross-examined.'

'Yes,' the judge said. She ordered a half-hour break.

Afterward, Chrysanthou focused on complications Mark endured. She said it wasn't true he had bone protruding from his leg, it wasn't true he had constant pain and spasms since the surgery. He denied each suggestion, but she kept asking the same question over and over.

'There was no bone poking out of your right stump straight after the surgery?'

'I don't know what to answer you, ma'am. I was there. It was my legs ... I had bone protruding out of my leg, ma'am.'

'Well, when you say, "protruding", what are you suggesting?'

'I mean protruding.'

'How? Can you explain that?'

'Exactly what the word means. Protruding.'

'What did it look like?'

'What does it mean to you, ma'am? Like it was sticking out of my leg.'

'How many centimetres?'

'Ma'am,' he said. 'I didn't ... I don't know the answer to that. I have just come out of having my legs off, having whatever else happen medically-wise. But to tell you that I had bone – I didn't pull up a ruler and measure my leg as to how much.'

'What shape was this bone that you say was protruding?'

'Again, ma'am, it's my leg. It's a bone. What shape is it? I don't know. It's roundish.'

'So it's round. Was it long? Did it look like a finger bone? What did it look like?'

'It looked like a bone protruding out of my leg, ma'am.'

'It's just false!' Chrysanthou shouted.

'Okay. It's not false. I'm telling the truth and if I'm telling a lie, then why would I have had more surgery from other surgeons, ma'am? I don't know what to say to that. I'm not lying. It's the truth.'

She branded parts of his affidavit as 'completely false', 'absurd', and 'ridiculous'. The more Mark said he couldn't remember dates, the more Chrysanthou peppered him with questions about specific years, months, days. The focus turned to the maggots toward the end of the day. She said there were 'no messages' where Mark sent the video and was ignored.

'Well, I don't agree with you.'

'There's no text, I want to suggest to you?'

'What am I supposed to do once I've sent videos of maggots in my legs? I didn't get the help I needed, and I didn't get the help I needed right from the get-go, as far as I'm concerned. But I didn't get the help I needed, so I searched out another surgeon.'

'And you say this happened at the end of 2019?'

'I don't remember the year, ma'am.'

'All right. Well, I want to suggest to you that this was a malicious lie that you made up about my client and Claudia?'

'No, ma'am. That's not true.'

Mark wasn't denying the timeline might be wrong, but he wouldn't be shaken on the bigger picture. His legs were infested with maggots on several occasions and the treatment he received was not good enough.

That night, I felt more physically drained than the first day of Chrysanthou's opening. I couldn't imagine how Mark must have been feeling. I started to question the value of the whole endeavour. If the job of journalists is to give the voiceless a voice, what happens when this is the end result? I had encouraged this man to tell his story, only for him to be accused of lying for hours on end, pounding his fragile trauma into the cold, hard pavement of the justice system. This wasn't a criminal trial, but it felt like one. I was losing sight of the bigger picture, and losing hope in the public interest of what we were doing. The cost felt enormous.

That night, JP called me to check in. I asked him again to push the lawyers to do more. I felt that we had thrown Mark to the wolves. 'Matt is looking non-interventionist,' JP told me, 'but there is a method to the madness. Mark's put on the affidavit. Sue's job is to say his evidence is not true. So far, Mark is coming across as truthful.'

The next day, I arrived at court early again. JP was already there.

'Mark's not in a good way, emotionally,' he said.

'Is it okay to go say hello?' I asked. JP nodded.

I found Mark in a small conference room. His face was totally drained of colour. He hadn't slept as his worst, most harrowing memories were pulled violently back to the surface. 'You're lucky I'm back,' he said.

After we left the room, Mark's friend told me he had demanded she take him to a bridge in the middle of the night. Mark was so rattled by the experience, he'd wanted to end his life. I apologised for everything and thanked them for being here, unable to say what I really wanted to say – that everyone could see he was telling the truth, and it will be over soon.

Mark wheeled himself back into the witness box as the clock ticked past 10 am. His utter exhaustion was clear in his voice, his words soft and wavering. But still, he didn't let Chrysanthou's strategy push him into changing his story.

'That's not the truth as I remember it, ma'am,' he responded to her baseless accusations. 'My truth is as the story – as I've told it.'

'Well, as you've told it here?'

'In the affidavit.'

'Are you sure you wrote that affidavit?'

'Ma'am, I don't know where you're going. Yes, ma'am.'

It went on and on like this. While Mark was deflated, he was certainly not defeated. He was sharp, spotting the traps Chrysanthou laid. The court was shown text messages where Mark had praised Dr Al Muderis. Mark spoke calmly, and kindly, about his former doctor. 'He's not my enemy still.'

Mark requested a toilet break in the first half-hour. The judge adjourned. Collins came over to me. 'This is callous. It's inhumane,' he said.

Hours into the second day of questioning, after Chrysanthou kept asking the same question, wanting a different answer, Collins stepped to his feet. *Finally*, I thought.

'Sorry, I object,' Collins said. 'These questions are not just becoming harassing. The witness has given his honest answer to the questions. He has not diverged one drop from …'

After a day and a half, the questioning eventually finished. Mark left the witness box and my jaw unclenched. I followed him out and saw he had tears in his eyes. 'Brutal … That was brutal.' I suggested we grab a coffee. We left the court building and found a spot in the sunshine on Macquarie Street. We locked eyes, and let out a collective sigh, exchanging exhausted smiles. We both knew how absurd this process was, because to us, the truth was obvious.

I apologised for putting him in that position and thanked him for everything. He said it was one of the hardest things he had ever done, that Chrysanthou's questions had made him doubt his very existence. He felt overwhelmed, confused, and unsure of every detail of his life. JP came to join us briefly and shook Mark's hand. 'You took a risk in speaking out, and Charlotte took a risk in telling your story, too,' JP said. He assured Mark that his evidence was solid and couldn't have gone better.

Mark, his friend and I sat on Macquarie Street for the best part of an hour, dissecting the cross-examination – the strange parts, the brutal parts, and the outright confusing parts. By the end of that conversation, Mark said he didn't regret sharing his story. He knew what Dr Al Muderis was up to was wrong and he was proud to have been a part of exposing that. His eyes started to fill with tears again, but this time they were happy tears. He thanked me for telling his story. 'I've done my bit. Now I can move on,' he said.

The conclusion of Mark's evidence was a huge milestone for the case. But there was no time to rest. There were six more patients due to give evidence that week alone, including my dad.

* * *

I felt more and more confident with the case as each day passed and new witnesses gave evidence. We heard from patient after patient, each with their own unique story of disappointment.

Thomson Geer arranged for patients from all around the world to travel to Australia to attend the Federal Court and sit in the witness box. Each witness was another brick in the wall of our truth defence, as one after the other confidently stood by what was written in their affidavits. Rachael Ulrich flew in from Texas, texting afterwards: *I think y'all have it in the bag!* Another American patient, Lisa Schaeffer, had her private text messages flashed onto the screen: *It's called karma and it's pronounced fuck you.* Lisa had been watching the trial, amazed that the public was finally getting to see the real Dr Al Muderis. She was also shocked by the new revelations the trial was unearthing. 'It's something that comes right out of HBO or Netflix,' Lisa told the court.

After Mark Urquhart, the person I was most anxious for was Dad. A few days after we had published the investigation, Dr Al Muderis's lawyers had sent a vaguely worded email alleging I had a 'serious conflict' that amounted to malice. They were alleging that my father's consultation with Dr Al Muderis in 2018 had impacted my impartiality and turned me into some kind of one-eyed devil.

Newsrooms around the world today are having conversations about impartiality, objectivity and the experiences and opinions of journalists in the social media age. Margaret Simons, who is regularly cited as an authority on media ethics, told me that objectivity is one of the worst understood concepts in journalism. 'We should bring ourselves to the reporting, all of ourselves, of course. But it's the process that is important.'

I was confident my personal connection to this story only strengthened the journalism. Having grown up as the daughter of an amputee, I was better equipped to understand the specific challenges they face. I understand the significance of things like phantom pain, neuromas, revision surgeries. I understand, on a visceral level, why it was such a big deal to go from being a below-knee to above-knee amputee. These things made sense to me in a profound, natural, innate way. They made me a better interviewer, and a better reporter. My personal connection to this story, and the understanding of disability that came with it, had no impact on the process I went through – of corroborating evidence, seeking out and presenting multiple perspectives, to ensure the reporting was accurate and fair.

From that very first letter accusing me of malice, I knew Dr Al Muderis's lawyers would try to spin the connection into something it was not. The mere threat prompted some editors in the newsroom to openly wonder if I really did have a conflict.

My father had been involved in several high-profile defamation cases during his career, from representing Bob Hawke to John Singleton. He started every defamation case with the same approach: by asking the complainant 'What skeletons do you have in the closet?' If their closet was crowded, he would always advise against suing. During his day, father-and-son team, both named Clive Evatt, were among the most talked about, and criticised, barristers, who read the newspapers each day to hunt for clients. 'Clive was the publisher's constant irritant,' Fairfax's old night lawyer Richard Coleman told *Justinian*. 'Clive was devious but never dull.' My father thought this case, like many of Clive Evatts', had been misconceived from the outset. He also hated Chrysanthou's style of cross-examination. I was worried his frustration with the legal machinations of the case could be misconstrued as hostility toward Dr Al Muderis and feed into the theory of malice on my part. I tried to persuade my father to keep his cool, but deep down I knew there was an immovable, unflinching stubbornness to him, an impulsive desire to do what he thought was right, that he simply could not and would not control.

I was still at home on the morning of his cross-examination when I spoke with my mother in the hallway. There was anxiety etched into her face after a mostly sleepless night. She had been nothing but supportive through this entire ordeal, but now, she was worried. 'I would hate for him to go through his entire life with an unblemished record and then finish his career with a negative credit finding,' she said. We both knew he was telling the truth, but one poorly answered question, one well-argued submission, and this could be a devastating moment for a King's Counsel at the end of his career.

I was already in the courtroom, listening to the cross-examination of a surgeon before him, when Dad walked in. He was wearing a freshly pressed suit and a red tie, his hair neatly combed in its usual fashion. His old colleague at the bar, Dauid Sibtain SC, was with him.

My hands trembled when Dad was called. I tried to make eye contact with our lawyers, to send one last message – *please protect him, do not let Chrysanthou get under his skin, be ready to object when necessary.*

'Is your full name Donald Edward Grieve?' Collins asked after Dad got in the box.

'Yes.'

'And you're a member of His Majesty's Counsel?'

'That's correct.'

'But retired?'

'That's right.'

When the cross-examination began, it felt like all my worst fears materialised almost immediately.

'Mr Grieve, you retired in 2019?' Chrysanthou asked.

'What is your question?' he responded. Silence fell over the courtroom.

'You retired in 2019 …?'

'What is your question?' he repeated. I turned to Dauid – a tight smile flashed across his face.

'Is that correct?' Chrysanthou continued.

'Yes,' Dad responded.

The next few questions passed normally, until Chrysanthou returned to her statement-as-question format.

'Now, you've spoken to your daughter, Charlotte Grieve, about this case, haven't you?'

'Yes.'

'And you've spoken to her about my client?'

'What is your question?' he bellowed again.

'You don't understand by the way I inflect my voice at the end, Mr Grieve, that I'm asking you a question?'

'No. You are making statements, not asking questions.'

'Mr Grieve, have you spoken to your daughter about my client?'

'Yes.'

After that, Chrysanthou was more careful with the structure of her questions. Dad was brief with his answers, standing by what his affidavits stated – particularly the conversation around phantom pain. After decades of preparing witnesses for trial, he knew the golden rule of short, honest answers.

'And I want to suggest to you, you don't have a clear recollection of that brief conversation?'

'Yes, I have quite a clear recollection of it.'

She turned her attention to his physical condition.

'You had very little pain at that time in 2018?'

'That's not correct.'

'You didn't have any chronic pain?'

'No. It comes and goes.'

'And I want to suggest to you that phantom pain or reducing pain was not of primary concern to you when thinking about osseointegration at that time?'

'No. That was the only – that was the only factor of interest to me.'

Then, Chrysanthou began taking my father through an email he sent – line by line – asking if he agreed the words were accurate.

'Yes. I should say the document speaks for itself,' he answered. This was another barb over legal tactics. He thought these questions wasted the court's time.

'Thank you for advice on my cross-examination, Mr Grieve, but could you please answer my question?'

'I just did,' he replied.

'No, you didn't,' she said, before correcting herself. 'Perhaps you did.'

The swagger and confidence that Chrysanthou had splashed all over the courtroom seemed to be cracking.

'You agree that, at the time of that letter 20 August 2018, you had no painkillers prescribed?'

'That's correct,' he said. 'Indeed, I have never had any painkillers prescribed so far as I can recall, other than on one occasion a few years ago, when I suffered some abnormally prolonged phantom pains.'

'And the reason you've had – other than that one instance – no painkillers prescribed is because you don't have a significant pain issue, insofar as your amputation is concerned?'

My anger returned at this. I knew as his daughter how much pain my father had endured over the years. I'd seen it.

'Well, I do experience phantom pains from time to time, of varying severity, but generally speaking they're not an overriding problem.'

As the questions went on, Chrysanthou beamed his private medical records onto the screen, livestreamed to YouTube for the hundreds of people tuned in.

He corrected her pronunciation of a prosthetist's name, then returned to correcting her questions, which soon arrived at the consultation in 2018.

'They asked you questions about any problems that you had had with your socket?' Chrysanthou asked.

'When you say "they", would you be good enough to be a little more precise? You've identified the existence of a number of medical practitioners. Are you suggesting to me that all of these individuals spoke to me?'

This was a common refrain my father used when he was at

his absolute wit's end but maintaining a façade of politeness. I've heard him say this many times in situations that send him into a tailspin – people interrupting a conversation, for example.

'One or more of them?'

'Well, I don't understand your question, I'm sorry.'

'One or more of the doctors present asked you about your mobility?'

'What is your question?'

'Is that right?'

'No.'

The court adjourned at 12.48 pm. Dad had lunch by himself at The Australian Club down the road, while Mum and her friend Elizabeth came up to the Thomson Geer offices for sandwiches. I asked the lawyers whether Dad bashing up Chrysanthou's questions was a problem. Everyone said no. They loved it, and thought it was going well. 'What an icon,' my sister said. She had been my guiding star throughout the process, one of the few people whose judgment I trusted entirely. Tess was born exactly 14 months before me, but took the role of big sister seriously, gently guiding me through life with encouragement, support and caution. From studying four-unit maths at school to scoring in the top one per cent of the New York Bar exam, she is almost always the smartest person in the room. When Tess said she thought it was going well, I relaxed.

After lunch, the cross-examination turned to the graph drawn by Dr Al Muderis during the consultation. Chrysanthou 'suggested' the downward line did not mean he would be wheelchair-bound by the time he was 80 years old.

'No, I don't accept that,' Dad responded. 'I have a very clear recollection of his statement to that effect.'

He said the doctor had 'certainly made it plain' that he would be wheelchair-bound within five years at most.

'I want to suggest to you that he said no such thing to you, Mr Grieve, and that you're mistaken?'

'Well, I don't accept that, with respect.'

Attention then turned to the letter sent to my father's GP. Dad called it a 'so-called letter' and said it contained several inaccuracies. Chrysanthou's hackles seemed to go up.

'Well, regardless of its accuracy, it's not a so-called letter to your GP. It was a letter sent to your GP and received by your GP at about the time of the consultation?'

'I accept that is so,' he said. 'But that does not vouchsafe its accuracy.'

This was a man who studied Latin at school, and whose daughter Madeleine spoke five languages, translated for two French presidents – their genes bound over a shared love of language and the endless ways to convey precise meaning. His use of 'vouchsafe' indicated he was in his element.

Finally, Chrysanthou turned to my correspondence with Dad about Dr Al Muderis, asking whether he understood I intended 'to write something negative' about the doctor.

'No ... I had no appreciation of precisely what my daughter was proposing to write about this matter.'

By 2.45 pm, he was dismissed. He walked out with his head held high. Later that night, a photo of him leaving the court building was published in *The Australian*.

'Old silk's jabs hit their mark in sparring match,' was the headline.

My father is usually the type to scowl in photographs, but in this picture, his eyes were relaxed, a soft smile swept across his face and the breeze ruffled his hair. He was in his happy place – leaving court after a solid day's evidence. My mother privately wanted to smack him over the head.

The Australian article described him as a 'critical witness' who gave 'combative evidence'. 'After a while, the patented Grieve niggle clearly got under Chrysanthou's skin.'

The article was written by Yoni Bashan, the same journalist who had written a previous article which, in my parents' view, falsely suggested my father had lied in his affidavit a few months earlier. Furious, my parents enlisted defamation lawyer Michael Bradley to fire off a concerns notice to News Corp. The newspaper was forced to amend the article, pay costs and publish the 'Donald Grieve clarification' in print and online, stating it 'did not intend to suggest that Mr Grieve had sworn false evidence'. This drew an important line in the sand in determining what *The Australian* could get away with, and was a reminder for News Corp not to take the word of background briefings from lawyers, nor their crisis communicator counterparts.

With Dad's evidence done, the sense of relief washed over me once again.

There would be 21 more trial days from that point, taking us to mid-April. During this time, I saw things I could never have imagined. I saw Dr Al Muderis intercept an elderly patient as she walked up to the witness box, in one last moment of intimidation. I saw a mother break down in tears, begging to know why her son was so mistreated. I saw Dr Al Muderis instruct his lawyers to pose wild conspiracies against his former colleagues. I saw Rowena Mattiske's evidence stretch days, during which she broke down in tears and needed multiple breaks so she could lay on the ground in pain. One after another, patients had intimate details of their health and personal histories probed and prodded in public under the full privilege of the Federal Court. They had nothing to gain but speaking the truth.

Unethical at best, dangerous at worst.

CHAPTER 16

International Patients

Billy Wynne flew into Sydney from Oklahoma with his wife to testify. We had only spoken once before, briefly, after the investigation was published. On day 31 of the trial, as he walked up to the witness stand, I saw his neatly pressed shirt covered burn scars that crawled down his arm and fingers, ending at his knuckles.

Billy trained as a paramedic as a young man and his first job was with one of the busiest emergency services in the south-western state. He worked 12-hour shifts, six days a week, excelled quickly, and was soon offered a position with EagleMed – a company that performs air evacuations. During one shift in 2013, ice flew into the helicopter's engine and the chopper crashed and burst into flames. Billy went down with it and was lucky to survive, but he was left with horrific injuries. Sixty-five per cent of his body was covered in third- and fourth-degree burns, and his bones were shattered throughout his body.

He spent six months in hospital, where he underwent 20-odd surgeries, including the amputation of his left leg, first below the knee, and then later above the knee. In hospital, Billy's limb swelled inside the burned skin and cut off the blood supply, so the doctors had to slice his limb to relieve the pressure. One cut was so deep it left a long scar, 'effectively a canyon', that ran from his hip to the end of his left stump.

Because Billy's stump was so badly scarred, it was difficult to find a socket prosthesis that fit. The socket was either so loose it slipped as he walked, causing him to fall, or so tight it rubbed against his delicate skin, creating wounds so severe he needed skin grafts. After three years, he started searching for alternatives. 'I began to feel desperate and to lose hope,' he said. 'I would have done anything for a better option.'

Billy discovered osseointegration around late 2017. Everything about the procedure seemed like it would work. When he found Dr Al Muderis online, he, like so many patients before him, was buoyed by the wall-to-wall glowing press coverage. 'I thought he must be an amazing surgeon because there were pages and pages about how amazing he was.'

Billy filled in the online questionnaire and was soon contacted by Claudia Roberts asking for X-Rays, then Fred Hernandez, who quoted him $US80,000. As they discussed the surgery and logistics of travelling to Australia, Billy started to regard Fred as a friend. He had no idea Fred had signed a confidential contract to receive a cash commission of $US1000 for every patient he sent to Dr Al Muderis.

Not long after Billy first got in touch with the team, he learned that Dr Al Muderis was visiting New Orleans for an osseointegration conference, and was holding a clinic on the sidelines to see patients. Billy booked a flight, eager to meet his new surgeon. When he arrived at the 'clinic', he was shepherded into a cheap-looking hotel room with several other patients, and instructed to take off his pants. Dr Al Muderis glanced over his stump.

'You're good, no problem. You got any questions?' he asked.

Billy had so many questions, and was surprised by how little the doctor explained the risks. He was most concerned about the scar tissue on his stump, and how this might respond to the osseointegration implant sticking out of it. He'd had problems with wound healing in the past, and was terrified this might happen again. He was told this wouldn't be an issue.

The appointment was over in minutes. Dr Al Muderis said Billy's surgery would cost around $110,000, but asked him not to tell other patients. Even at the time, Billy noticed red flags – the hotel room, other patients stuffed into the room, the short consultation, the lack of discussion. *He's from a different country,* Billy told himself. *Maybe things in his world are so different and maybe that's just normal in Australia.* Billy wanted to find a solution so badly, he tricked himself into ignoring his unease.

Before he arrived in Australia, Billy had transferred $84,000 for the surgery and paid the rest in instalments. When Billy informed the team of the financial strain the surgery created, Claudia Roberts told him Dr Al Muderis 'kindly' offered the payment plan but could not reduce the implant price 'because the implant company is not as compassionate and cannot lower the cost'. She didn't mention that Dr Al Muderis was the sole shareholder of that company.

Dr Al Muderis acted like they were meeting for the first time when Billy went to the Macquarie University Hospital offices. 'Is osseointegration something you'd be interested in?' he asked. Billy thought it was a joke. He'd just flown halfway around the world, drained his savings, gone into debt and the surgery was just a few days away.

'I'm here for the surgery. I have a surgery date,' Billy responded, dumbfounded. As Dr Al Muderis started looking through his papers, Claudia walked past.

'Claudia, who is he?' Dr Al Muderis called out.

'This is Billy, the one you met in New Orleans,' Claudia responded.

The red flags had now morphed into giant flashing stop signs.

'Oh, of course I know who you are,' Dr Al Muderis then said.

Dr Al Muderis asked if Billy had any questions. Nothing felt right, but Billy tried to stay positive, so desperate and hopeful that this procedure would change his life. He explained, yet again, that his biggest concern was his scarring.

'You're fine,' Dr Al Muderis reassured him, showing a few photographs of other burns patients who'd had osseointegration before changing the topic.

'I remember thinking to myself at the time, either Munjed is incredibly talented and confident, or he is a reckless fool,' Billy said.

A few days later, Billy was admitted to hospital for osseointegration. He remembers the pre-operative appointment lasting only a few minutes, the shortest he had ever experienced over dozens of operations. When he woke up, he was groggy, and put the pain down to normal post-operative pain. When the bandages came off, his leg was bloody, warm and red, and became more swollen and more painful by the hour. He raised concerns with Dr Al Muderis and Roberts, but they assured him everything was normal.

The following day, red blood blisters had formed and his skin had turned black. Billy's training and experience taught him this meant the skin was dying. *This is exactly what I had told Dr Al Muderis I was worried about,* he thought. He contacted the doctor and his wife only to be dismissed once again. The pain got worse, and Billy suspected infection. He texted both Roberts and Dr Al Muderis, but each time was dismissed or ignored. The pain became unbearable, to the point where Billy thought he was dying. Eventually, a pain specialist visited Billy's hotel. He arrived with a duffel bag and administered an injection in Billy's spine, on top of the blood-stained hotel sheets. The injection didn't work. When Billy threatened to call an ambulance, Dr Al Muderis organised a room at Macquarie

University Hospital. 'You figure out your own way there,' Dr Al Muderis told him.

Billy ordered an Uber, his leg bleeding all over the car. He was given a ketamine infusion at the hospital, which finally dulled his pain for a few days. He barely remembers the rest of the stay. Everything felt out of control. When he stabilised, he wanted to get out of Australia immediately.

During his final appointment in Australia, Billy felt depleted, like all of his worst fears had come true. Dr Al Muderis did not ask about his doctors back home, and there was no plan to oversee his care. Back in America, Billy continued to have problems. He had several infections, so severe that he went to the emergency room twice. 'Despite Dr Al Muderis's assurances that my wound would heal quickly, it took two and a half years for my stump to completely heal following the osseointegration procedure,' Billy deposed. 'The wound was open that whole time.'

To this day, Billy still deals with fluid leakage and a gap between the scar tissue and implant – problems Dr Al Muderis never discussed with Billy. Though Dr Al Muderis said the surgery would help with phantom pain, he is still regularly hospitalised for pain. Despite all his suffering, Billy is now more active than he ever was using sockets, and he remains a strong advocate for the surgery, which, he said when done properly, can be life-changing.

In the witness box, Chrysanthou asked Billy what seemed to me to be mind-boggling questions.

'You were having a great time in Australia?' she asked.

'No, that couldn't be further from the truth.'

Chrysanthou presented scraps of evidence she thought were smoking guns – photographs of happy moments in Australia, supportive emails to Dr Al Muderis. But each time, Billy responded with clear-headed confidence, shutting her down. He explained that his determination to remain on good terms with

Dr Al Muderis came from a place of fear. He felt he needed to keep the doctor on side if problems arose. He stood firm in his view that Dr Al Muderis should have listened to him.

Toward the end of Billy's evidence, I got a work call that I had to take. I was lingering in the hallway, speaking in hushed tones, when Billy emerged with his wife. I hung up and walked over to introduce myself and thank them for coming all this way.

'I don't think we'll be coming back to Australia,' his wife said. 'I love it but we won't be back.'

We shook hands and parted ways.

* * *

Blythe Warland flew in from Queensland to give evidence on 15 March 2024 – Day 34 of the trial. In Chrysanthou's opening, she triumphantly revealed records that supposedly proved Blythe was wrong about every aspect of his life – chief among his lies was Blythe's claim that he had developed Complex Regional Pain Syndrome (CRPS) *after* the surgery. This was a critical point to Blythe's story, one that he repeated many times to me. Blythe said he had developed CRPS after osseointegration, a condition so all-consuming that it totally destroyed his life. He was never warned of this potential complication, and said if he was, he might not have gone ahead with the surgery.

For Blythe, the main aim of osseointegration was to rid himself of pain medications so he could clear his mind and return to work, but the crippling and little-understood syndrome saw him end up on more painkillers than ever before. In the article we published about Blythe, he was quoted as saying the pain was so severe he'd lost his business, his wife and his house.

Chrysanthou's team had gathered corporate and property records that showed, in fact, Blythe lost his business, house and marriage *before* the surgery. More concerningly, she also revealed a pre-surgery questionnaire that showed Blythe had ticked 'yes' to 'CRPS' before the operation, which indicated it was something he experienced at the time. While the timeline of losing the house, wife and business may have been more complicated than Chrysanthou made out, the questionnaire totally floored me. Suffering CRPS after the surgery was Blythe's key complaint about osseointegration. We'd had countless conversations about how this unexpected complication had impacted him – yet he'd ticked 'yes' to having it before the surgery. How could he get that so wrong? Did I misunderstand something? I was prohibited from calling him to ask, so eagerly – and anxiously – awaited his evidence.

I arrived at the Federal Court earlier than usual and waited for Blythe to arrive. I spotted him walking toward security and briskly walked over to say hello. He had the same wild beard and bright eyes as the first time I met him, almost two years ago.

'How are you?' I asked.

'Not good,' he responded. His leg had been playing up and he had been awake since 3 am. 'No amount of coffee could wake me up.'

We made small-talk as we headed to the lifts. When it came time for Blythe to get in the box, he took a deep breath as he braced for tough questions. As Chrysanthou went through the chronology, she made some mistakes, and laughed them off – 'it's been a long week' – as she jumped around in time. Eventually, she arrived at the questions I was most interested in.

'In 2015, do you recall that you believed you developed CRPS?'

'No. I know I've ticked the thing there and – I'm slightly dyslexic, and when I was ticking the tick box ... I only worked this ... because I could not work out how I would have ticked "complex regional pain syndrome" if I've never heard of it before and ... Not yesterday, the day before, I was going through my notes and I actually read it as "chronic regional pain syndrome" – "chronic pain" – and I ticked it because I read it wrong.'

This was not the answer Chrysanthou wanted. People tick boxes incorrectly all the time, including in matters of legal importance. In this case, Blythe had made an entirely understandable mistake and his answer perfectly explained it.

'We will come back to that,' Chrysanthou said, and changed topics.

The cross-examination only offered a deeper insight into the trauma that hung over Blythe's life. He spoke of how he'd woken up in the operating theatre when his leg was first amputated, causing him to suffer PTSD. That experience was more traumatic than the injury itself, he said, leaving him with insomnia and serious depression. He suffered intrusive thoughts, unable to escape the image of his leg being cut off. On top of the mental pain, he underwent dozens of surgeries to remove the neuromas. His marriage was tumultuous, plagued with fights and eventually ended in divorce. 'Being with someone that's always aching and grumpy is pretty hard,' he said. He talked about how desperately he valued his mobility, and how he approached life like a 'bull at a gate'. Being told to use a wheelchair was like 'a death sentence' to Blythe.

Chrysanthou returned to the questionnaire with the CRPS box ticked. 'I want to suggest you thought you had that at that time?'

Blythe was steadfast.

'No. No, because I had never been diagnosed with it. It was new. That's where I said, "I have got dyslexia" and because that has been messing with me. Like, why did I tick something that I have never been diagnosed with. It was only when I was talking to—'

Chrysanthou cut in. 'Dr Ho?'

'No. Sophie with my affidavit that I actually read it as – how I can only imagine I read it then.'

Sophie Meixner was another one of the solicitors working on the case, forensically and sensitively, supporting witnesses through the trial. Chrysanthou showed Blythe his social media posts, which, she suggested, captured him having a great time. 'I always try to be upbeat on social media. You know, everyone has a perfect life on that. I was going out of my brain,' Blythe said.

Throughout his evidence, Blythe described difficulties and blow-ups from Dr Al Muderis, but also stood by his earlier praise of the doctor. He maintained that Australia's boat turnbacks were bad policy because they meant people like Dr Al Muderis were kicked out. This was another patient who clearly had no vendetta and, in many ways, had a positive experience with osseointegration. His problem was that Dr Al Muderis had ignored his concerns, time and again. The more Chrysanthou denied experiences that dominated Blythe's life, the firmer he became in pushing back. This came to a crescendo when Chrysanthou denied Blythe's infections.

'You didn't have a series of long-lasting infections after osseointegration. That's false?'

'Okay, then have a look at the doctor's report. I've got the doctor's report. You've got it. You've got my doctor's report. There's 160 pages, and that outlines how many infections I've had just from one doctor. So, I'm sorry, but you are incorrect. You can say what you like,' Blythe said firmly.

Chrysanthou accused Blythe of telling outright lies, but he stuck to his guns. He told the court that his relationships ebbed and flowed, and that he had to completely shut his businesses after the surgery. He knocked back the accusations one by one, leaving the triumphant revelations from Chrysanthou's opening in tatters.

'And you had no problems at all with Dr Al Muderis until you spoke to Charlotte Grieve in June 2022?'

'No. I've already said I had had issues.'

'No further questions, your Honour.'

That night, the Quill Awards, Victoria's most prominent journalism awards, were held in Melbourne. I'd been nominated for my reporting about the over-use of shackles on patients experiencing mental illness, so I had to leave the court early to catch a flight. As I drove to the airport, I plugged into Blythe's evidence on YouTube, hanging on every word, waiting for it to fall apart. But it never did. The questions ended without me, Blythe or the case sustaining a single wound.

Matt Collins had once given me the analogy of our court case being like a swan. Above the water, it glides elegantly with beauty and grace. Beneath the surface, its legs are pedalling frantically, batting away reeds, pushing against currents, furiously driving it forward. While I was worried Blythe's evidence might be damning, everyone's hard work behind the scenes meant it was just another day.

When I landed in Melbourne, I changed into a cocktail outfit in the airport bathroom before jumping in an Uber, where I called Blythe for a debrief.

Blythe said he'd thought about how to behave in the box. 'When I was a kid at school and kids were giving me shit, I was the class clown. I approached it light-heartedly and didn't let it affect me. So any point I was able to inject humour into it, I did. I thought if I antagonise – it's going to escalate up. I didn't get my back up until when she said I was lying about infections. That's when I hit her between the eyes. It's 160 pages from my doctors.'

Blythe said he had been preparing for a serious stoush, but felt the questions were easy at times, incoherent at others. In all, he was glad it was over.

'Thank you for calling and helping me make sense of that weird two and a half hours,' he said. 'I hope you guys win, I do.'

**

Eang Srey Da grew up in a rural village in Cambodia, surrounded by rice farms and sugar plantations. When she was still a teenager, she was carrying water on her shoulder when she fell and sprained her ankle. She was taken to a village doctor, who treated her with traditional medicine, but her leg continued to swell. Eventually, her parents took her to a mainstream doctor, who told her the injury had not healed properly and the bones had deformed.

Her family could not afford the hospital fees, so took her back to the village for treatment. Her injury got worse and, eventually, doctors said her leg needed to be amputated above the knee. Eang Srey Da was taken to the Khmer-Soviet Friendship Hospital, a publicly run hospital in Cambodia's capital, Phnom Penh, where she spent two weeks for the amputation and recovery. After she was discharged, she used walking sticks before a local clinic gave her a prosthetic leg. The prosthesis was simple, strapped on by a belt tied around her waist. It was painful to wear and the leg slipped off as she walked. She couldn't wear it for long stretches, and sometimes needed crutches too.

She put up with this for five years, until in 2015, Eang Srey Da was told about a new surgery being offered to amputees by a charity-funded hospital in Phnom Penh, that could fix her problems and give her a whole new leg. She was thrilled, and travelled to the hospital to learn more. There, she was shown videos of osseointegration patients walking with ease and was told the surgery would help her walk.

Also in the hospital that day was a young man named Pril Sina. He was a widower and farmer, raising chickens and ducks from his home in a rural village to the north. That year, Pril Sina had a bad motorcycle accident and broke his left leg in several places. He was told the breaks were so bad the leg would need to be cut off. Desperate to save his leg, Pril Sina sought treatment from a traditional doctor, who only confirmed that the leg had to go. Pril Sina was taken to a government-run hospital where his left leg was amputated above the knee, and he was also given a simple prosthesis. Several months later, he learned about the new surgery that would see him walk again.

Pril Sina and Eang Srey Da each met with a Cambodian doctor, who explained how the surgery worked and promised the wounds would heal. They were told the operation would be performed by a doctor from Australia, and were given basic information about risks, such as further surgeries or death. They both remembered meeting Dr Al Muderis briefly while he was in Cambodia, and then never again. The operations left both Pril Sina and Eang Srey Da with rolling, permanent, unforeseen complications, and both regretted going ahead with the surgery.

When Dr Al Muderis launched his litigation, I was keen for our case to include Eang Srey Da and Pril Sina. To me, their experiences spoke volumes about the disconnect between how Dr Al Muderis portrays himself as a global humanitarian, trotting from one war-torn country to the next, and the reality. These were some of the most disadvantaged people on the planet, and this surgery had made their already difficult lives even harder. But by late April, less than five months before the trial was set to begin, the legal team hadn't been able to get hold of them. Neither were answering their calls, and later, their phones were disconnected all together.

'We haven't had any success in speaking to our Cambodian witnesses,' JP emailed me on 25 April. 'Do you think there is any way you can get through to them and tee up some calls? Then we'd need to get the statements witnessed on Facetime like I did with you. We can literally make any time work if you can get through to them.'

This was one of the points in the trial where I realised a solicitor's skill set is, at times, not dissimilar to a journalist's. They need to track down sources and ask them to participate in unfamiliar processes to share their story for no benefit other than the importance of the truth. Both solicitors and journalists are forever at the whims of their witness/source's mood, availability and courage in speaking out. In short, these people owe us nothing. Getting two Cambodian villagers into a news story, let alone a courtroom an ocean away, was a mammoth task.

I emailed Dr Jim Gollogly again, the gruff-talking American who initially put me in touch with the Cambodian patients, asking if he had updated contact details for either patient.

Jim responded the next day, to my surprise, but any spark of joy was short-lived. His assistant had tried to call the patients but couldn't get through. Another dead end.

I reminded the lawyers about the Cambodian journalist, Kourchetta, who completed the original interviews with Eang Srey Da and Pril Sina. A young law graduate reached out and asked Kourchetta to set up a phone call with the patients to 'take a quick statement'. The journalist said in response he had recorded the interviews, but wasn't sure if he still had them and promised to check his computer. It would take another month for Kourchetta to finally locate and send the recordings, and countless more meetings and phone calls to track down the patients. But eventually, through sheer determination, they got through. Both Eang Srey Da and Pril Sina filed affidavits in Khmer, which were translated to English, and both agreed to give evidence in court. Now this was a miracle.

Day 39 of the trial came on 22 March 2024. Both Pril Sina and Eang Srey Da had been transported from their villages to a small law firm in Phnom Penh to give evidence by video link through a translator. I could never have imagined this would be the way I would first see their faces.

I was sent their affidavits that morning. Each line matched what Kourchetta had sent me, and what was published. The chain of communication between different countries, languages and cultures held up. A wave of relief passed over me. Also contained in the affidavit were disturbing new details.

'I was told the operation to put metal in my leg would be done by a foreign doctor who volunteered at the hospital,' Eang Srey Da deposed. 'I did not ever meet this foreign doctor [prior to surgery]. By the time he came into the operation, I had been given an anaesthetic and already fainted.

'After one week the doctors asked me to walk. The leg is not straight. My wound has never healed. From the time of the operation I have had pus and fluid come out of my leg every day ... I have been to my local hospital to try to get help. They told me they cannot help because they cannot conduct this operation.'

Eang Srey Da said she made around ten trips back to the hospital for help. 'Each time the doctors tell me my leg is okay, but I know it is not okay. About six months ago I saw Dr Jim and asked him to remove the metal. I am very worried that the wound has not healed. He said he cannot remove it as the metal is too tightly connected to the bone so he cannot take it out. He said he can only take it out if it becomes loose. I wonder when can it become loose? I am worried what will happen when I get older and if I get diabetes or something what will happen to the wound. I want someone to fix my leg and take the metal out.'

Eang Srey Da was first to give evidence. When I saw her face for the first time, I was hit by the reality that we were so close in age, yet our lives had been so different. She was wearing a green buttoned shirt, her dark hair brushed neatly into a ponytail and tucked behind her ears. She read from a Khmer version of her affidavit and the questions were translated by an interpreter. Chrysanthou took her through her accident, her amputation, the problems she had with her socket prosthesis, and the process she went through before getting osseointegration, speaking with the Cambodian doctors before Dr Al Muderis arrived.

'Did you ask any questions?'

'Yes. I only asked a question, whether it's going to heal, and said, yes, it will heal,' the interpreter said slowly.

Chrysanthou interrupted Eang Srey Da before she finished another answer, and the judge reminded her not to interrupt. She qualified her responses by saying the surgery was a long time ago and she couldn't remember exact details. She did remember a camera crew that had come to follow Dr Al Muderis, and asked that they not film her.

Next, Pril Sina took the stand. His skin was darker and his jet-black hair was cut short. He chose to give a religious affirmation, and swore to tell the truth. Chrysanthou started again with questions about the accident, before turning to the difficulties Pril Sina had experienced with traditional sockets. He had often had to use crutches, until he too heard about the foreign doctor promising to help. Pril Sina said he also remembered being shown videos. When Chrysanthou asked if he was shown photographs of the metal coming out of the leg, Pril Sina said no.

'I didn't see the metal coming out,' he said, through the translator. 'I saw the legs.'

Later, he said he couldn't remember exactly what was said. 'It's too long. All I remember is I went into the room, and I watch a video with him, and he ask me, "Is it okay? Are you accept the surgery?" and I said yes, and then the surgery started.'

In re-examination, Collins had only a few questions. He asked Pril Sina what risks exactly was he warned about prior to the surgery.

'Like as I mentioned before, if there is a problem, they might cut my leg again, and the worst scenario is I might die.'

'And any other risks, apart from cutting your leg again or dying?' Collins asked.

'I don't remember,' he said.

After the livestream from Cambodia cut out, the judge asked whether she had correctly noticed that Pril Sina was using a walking stick. He was. She made a note.

Chrysanthou thanked the interpreter for her 'excellent assistance in trying circumstances'.

'No, the way you phrased the question is very easy for me to interpret,' she responded.

'That has never been said to Ms Chrysanthou before. You will have to frame that transcript,' Collins quipped.

The day was over.

CHAPTER 17

The Good Doctors

The month after our first stories were published about Dr Al Muderis, I received a Facebook message from a woman named Sonya Haskett. She wanted to speak with Mark Urquhart or Brennan Smith, but didn't know how to get in touch. It was clear she was nervous when I called. Dr Al Muderis had performed osseointegration on her son's arm and they'd had nothing but problems since. She was considering suing for medical negligence, and wanted to speak with anyone who could help. The conversation was brief and I didn't hear from her again. Little did I know, our lawyers had been beavering away in the background, and on 26 March 2024, day 41 of the trial, both Sonya and her son, Shannon, would testify.

I learned Shannon's life story through his affidavit. He grew up in Perth and enrolled in the military as soon as he finished high school. He was deployed to East Timor for a year, but returned to Darwin for more training so he could go to Iraq. These plans were brought to an abrupt end when Shannon had a devastating motorbike accident, severing his left arm above the elbow on impact and badly injuring his whole body. He was lucky to survive and spent weeks in intensive care, where his leg was also amputated above the knee. He emerged from hospital a bilateral amputee.

He moved back to Perth to live with his parents, where an orthopaedic surgeon hatched a plan to lengthen his residual leg bone so he could use a socket prosthesis. This involved encasing his leg with a metal brace, which screwed into his bones. He tightened the screws each day, causing excruciating pain. After 14 months, the torment paid off – the bone had grown eight centimetres, allowing Shannon to use a socket prosthesis. But his problems were far from over. With only one hand, it was hard to put on his prosthesis each day, and when he did manage to get it on, it would slip off when he sweated. As for his arm, there wasn't enough muscle to connect a myoelectric arm and every prosthesis he used failed. He eventually gave up and adapted to what he had. He found ways to cut tomatoes, and even reload his guns. Shooting was his passion.

Shannon discovered osseointegration in 2012. Orthopaedic surgeon Dr Richard Beaver performed the procedure on select patients in Perth and thought Shannon might be a good candidate. Dr Beaver took the time to explain the many risks and complications, during monthly then fortnightly appointments over six months. Shannon's family also attended the consults, exhausting all their questions until they had a deep understanding of the road ahead. The procedure was performed in a two-stage surgery and Shannon was closely monitored through the rehabilitation and recovery. He was told to pay close attention to any discharge from the stoma. If it looked gluggy, or snotty, Shannon should be on high alert for infection. Slowly, but surely, the wounds healed and he walked.

He met Dr Al Muderis in mid-2017 by chance. Shannon's usual prosthetist was out of town, and he needed a small part of his osseointegration leg fixed. Dr Al Muderis was attending a conference in Perth, and offered to help out.

'Why don't you have a prosthetic arm?' Dr Al Muderis asked.

Shannon explained the problems he'd had with myoelectric arms, how there was not enough muscle for the sensor pads to work.

'Is the Department of Veterans' Affairs covering your medical expenses?' Dr Al Muderis asked. 'I could have a robotic prosthesis fitted which would connect with and be controlled by your nerves.'

Shannon was told this would give him far greater functionality. Dr Al Muderis said he was one of three surgeons worldwide who could do the surgery, and the only one in Australia. Shannon was interested. He spoke to his insurer and set up a consultation.

The next time they met, Dr Al Muderis's mood had shifted. Shannon felt like the doctor was in a rush, and the appointment lasted only 30 minutes. He felt Shannon's stump, whizzed through some risks and quoted him $18,939 for the procedure. Dr Al Muderis told Shannon he was 'low risk' of infection.

'You're a young, healthy guy, I don't see it happening for you,' Dr Al Muderis said.

Within four months, Shannon was admitted to Macquarie University Hospital for surgery. He said the pre-operative consultation was 'very short and abrupt' and Dr Al Muderis 'seemed in a hurry to leave'. Shannon was anxious. Unlike when he'd had osseointegration on his leg, where every step was carefully considered and explained, this time everything had been so quick, and he still had so many questions. He brushed these feelings aside. *I'm here now, I might as well go ahead*, he told himself.

Shannon was taken to the rehabilitation centre after the surgery, where the alarm bells only got louder. There wasn't a proper part available for him to start the loading process, and the plastic replacement they gave him tore and broke each time he used it. Dr Al Muderis was nowhere to be seen, and only visited after Shannon complained. When Shannon asked when the robotic arm would be connected, the answer was disturbing.

He was told it wasn't available, and given no timeline for when it might be. To make matters worse, Shannon was told he would need a second surgery, which wasn't yet approved by the relevant body, so he would have to use muscle stimulant pads to activate the arm. This had been the problem in the first place: Shannon didn't have the muscles to do this. Now he had an implant poking out of his limb for no reason. He was furious.

'I didn't need to have it done now. What's the point in me having this if I can't operate it? You said you were going to make me half-man, half-machine, what am I meant to do now?'

Dr Al Muderis's face was blank. The conversation was heated, and the doctor left without offering any answers. Shannon was discharged and travelled back to Western Australia. No telehealth calls or follow-ups were scheduled.

Shannon saw his normal prosthetists back in Perth, who had no idea what to do. They'd never seen the implant design before and had no clue why Dr Al Muderis had put it in if there was no connector for a robotic arm. Dr Al Muderis had put 100 staples close to Shannon's armpit, meaning even the slightest bit of sweat ran straight into the stoma, presenting a major infection trap. Shannon suffered serious infections over the next two years. Ooze and pus was constant. Then came the terrible smell, which was impossible to live with. He stopped seeing friends or even leaving the house. Shannon called and left messages for Dr Al Muderis, but rarely got a response. When he did get through, he was told everything was fine. It clearly wasn't. The skin started to recede around the implant, exposing the bone.

Shannon was severely depressed by late 2019. His stepfather and prosthetists were now also emailing Dr Al Muderis, desperate for a solution. Shannon flew to Sydney with his stepfather to demand answers. Dr Al Muderis was the expert. Surely he would have a solution.

The appointment lasted no more than 15 minutes. Shannon sat there profusely sweating from an out-of-control fever, as pus dripped from his implant. 'It is not necessarily infected,' Dr Al Muderis maintained, without taking any swabs, blood tests or even examining Shannon's arm. His parents demanded to know when the promised robotic arm would become a reality.

'I am not an engineer. I have done my part,' Dr Al Muderis told them. 'I will get you to see my engineer. He will tell you.'

They were sent to William Lu, a young researcher whose career was bound to Dr Al Muderis like bone binds to titanium. He told the family he would send a connector to Shannon's prosthetists in Perth. This never happened.

Shannon saw new surgeons back home, who debrided the wound and took swabs of his arm. The results confirmed it was crawling with bacteria. His leg, which had never before been infected, started hurting. He was diagnosed with osteomyelitis in the leg and the osseointegration implant had to be removed. Shannon spent a week in hospital and was discharged with intravenous antibiotics. The skin kept receding on his arm, and eventually, three years after Dr Al Muderis had performed the surgery, that implant needed to be removed too.

After all this, Shannon's arm was significantly shorter than when he first met Dr Al Muderis. He had hoped to compete in the Paralympics in shooting, but could no longer load the pistol. His leg stump was also too short for a socket prosthesis, confining him to a wheelchair.

It was a devastating story from start to finish. As I reflected again on Dr Al Muderis telling Tom Steinfort that we had spoken to the 'handful' of 'disgruntled' patients, when he knew this was not the case, I became angry again. *Unethical at best, dangerous at worst.*

* * *

Shortly before the hearings started on the 41st day of evidence, I saw Shannon sitting in a small conference room near the courtroom. We had never spoken before, and at that point, I still really didn't know the details of his case. I entered the room and introduced myself.

'I hear you're going to be raked through the coals soon,' he said.

'That's right,' I said. 'But I'm not nervous. The more I learn about Dr Al Muderis, the worse it gets. I can't understand why he's pursuing this case. They say the stories were misleading, I don't agree.'

'When I was watching, I thought, thank God. This is the first time someone has told the truth about him.'

I told Shannon I didn't know the full extent of his story, that I'd only spoken to his mother briefly, but I understood he'd been through the wringer.

'It is what it is,' he said, in a refrain I'd heard often from amputees.

Shannon, then aged 38, was a good-looking man who should have been at the peak of his life. His brown hair was an overgrown crew cut. A snake tattoo crept down his forearm, and his eyes displayed an inner strength. He'd been through a lot, but didn't want to wallow in what could have been.

Shannon wheeled himself up to the stand. As the court assistant crowed 'all stand' and knocked the hammer on the wooden bench, Shannon shot right up, balancing on one leg. His black pants leg was pinned under his thigh, and the white shirt sleeve of his left arm was empty.

Chrysanthou's tone was polite that morning. She took him through his first meeting with Dr Al Muderis, who used a drill to change his prosthetic part, which hurt Shannon at points.

'You're not suggesting he was intentionally causing you pain?'
'No.'

As Chrysanthou went through the chronology, Shannon stopped to pause and think, retracing the lines of his memory to answer as accurately as he could.

'Do you remember telling Dr Al Muderis about trouble using sockets?' she said. 'You hoped to have some functionality?'

'That was the whole reason of having it done,' he said. 'Yes.'

Shannon re-enacted the moment Dr Al Muderis first examined his arm. As he lifted his limb, the empty shirt sleeve flopped and crumpled. It gave the courtroom an up-close look at how residual limbs move, an almost jarring display of what it's like to be an amputee. 'He gave me a quick glance, said there were risks,' he said. 'But my age, how fit I was, those risks wouldn't really impact me.'

Shannon said again that Dr Al Muderis explained there was a 'very, very low chance the risks would impact me'. The judge scribbled something down on her pad as he was speaking before fixing her gaze again on Shannon.

'I suggest to you that he actually explained the risks in more detail?' Chrysanthou said. Shannon scrunched his face, and shook his head.

Chrysanthou went through each risk one by one, insisting Dr Al Muderis had warned him about it. Shannon answered no, no, no. Each denial was like a shot into the bullseye of our truth defence.

The barrister spent the next hour accusing Shannon of describing events that 'never occurred', conversations that 'never happened', or getting things 'completely wrong'. He knocked each accusation back, calmly, consistently. 'I was in the room,' he explained. Then, Chrysanthou suggested that the key conversation in the rehab centre, where Dr Al Muderis had admitted a robotic arm could not be connected, didn't occur.

Shannon's tone hardened. 'It did happen,' he said. Shannon then took a deep breath, grabbed the glass of water in front of him and took a sip. Chrysanthou asked if he needed a break. He said no, and the judge asked if he was sure. The whole courtroom could feel his frustration.

The questioning went on. Chrysanthou returned to the same conversation, saying Shannon was wrong because, in fact, her client never even attended the rehabilitation centre. Shannon's anger was palpable now. His voice was rising.

'That is,' he said, simmer coming to boil. 'That's,' he repeated, as if remembering Marlia Saunders' advice to stay calm, 'not correct.'

As the evidence went on, Shannon expanded on certain conversations in his affidavit with ease and specificity. Not only did his answers line up exactly with what was written, he also provided fresh details.

After a short break, the questions kept coming, zooming in on specific periods when Shannon had been very ill, seeing many specialists, undergoing many surgeries and on many drugs. He reached into his pocket and pulled out a handkerchief to dab his forehead. His answers reduced to 'I don't know'. Collins cut in to see if Shannon was okay. The judge noticed too. 'You're looking a bit …' the judge said.

'Yes, a bit flustered,' Shannon supplied. 'Just a lot, a lot of dates being thrown at me. When you're throwing dates at me, I can't … There was a lot going on.'

Chrysanthou changed focus for one last question.

'Do you recall your mother told you at the beginning of last year that she spoke to a journalist called Charlotte Grieve?'

'I remember she said that she watched a *60 Minutes* program and that I should watch that and—'

Chrysanthou cut in. 'Did your mother tell you she spoke to a journalist called Charlotte Grieve?'

'No.'

Shannon was dismissed. As he wheeled himself out of the courtroom, I stood, bowed to the judge and followed him. Marlia came too, and we packed into the small conference room. 'You were great, very believable, so firm on all the points she challenged you on,' Marlia told him, flashing a big, comforting smile. 'Don't worry about the dates.'

There was a thin sheen of sweat on his forehead, and he was shaking his head. He seemed to be having a physical reaction to the anxiety and frustration. 'I almost lost it at one point,' he said. We both knew exactly what point he meant. 'But I took a deep breath. There's a time and a place.'

I smiled at him. 'You nailed it. Thank you.'

After Shannon, his mother was up. Straight out of the gates, you could hear the fury of a wounded mother in her voice.

'He did not seem interested in the infections that my son had, that my husband saw, that I saw,' she said, the sentence heavy with despair.

Sonya told the court how unwell Shannon had been. She couldn't get him off the couch, he was so sick, profusely sweating all the time. 'The smell that was coming out of his arm was … Disgusting,' she said. 'The fluid, thick white fluid was coming out of his arm, he would have gauzes everywhere. His clothes were stained. It wasn't appropriate.'

She closed her eyes briefly and paused as if reliving the ordeal.

'I want to suggest the symptoms you described are exaggerated?' Chrysanthou said.

'No.' She hit straight back, staring Chrysanthou directly in the eye. 'And his mental state was worse.'

Sonya could not understand why Dr Al Muderis performed the operation, why he lied about what he could do, why he didn't help them, why her son's problems kept getting worse. She was at her wit's end.

'If I could say to Dr Al Muderis,' she said, sobbing now, 'why did you do that to my son? What misery he has caused my son, my family and my husband …'

Tears still falling, she compared the care given by the surgeon in Perth who took a year to perform osseointegration on his leg. 'He did as much as he possibly could. He took his time. He made sure of what he was going to do. He didn't just think that he could do something. He did it.'

Chrysanthou's questions only unveiled new details about the depths of Shannon's sickness. Sonya described his body covered in rashes, his depression, the antibiotic drips in the hospital, then at home. It was a nightmare.

'Why would he do surgery on my son knowing he has an osseointegration leg and it could have caused some kind of infection to put him in a wheelchair? Why? His thought process of doing that … I don't understand. I honestly, I clearly don't understand.'

* * *

The first call I received on day 50 of the trial was at 7.40 am, from solicitor Sam McGeoch. She was chasing a document from July 2022 that the other side had asked for. It was Eid that morning and I had breakfast with my partner's family, where I was treated to home-cooked seviyan and warm conversations. The traffic going into the city was a little heavier than expected, and I anxiously tapped my foot in the Uber, compulsively checking the time. I wanted to make sure I was in court before Dr John Anstee began his evidence.

I made it in time and rushed to level 18 to find Dr Anstee sitting in a small room with JP and Collins. His face lit up. 'So lovely to see you,' Dr Anstee said. 'You know, if you had told me this would happen at the beginning of this,' he continued, pausing for effect, 'I would do it all again.'

That was exactly what I wanted to hear. 'You're not wearing your signature bow tie,' I said.

'I thought if I stopped dressing like a wanker, I wouldn't talk like one.'

Everyone laughed. We chatted briefly about how long the case had gone for. By this point, it felt like an eternity. 'Why is he doing this?' Dr Anstee asked, genuinely.

'I don't know,' I said. 'Perhaps he thinks he hasn't done anything wrong.'

While Dr Anstee cracked jokes and made small talk, I could see he was nervous. He said he regretted criticising Dr Al Muderis's boats and cars. I reminded him those comments hadn't been broadcast and, in any event, everyone is entitled to an opinion. Wary that the conversation was straying close to the line of discussing evidence, I changed the topic.

Before long, solicitor Issy Gwinner pointed out the time – the hearing started in three minutes. As we jumped up and shuffled into the courtroom, I flashed Dr Anstee one last smile.

Dr Anstee was the last person to give evidence for our truth defence. As the only on-record expert in the media investigation, I relied on Dr Anstee's opinion. His career as a plastic surgeon, his expertise in osseointegration and the reasonableness of his views gave the stories integrity. The fact that Anstee was prepared to allow cameras into his family home, to put his face to my investigation, had been critical to the story going ahead.

Dr Anstee had spent his career performing some of the most marvellous surgeries – full reconstructions of missing appendages on patients who had been through severe traumas, including a woman whose face he rebuilt after she was shot in the head. He had performed osseointegration surgeries for almost two decades when he first heard of another surgeon entering the space – Dr Munjed Al Muderis. 'Sometime after that I started to see patients coming into the Alfred who had received osseointegration surgery with Dr Al Muderis, and who had experienced complications with their osseointegration performed by Dr Al Muderis. Many of these related to problems with the patient's stoma.'

In Dr Anstee's view, the main risk with osseointegration surgery is infection – and that risk is directly tied to the quality of the stoma. If the skin is not tightly wrapped around the implant, the risk of infection increases. Dr Anstee believed that plastic surgeons should manage the stoma – not orthopaedic surgeons, like Dr Al Muderis. In his affidavit, Dr Anstee said he was very concerned to learn that Dr Al Muderis had also been performing TMR surgery – the nerve surgery that promises to help with phantom pain. This is a 'very delicate procedure', he wrote, one he thought should only be performed by highly qualified plastic surgeons.

Sitting in the witness stand, Dr Anstee's white hair was neatly brushed, glasses propped on his nose as he looked across the courtroom. Before the evidence had even begun, my phone lit up with a text from JP: *Anstee. What a legend.* I responded immediately: *Seriously*, with a gold medal emoji. The surgeon pledged to tell the truth and the questions began.

Chrysanthou started by asking about the surgical trips Dr Anstee had performed overseas, where he travelled with an organisation called Interplast to provide cleft palate and lip surgeries to under-resourced communities. These operations were performed in a makeshift hospital, Dr Anstee said, and local staff handled most of the post-operative care. It was obvious why Chrysanthou was bringing this up – an effort to make the case that Dr Al Muderis's surgical trips to Cambodia and Iraq were no different. *Apples and oranges*, I thought. Next, she turned her attention to what she called Dr Anstee's 'long-running public feud with AHPRA'.

'You've spoken publicly in the past about your discontent with that organisation?'

'I have.'

Dr Anstee agreed he wrote a letter to *The Age* in 2016, criticising AHPRA. One of his key criticisms over the years has been the regulator's poor protection of the title 'surgeon', particularly when it comes to cosmetic surgeons.

'Yes,' he said. 'I object to non-surgeons calling themselves surgeons, that has been at least partly redressed recently. My main argument with AHPRA is their complete failure to care for a very vulnerable section of the community so that they're exploited financially and medically, and AHPRA are still not facing up to that problem.'

Next began a bizarre and stomach-turning series of questions about maggots. Dr Anstee said he had never seen maggots in a human before I showed him the video of Mark's legs. He had only seen them in sheep, where maggots ate through dead flesh, then started on the live flesh. 'When maggots have cleaned up all the dead tissue, they don't then commit suicide and drop off,' he said. 'It's a significant problem. Uncontrolled maggot infestations are not good for wounds.'

Chrysanthou tried to use technical information about maggots to suggest that Dr Anstee didn't know what he was talking about. But the more she explored this topic, the worse it got.

'And you agree that maggots can infest any piece of meat?'

'Yes, I do.'

'And that normal fly maggots do not continue to feed on living tissue, to your knowledge?'

'Which are normal fly maggots?' Dr Anstee asked. 'Which breed of maggot are we talking about? There are different flies and different maggots, and the one that sheep farmers fear is different from the common blowfly in Australian houses.'

'And the one that sheep farmers fear, I think, are called the horsefly. Is that the one you're talking about?' Chrysanthou asked.

'No,' Dr Anstee responded.

'Which one are you talking about?'

'The horsefly is a different animal. I forget the name, but they go on feeding 'til the sheep is dead.'

These disturbing questions went on, exploring whether certain types of maggots ate dead flesh. I couldn't believe what I was hearing. How did this assist her client? Was it better if the maggots in Mark's legs only ate the dead flesh? How could she even prove that? Why would it matter? Dr Anstee grew tired, and brought the court back to reality.

'I can't answer that question,' he said. 'I would not tolerate maggots in any wound of any patient that I had. I can't see them doing any good, it must be absolutely horrifying to the patient and anybody else who has anything to do with it. It is, I view it as a failure of management.'

Chrysanthou tried to suggest maggots were actually the patient's fault, caused by bad hygiene. Again, Dr Anstee came down firm.

'I don't think it has anything to do with whether the patient washes his or herself. What you need for an infestation of maggots is an open wound, preferably with dead flesh in it, and a few seconds of a fly. I don't know whether the patient washes the rest of himself, I don't think it makes any difference.'

Over the course of the day, Dr Anstee was extraordinarily humble. He was quick to admit any mistakes, and never shied away from criticising himself or acknowledging he was a conservative doctor. On the key points of the case, such as how to deal with infection, he spoke with authority.

'It must be taken seriously,' he said. 'Because any sign, any significant sign of infection, pain, redness, swelling, discharge, particularly pus, warrants a culture. Get hold of some of the fluid and culture it.'

Dr Anstee rattled off a list of tests that should be performed if a doctor suspects infection. He said if any come back positive, the patient must go straight to hospital. 'You never die of embarrassment,' he said, because if it progresses to osteomyelitis, 'it's a real problem'.

Later, Chrysanthou focused on TMR surgery, the nerve procedure Dr Al Muderis used to treat phantom pain. She motioned to the whiteboard and asked him to draw a diagram. 'So that we understand the difference when we're reading about it, late into the night, alone?' Chrysanthou joked.

The judge appeared to tighten her jaw and give a clenched smile. Dr Anstee jumped to his feet, quickly commanding the room. He explained the surgery simply, using colloquial language like 'malevolent little nerves' to ensure lay people understood.

He seamlessly switched between drawing on the board and turning to explain to his audience. The courtroom hung on his every word. You could see he'd spent a lifetime educating the next generation of surgeons, excited and energised by helping them understand. He marvelled at the progress of nerve surgery and the 'wonderful' technology that allows patients to control their prosthetic hands using computers.

'And this is fantastic because now patients can build block towers with an artificial hand,' he said. 'Next year it will be better, and the year after that even better.'

He was still standing as he delivered this last line, a twinkle in his eyes that revealed the depths of his passion. As I watched, I was filled with immense joy. I was right to trust Dr Anstee. This was not a doddery old man determined to stifle medical innovation, as Dr Al Muderis had sought to portray him. He was a principled surgeon whose life's work had been helping others. Dr Anstee was a good surgeon and a good person, and the court could now see that.

Chrysanthou spent the rest of the cross-examination taking Dr Anstee through each patient, one by one. He explained gently how Dr Al Muderis failed each person. As the clock struck 3.04 pm, Chrysanthou concluded the cross-examination. 'No further questions.'

Collins stood up. He asked about patients taking out payment plans and loans for surgery. Dr Anstee said he didn't think we should live in a world where healthcare is dictated by money.

'Osseointegration surgery can help people enormously, and I don't think, in this society, patients should be restricted on grounds of cost.'

Then, Collins asked about surgeons who use implants they have a financial interest in. 'It doesn't pass the sniff test, does it?' Dr Anstee said.

Finally, Collins turned to Dr Anstee's first engagement with me.

'I was a bit hard on her,' he said with a smile.

'A bit hard on Ms Grieve?'

'On Ms Grieve.'

'What did you consider to be missing from the publicly available information about him at the time you were speaking to Ms Grieve?'

'Nothing ever goes perfectly all the time, and I think that we, as surgeons, should appraise the public of that. We don't ever want my profession or your profession to be regarded as a conspiracy against the public, and the way to avoid that is to have the public fully informed. Yes, you can have this operation. Yes, there are complications. You can die, or it could be worse. These are the odds. Think about it for a week, not advertise and then operate the same day.'

I wrote a note to myself in all caps. THIS IS THE KEY POINT OF THE WHOLE THING. PUBLIC INTEREST.

With that, Dr Anstee was dismissed. The truth defence part of our case was over.

I walked with Dr Anstee down to Macquarie Street as he waited for a taxi to take him to the airport, suitcase in one hand, suit-holder in another. Autumn had arrived, and there was a cold gust in the air. I shook Dr Anstee's hand, thanked him for everything. 'We couldn't have done it without you,' I told him.

Dr Anstee stared me straight in the eye. 'It's what we ought to have done. What I ought to have done and what you ought to have done. It was the right thing. We should be proud.'

CHAPTER 18

Sandip's Bootcamp

I was sitting in a large conference room on 14 March 2024 at the Thomson Geer offices after another long day in court. There was a storm brewing over Sydney Harbour and I could see an Australian flag flapping violently in the wind. It might sound clichéd, but the change in weather reflected my darkening mood.

'Charlotte, you've got a lot of work to do,' JP said.

We were there to discuss what I needed to do to prepare for the next round of cross-examination. The victory in the confidential source battle had unlocked the public interest defence. This rested on proving we'd acted reasonably to form a genuine belief the stories were in the public interest, which meant putting my every move under a microscope. Every step I took, every phone conversation I had, every email I sent, every document I read, and even my thoughts and feelings, were now open to intense scrutiny.

Barrister Sandip Mukerjea had been briefed to help prepare me, Tom and Natalie for the box. He beamed into that meeting from his chambers in Melbourne, joining JP, Sam McGeoch, and Nine's in-house lawyers, Larina and Kiah. Ahead of the meeting, I was told we needed to map out how to prepare for potential lines of attack. These ranged from the various iterations of the concoction theory, to allegations our sources lacked expertise, and my 'lack of experience' as an investigative journalist. As I contemplated these attacks, the stress headaches I'd been having returned. It was another reminder that the end was still a long way off, and the journey ahead would not be easy.

'You're going to be called a liar who deletes records,' JP said.

'She'll try to portray Charlotte as green, a cub reporter doing this big investigation,' Larina said.

Kiah agreed. 'She'll say Charlotte was far too inexperienced, was given huge responsibility … She'll try to get you to admit that you're not experienced.'

Perhaps noticing my change in mood, JP assured me these were not strong arguments. 'We're not worried. Your investigation speaks for itself.'

I remained largely silent throughout the meeting, taking notes and thinking about ways I would respond. Journalists are among the most neurotic of professionals, constantly doubting their ability, questioning information given by sources, thinking everyone is trying to screw them. Every day is a competition, with the value of your output measured by your story's position in the newspaper, the impact it has in the real world and the response from the public.

Seeds of doubt started to enter my mind. I *was* inexperienced, technically speaking. I *did* delete records. Mistakes *were* made. JP said my memory had proven to be on-point, and that the best way I could prepare was to familiarise myself with all the material that could be used against me. This included rewatching the raw footage of all the interviews, re-reading all the relevant affidavits, going through as many of the subpoenaed documents as possible. Sam gave me a hard-drive with the thousands of documents I'd handed over in the discovery process, which Dr Al Muderis's lawyers would have spent late nights trawling through, looking for smoking guns.

'We can never tell you what to say,' Sandip said. 'But what we want to do is canvass topics on which you'll be cross-examined on to give you the opportunity to consider your answers.'

When the meeting finished, I had less than three weeks before I was supposed to give evidence. I was juggling multiple investigations for my day job, while trying to show up in court for as many witnesses as possible. Each night, I spent a few hours reporting before turning my attention to the mountain of documents. I took the hard-drive everywhere, whipping out my laptop at every available moment to scroll through another mass of documents. It was headache inducing, but as I read through the endless pile of text messages, emails and notes, I noticed details that helped jog my memory. There were more sources that corroborated key pieces of evidence than I had remembered. I noticed important details I'd forgotten.

On Easter Monday, less than two weeks before I was scheduled to give evidence, I flew to Melbourne for three intensive days of preparation with Sandip and Sam. I was sitting at the airport gate waiting to board just after 7 am, reading over my old notes of a conversation with a confidential source, and one passage jumped out. 'Everybody is fully aware of the situation,' this person told me. 'He believes in his own reality. But his reality doesn't match the rest of the world.'

Up until now, so much of this trial had been focused on presenting evidence to prove the truth of what had happened. What if Dr Al Muderis was in denial about the truth? In 1998, Harvard biology professor Ruth Hubbard coined the line, 'truth is in the eye of the beholder'. Her argument was essentially that truth, like beauty, is subjective – influenced by a complex intersection of individual perspectives, experiences and emotions.

I spent a lot of time contemplating Dr Al Muderis's motivations. Money? Fame? Power? The thrill of complex cases? The desire to help amputees? It felt like a combination of all of the above. The trial had led to an exhaustive inquiry into

Dr Al Muderis's practice and unearthed shocking new facts. And now, more than ever, I was confident this early warning was right, and the doctor really was living in his own reality.

In Melbourne, I took an Uber to Sandip's chambers on Queen Street in the CBD. The city was a virtual ghost town. The sky was grey and the wind was laced with the unpredictability of Melbourne's chill. Sam collected me from the street, still carrying my luggage, and escorted me to the 27th floor, into what would become my own private hell for the next three days – a room at the centre of the office with glass walls and no natural light. It was like being stuck in a fishbowl, where time was frozen and the lines of attack were endless.

Sandip opened the first session by setting the terms for the battle ahead. Essentially, he explained, the public interest defence involved two competing ideas. I held the subjective belief that these stories were in the public interest, and the court process was designed to establish an objective test of whether that belief was reasonably held.

'If a journalist knows 50 per cent of what they have published is false, but still publishes the information, the defence is lost,' he said. 'That's why we have to go into chapter and verse about your reasonable belief this was in the public interest. Why was this in the public interest? And what were all the reasons that view was reasonable?'

Sandip said Chrysanthou would try to magnify any small inconsistencies between the stories and evidence that had surfaced during the trial to portray the entire investigation as riddled with errors. 'If you had known these facts were false, would that change your view that these stories were in the public interest?' Sandip asked. This was a question I would come back to time and time again, and every time, the answer was no. The 'errors' Chrysanthou had pointed to were insignificant details that didn't change the thrust of the story, and certainly didn't shake the public interest of the series. Like how Nick McKenzie got the date of one of Ben Roberts-Smith's murders wrong – that didn't change the fact he was a war criminal.

In that empty corporate office, Sandip went through every detail of my investigation. By this point, he had a firm grasp on the material, the timeline of people I had spoken to, and documents I had seen.

That day, we went out for lunch. 'Italian or Japanese?' Sandip asked as we waited at the lifts. 'I know they're your two favourite cuisines.'

The hawk-eyed barrister had picked this up from a private text message exchange between Mark Urquhart and myself that I had long forgotten about. I laughed it off, but it again triggered that uneasy feeling in my stomach. I was so exposed. As we ate, Sam noticed that I looked deflated. She leaned over. 'Charlotte, I hope this isn't going to make you give up on journalism. You should remember that this is not normal. Most journalists don't ever have to go through anything like this.'

The preparation with Sandip was tough. It seemed like I was being held accountable for decisions way above my pay grade – or outside the scope of my work. I was grilled about the front-page headline, for example, which wasn't even shown to me before publication. Decisions and steps I had taken almost two years ago could be picked apart and twisted to portray me as some kind of crazed and evil liar, hell-bent on bringing Dr Al Muderis down.

One night after a long day of intense preparation, I met my partner at a bar. He kindly offered to buy me a glass of wine. 'No,' I snapped. 'I can't drink. I need my brain to function.' Afterward, we went to a Pakistani restaurant for dinner with a friend. It was Ramadan and the place was heaving. As everyone broke their fast, my mind kept wandering to the potential questions I might be asked.

One of the most upsetting lines of attack I braced for was that Dr Al Muderis might accuse me of racism. Before we published the story, the Iraqi Medical Association sent a letter to our editors accusing the entire team of a lack of diversity and racism in the reporting. In public speeches and in his memoirs, Dr Al Muderis had spoken frequently about how the overwhelmingly white medical fraternity had been racist toward him, and attributed the criticism of his practice in part to his race. Through my reporting, I did hear racist comments about Dr Al Muderis – innuendo about his medical training from Baghdad, or remarks that things are 'done differently' in Iraq.

I had written about the prevalence of racism in Australian hospitals while investigating AHPRA. I learned through interviews and documents how Indigenous doctors received disproportionate complaints about their practice or racist slurs from patients. We know from countless royal commissions and coronial inquiries that racism in healthcare causes patients to die when critical decisions are based on harmful stereotypes. There is no denying Australian society is steeped in racism, and this includes the media. A lack of diversity has resulted in real, tangible problems with journalism and how society understands the world. I understand how racism, and also unconscious bias, impacts all levels of media reporting, including my own workplace. It brought me no joy to be accused of racism in court. Even though I knew the suffering of Dr Al Muderis's patients was unrelated to racism, the prospect of having to defend myself, as a privileged white journalist, of that charge was deeply disturbing.

Another line of attack that kept me up at night was the suggestion that I had become too close with the patients, and had lost objectivity as a result. It was true that I had put significant effort into building relationships with the patients, particularly those who agreed to go on the record. I needed them to trust me as much as I needed to trust them. Many of the patients had experienced complex trauma, or mental illness. Journalists have no psychological training, so must decide how to deal with sources based on instinct. I established barriers when necessary, but spent time building relationships too. I genuinely cared about the patients' welfare and sometimes checked in just to see how they were going. It was true that this felt like more than just a story to me – rather, it was an opportunity to empower patients to share their experiences in the hope of triggering positive change.

The most damning scrap of 'evidence' that I was too close with the patients was what my lawyers would come to privately refer to as 'underwear-gate'. Sometime toward the end of the investigation, Carol Todd was in dire straits. She was in and out of hospital due to rolling infections, and dealing with crippling pain. Her doctors had told her she might never walk again and she confided that she was feeling suicidal. She mentioned that she'd been stuck in the same pair of underwear for days. Her normal underwear no longer fit, she didn't have the energy to get to the shops. She didn't know how to shop online. It was a brief comment that caused my journalist mask to slip. I asked what kind she needed, logged onto the Bonds website and ordered a few packs to be delivered to her house. I used my personal bank card and thought nothing more of it.

This split-second decision would come to be yet another source of drama during the trial, another reed wrapping around the swan's leg. Dr Al Muderis's lawyers demanded invoices for any other 'gifts' given to patients (there were none, aside from two separate meals given to Mark and Brennan after we filmed their interviews). I could see how this could be weaponised against me but, on oath, did I really regret buying the underwear? By the time I made the purchase, Carol had already agreed to go on the record, her photograph had already been taken and the story was written. They couldn't say the underwear was an inducement. Should I have done it? Probably not, but I still couldn't bring myself to say that I would do anything differently.

After chewing over potential answers, I settled on the most truthful. If asked about underwear-gate, I would say that it was a human reaction to a distressing situation that had no impact on my reporting. Whether the judge would make an adverse finding on my credit, or my role as an independent, impartial journalist, was for her to decide – that was my truthful answer.

We continued to plough through my affidavit, Sandip grilling me on various lines. Sam reassured me again at one point. 'I know you're putting your heart and soul into this,' she said. 'We're focusing on the bad stuff only. Don't forget your entire affidavit that shows all the people you spoke to, all the information you gathered.'

As the questions continued, and we went through bundle after bundle of the thick stack of documents, I started to feel more confident. I kept poring through the documents at home, studying the contents, thinking deeply. There were going to be uncomfortable questions, but as time went on, I felt ready for them. I was like a boxer preparing for a bout, learning how to strike, when to duck, constantly on my toes. After three straight days with Sandip, I felt ready – or as ready as I ever could be.

At the end of the final day, I asked Sandip: 'We've been so far in the weeds, but what does this case really turn on, in your opinion?'

He took a few moments to collect his thoughts before summing it up. Chrysanthou's case would be that my mind was set from the very beginning about what this story would be, he said, and that I systematically collected negative information and disregarded positive information to paint Dr Al Muderis in the worst possible light. She will try to get inside your head, he told me, to reveal why you discounted some sources and valued others. She will piece together a string of mistakes and build it into a picture of an article so wrong it must be banished from the public record, immediately. 'You need to prove that's not true,' Sandip said.

'Do you think we're in with a chance?' I asked meekly.

'Yes,' he responded. 'A decent chance.'

***

After the training bootcamp, I returned to Sydney for the remainder of the truth evidence. I was to have one more session with Sandip, but otherwise, it was over to me. Everyone kept saying they didn't want to 'over-prepare' me, but I felt like there was no such thing. I continued to scroll through the endless documents – emails, texts, notes, reports, draft scripts, trial transcripts – noticing new facts that I would arm myself with to defend the work.

Deep in this process, I found myself re-reading the transcript of Chrysanthou's opening. I had used the word 'mutilated' to describe some of the patients. During the investigation, I had seen countless photographs of stomas gone hideously wrong, flaps of sliced skin hanging at alarming angles, gnarled and lumpy stitches, broken-down wounds, bloody and bruised flesh, jagged bones visible to the naked eye. I remembered hearing Shona describe Mark's legs being taken out of the operating theatre in plastic bags, and her horror as it dawned on her just how experimental this procedure really was. I was confident the word 'mutilated' was accurate.

The word stuck in my mind. While I was studying Chrysanthou's opening, I noticed her summary of Dr Al Muderis's work as a junior doctor in Iraq. 'That is until an incident at the university medical centre in Baghdad where members of Saddam Hussein's Ba'ath Party brought deserters into the hospital and ordered surgeons to *mutilate* the soldiers by amputating parts of their bodies.' The word jumped off the page. It appeared even Chrysanthou had deemed unnecessary amputations as mutilation. I knew I was deep in the weeds, and this observation likely meant nothing, but the deeper I got, the better I felt.

As my cross-examination drew closer, I decided to put a pause on my day job. I called my boss and said I wanted to postpone the story I was working on, a story for the weekend papers about a man trapped in immigration detention on spurious police intelligence. New details kept cropping up that I needed to iron out. I didn't want to rush it, and I wanted to clear my schedule and focus purely on preparation. 'If you don't mind, I think I'll just focus on this,' I told then-investigations editor Mat Dunckley. 'Yes, because "this" is pretty big,' he responded.

The trial had zapped me of so much energy by this point. My head ached constantly. I didn't want to drink, or even eat. Family members remarked I had lost weight. My dreams became dominated by the trial. I maintained the strict regimen of going for a short run in the morning, listening to the same soundtrack my partner had prepared for me, forcing myself to eat a single slice of toast and limiting my caffeine to one coffee in the morning, one glass bottle of coke at lunch.

As the day neared, I became increasingly eager to get on the stand. I felt like I was living the plot of *Frost/Nixon* – a movie in which one man must lose, famed interviewer David Frost or Richard Nixon – but in this case, it was me versus Dr Al Muderis.

This all continued until 5 April 2024, the 47th trial day. I was match fit and itching to get in the box. I felt desperate to get it over and done with, to have my time back, to stop feeling my every move was being monitored. The end was so close I could touch it. Then, in the space of a few minutes, it was snatched away.

Barrister Melissa Marcus was representing me in court that day as debate was unfolding that threatened to push my cross-examination back by a month. Melissa said any further delays would be 'incredibly draining' on me 'psychologically and emotionally'. Hearing this, something in me cracked. I had told the lawyers the reason I wanted to stick to the original schedule was because I had carefully reorganised my work and personal life to be ready, in Sydney, now. I never mentioned any stress or psychological toll. Making that argument now felt like it flew in the face of every effort I had taken to put on a brave face. Since day one, I had bristled at any suggestion I was not coping and quickly changed the topic if anyone called for a 'welfare check'. I was a serious investigative journalist. This was part and parcel of the job. I could handle it.

I called JP first, but he didn't answer, so I immediately called Kiah. I told her firmly that my desire to give evidence next week had *nothing* to do with emotions, but rather practical logistics. I had put everything on hold for five weeks so I was ready to go. I knew that the more I protested that emotions had *nothing* to do with it, the more obvious whatever I had been suppressing became, but I didn't care. Kiah told me she understood, insisting no-one thought I was fragile, but reminded me of the stress that all trials put on journalists. 'You're not the first, and you won't be the last. It's not fun for anyone.'

When JP called back, I made the case again. He said nothing could be done. The judge wanted to delay the evidence, and this way there was a neat delineation between the truth defence and the public interest defence. Rushing the cross-examination of a key witness, being me, could even be grounds for an appeal. JP acknowledged it was annoying, but said we needed to focus on the main game – winning the case. And we were on track to do just that.

The court had heard evidence that day from Stephen Ruff, a medical expert who calmly and concisely explained exactly how Dr Al Muderis had engaged in medical negligence. JP said Ruff was one of, if not the, best witness he'd ever seen over his whole career. He felt like he was holding the winning lottery ticket, watching the balls being drawn from the spinning glass sphere one by one. Each time Ruff delivered another killer blow, the woman in the sparkly dress drew a winning ball. 'The truth defence is going very strongly,' he said. 'The judge will likely deliver us a victory. She's trying to give Sue procedural fairness to avoid an appeal.'

His explanation about the delay made sense, but didn't stop the sheer disappointment and despair I felt. I was so close to being freed from the grips of this trial, and wanted so badly for it to be over. I put my sneakers on and drove down to Bondi Beach in the rain. The sea was wild, the wind gusty and cold. I felt like I was acting out a dramatic scene in a movie, and leaned into the character. I posted a video on Instagram of birds flying against the wind. Some friends responded that it was arty, but only my mum understood. *Free soon!* she responded.

I spent the next month trying to push the trial out of my mind. I ploughed my energy into an investigation into a global cryptocurrency fraud. I spent time with friends, went for long walks, and spent short bursts of time refreshing my memory of the trial material. Finally, after the five-week delay, the day arrived. The night before, I met the lawyers for one last meeting. Matt Collins did most of the talking. He looked me squarely in the eye and reminded me that the most important thing was to tell the truth and stay focused on the bigger picture – the public interest.

* * *

The morning of 7 May 2024, I went for my usual run, listening to Kendrick Lamar. My legs were pounding the pavement faster than they ever had. As I reached Rushcutters Bay, Marlia texted me a photograph of a rainbow and said it was a good omen. Back home, I read my 'beliefs' one last time – the ten pages of dot points at the end of my affidavit that outlined why I believed these stories were in the public interest. They included:

> 'I believed the patients were not properly informed by Dr Al Muderis of the full spectrum of risks of osseointegration surgery.

'I believed Dr Al Muderis does not himself have an accurate understanding of the risks of osseointegration as his research team was not collecting appropriate data.

'I believed patients sign up for osseointegration surgery with Dr Al Muderis with unrealistic expectations of the outcomes.

'I believed Dr Al Muderis's AHPRA profile does not accurately represent his record on surgical performance.'

If the rainbow was a good omen, I hoped the burst of heavy rain as we entered the court building was not a bad one. As I waited to be called, I sat with damp clothes and shaking hands. My face was hot and chest tight. *Shitting myself.*

I worked to calm myself as Chrysanthou argued about how unfair it was to argue that Dr Al Muderis's experts were commercially reliant on him. She went on and on, trying to claw back her client's reputation. Her rising voice, to my mind, only signalling a level of desperation. As Chrysanthou became louder and louder, the judge grew frustrated. Her eyebrow firmly raised, the judge took deep breaths and rolled her eyes, before she finally intervened. 'You don't need to yell,' the judge said to Chrysanthou.

'Sorry, your Honour,' she said, volume at the max. 'I'm not yelling.'

After fierce debate and a short break, it was time.

'May it please the court,' Collins said. 'We call Charlotte Dixie Grieve.'

CHAPTER 19

The Longest Cross-examination

Stepping into the witness box before Justice Abraham was surreal. Having scrutinised her face from the back of the courtroom and over the YouTube link, suddenly I was looking directly into her eyes. I could see the colour of her lipstick, the light shining off her hoop earrings, the strands of her spikey hair. Everything seemed to move in slow motion, while my hands trembled. Collins asked whether the affidavits were mine and I responded 'yes', speaking into the same microphone I'd seen all our witnesses use. My voice sounded louder, and more metallic, than theirs ever did.

As Chrysanthou got started, I couldn't understand what she was asking. I asked her to repeat the questions, over and over. She could smell my fear. She looked me dead in the eye, her voice raised.

'You don't understand a lot of things to do with medical matters, do you, Ms Grieve?'

'I disagree with your proposition.'

'You were wholly, wholly inexperienced when you published these articles, in any issue to do with medical matters?'

'I disagree.'

Chrysanthou beamed a copy of the print articles onto the screen, and took me line by line through what had been published.

'Now, where you say in your article that my client left some people mutilated, what did you mean by the word "mutilated"?'

'Deformed in some way.'

'Which patients, who you spoke to, or were aware of prior to this publication, were left mutilated by my client's failures as a surgeon?'

'Mark Urquhart, for one.'

'In what way do you say he was left mutilated?'

'Dr Al Muderis had amputated both of his legs.'

'So you are saying a planned surgical amputation is a mutilation?'

'If it's not necessary or well advised, yes.'

'You understand, don't you, that's not the ordinary meaning of the word "mutilated"?'

'I don't understand that, no.'

'The ordinary meaning of the word mutilated is to leave someone grossly deformed?'

'I accept that.'

'And no person would understand that the ordinary result of a planned surgery could be described as a "mutilation"?'

My mind returned to Chrysanthou's opening, where she declared Dr Al Muderis's colleagues had 'mutilated' the soldiers' ears. Those men didn't consent to that surgery, but arguably, neither did Mark.

'I would say that an unnecessary amputation of someone's legs is a mutilation. I stand by that.'

Then, she accused me of having 'no basis' to say the maggots in Mark's legs were ignored.

'I did have a basis.'

'You knew it to be a highly sensational or evocative claim, didn't you, that a person is left sitting there with maggots?'

'I disagree with your choice of words.'

'Well, how would you describe how you understood, or how you intended the reader to react, to a claim that a patient was left, ignored, with maggots in his leg?'

'It's a distressing situation of an unforeseen risk of this surgery that was not tended to in an appropriate time or manner.'

'Well, it's grotesque, isn't it?'

'It is, yes.'

She accused me of 'deliberately' diminishing the benefits of osseointegration surgery, writing 'wholly misleading' descriptions of the procedure, highlighting only 'horror consequences' and publishing 'wholly unchecked, unverified allegations', 'grubby', 'not legitimate', 'grotesque tabloid' journalism. Each time, I disagreed.

Then her questions turned personal.

'Do you agree that the fact that Dr Al Muderis owns an expensive house and car is wholly irrelevant to what your article was about?'

'No.'

'You understand, don't you, that some people make a lot of money?'

'Yes.'

'That doesn't mean they're ripping off their customers or their clients, do you agree?'

'Yes.'

'Right. You've got two barrister parents, don't you?'

I shot a death stare at Collins, hoping he would object. My family had already been so exposed in this trial, this felt deeply unfair. He stayed quiet.

'Sure. Yes.'

'A highly paid profession?'

'Yes.'

'And because a barrister drives around a Bentley, doesn't mean that he's ripping off his clients, do you agree?'

'Yes. I don't think we were making the point that he was ripping people off.'

'Well, why else would you include the fact that he can afford expensive things?'

'It was relevant to the story insofar as patients had expressed to us concerns that he was presenting himself as purely altruistic, purely motivated by humanitarian work, and was often doing a lot of these surgeries for free, when we knew, through US court documents at least, that he was making significant profit margins on osseointegration. So, it was a relevant point in the story because a number of patients had mentioned this seeming contrast between the public image he portrays and the private reality that he lives.'

Chrysanthou seemed to hate this answer. She noted that Dr Al Muderis wore a Rolex on the front cover of his memoir (a detail I had never noticed) – evidence he never hid his wealth.

'And you had no basis, did you, to say as you just did, that my client somehow presents himself as someone that isn't making money?'

Collins interrupted. 'That's not what the witness said.'

The judge agreed. 'That's not what the witness said. It's not. So don't give me the look. Ask the question properly.'

'I was just about to … I withdraw it, your Honour,' Chrysanthou said.

The nerves I felt had evaporated toward the end of the first day. In the boxing ring, I kept my gloves over my skull when she tried to land a hook. There were moments where I was clipped, lost balance, but then regathered and stayed steady. I didn't feel Chrysanthou won a single point. In fact, some questions made me think Chrysanthou was under-prepared.

I left the courtroom after that first day high on adrenaline. I put my AirPods in and walked through Hyde Park blasting 'All Falls Down', the soundtrack to this time of my life. My partner called and said it sounded like I was in a good mood. I warned him I couldn't discuss the day, but said I was feeling as good as I could. We spoke for a few minutes, then I continued through the park and along Oxford Street, all the way home. When I walked in the door, the adrenaline had worn off and I was hit with a wave of exhaustion. I've never felt the physical aspects of tiredness more than during this trial. My body felt physically heavy, and my head constantly ached. I got into bed still wearing my court clothes, and pulled the covers over me as I started refreshing the news to see what, if anything, had been written about the day. News Corp had written nothing, which I'd come to view as a sign things were going well. The *Herald* article captured the moment Chrysanthou yelled about not yelling. I chuckled and closed my phone.

By the second day, I was much less nervous. Chrysanthou started the morning with bigger-picture questions.

'You understand, don't you, having worked in media for a number of years now, that, in your position as a journalist working for a national media corporation, you have, or you are in a position of power to utterly destroy a person?'

'I disagree with utterly destroy, those words.'

'Well, utterly destroy their reputation?'

'I disagree with your choice of words.'

'What do you disagree with?'

'I understand that these stories can have impact, and I'm aware of the serious nature of the allegations, but it's not that we are going out to destroy someone's reputation. We're just reporting what we believe in the public interest.'

She tried again and again to get me to reveal information about my confidential sources, but I deployed the journalist privilege over and over. Next, she asked me about deleting the Facebook messages.

'As I said in the last application, I did that as a knee-jerk reaction to protect the sources. And in hindsight, I probably shouldn't have done it because I have nothing to hide, but I ultimately don't regret hiding the messages.'

'Don't you think that it was wholly dishonest of you to delete those messages?'

'No.'

On the third day, just before the lunch break, the questions turned to nurse-turned-whistleblower Shona. The barrister tried to bait me into saying that Shona was 'untrustworthy' because she had shared emails with me, which included patient names. Chrysanthou said this was a breach of medical ethics that should have made me cautious of Shona's credibility. The emails were never for publication and only shared because I kept badgering Shona for paper trails to verify her claims. I had no doubt that Shona was an ethical nurse and now lawyer, who wanted to help people, so I pushed back firmly.

Chrysanthou kept asking the same question, over and over, worded slightly differently each time. 'You held concerns, didn't you, about Ms Stewart's credibility and reliability in circumstances where she was such a person to freely engage in such breaches of confidence toward patients?'

'No,' I said. 'I was asking her to provide information that supported what she said, and she was doing that, so if anything, it increased her credibility in my view.'

Chrysanthou then introduced a new claim to prosecute this further. She accused me of deleting Facebook messages with Shona to conceal what she was now openly calling – without evidence – unethical conduct. She triumphantly showed me two versions of our conversation logs as evidence I'd deleted messages. I was confused.

'I will have to check my phone but I honestly don't recall. I must – might have done it on the spot.'

'Why would you delete messages from Ms Stewart?'

'I don't recall. I don't recall doing that,' I said, racking my brain.

'Is it because you knew that it was obvious, from the content of those messages, that she had unethically provided you with patient names in breach of her obligations as a nurse?'

'No.'

'And that you were trying to protect her, perhaps, from scrutiny from this court by the fact she had engaged in that conduct?'

'No.'

The judge called the lunch break and I pulled out my phone to check. The messages were all there. I triumphantly raced over to JP and Sam, displaying the messages: 'See! They're here!' They were already all over it. I left the courtroom feeling elated. Chrysanthou's smoking gun was just another misfire.

Each day, I had to spend the lunch breaks alone. I took a plate of food from Thomson Geer's conference room then stayed in my own private cell. As I had been warned, everyone avoided eye contact with me and no-one said a word. I forced myself to swallow the food, even though eating was the last thing I felt like doing. I watched the city below, sometimes laying on the office floor. My partner remarked I had turned into their little pet – they fed me, kept me alive, only to walk me to court each day.

When we returned after lunch, Chrysanthou returned to the same subject. She tried to put the 'chronology' of messages between Shona and myself, and accused me again of only handing over some of the messages on purpose. She kept asking about specific messages sent at specific dates, but like the patients before me, I couldn't remember those minor details. All I knew was that I didn't delete any messages with Shona, and now I had the proof to back it up. This time, I was the angry one.

'I have just checked my phone, and all the messages were there. Whether you have them or at what point they were discovered, I am not sure, but we – I produced all the messages.'

Still, she couldn't let it go. Her questions grew increasingly convoluted, going round and round. Finally, something in me snapped.

'Sorry. I am not following your line of questioning. But you accused me of deleting messages. I never deleted the messages. I handed them over. I am not sure where they are, but they should have been discovered,' I said, my voice sharp now.

'So do you have any idea why the document that was produced to us by your discovery and as exhibited to your affidavit appears to quite deliberately exclude the 10 June messages?'

'No. And it wasn't deliberately. As I've maintained, I handed over all the messages. They're there in my phone. I have nothing to hide. There was no deliberate effort to conceal messages or to conceal evidence. I don't know what happened with the lawyers, but I've told you what has happened with my messages.'

'So you don't know why ... it would appear the 10 June messages have been deliberately excluded?'

'I believe I've answered that question.'

Collins objected. 'The question has now been asked three times and there's no basis for putting to this witness it has been deliberately – in circumstances where she said she has had nothing to do with it.'

'The witness repeatedly says—' the judge said, before Chrysanthou interrupted.

'Your Honour, it's her discovery and it's her affidavit.'

'I understand that,' the judge said. 'But you've asked the question numerous times.'

Finally, Chrysanthou gave up and returned to Shona again.

'Do you remember she made an admission to you or a claim that she had forged scripts?'

'At the instruction of your client, yes.'

'You found that to be quite a startling allegation?'

'Yes.'

This allegation was never published. Chrysanthou wanted to know why. I couldn't understand why she would willingly bring this damning allegation about her client onto the public record, under the full privilege of the court. But she did. Chrysanthou said if I thought it was credible, I would have pursued it.

'No,' I said. 'At that point, there were so many serious allegations being raised about your client to me that one somehow fell by the wayside.'

'Did you consider it a serious act of dishonesty for a nurse to forge pain medication scripts?'

'At the direction of your client,' I repeated.

She did not accept my answers. I was so desperate to put Shona in front of the cameras, Chrysanthou declared, that I overlooked any red flags about her credit. I disagreed.

'The main issue that I had with her credit that I was trying to explore was the impact of the sexual relationship that she had with Dr Al Muderis, and I tested her a number of times on that, whether that could be clouding her view, whether that could be clouding her judgment. That was the part of her credit that I was concerned with. This didn't concern me.'

'And what I am putting to you is, you didn't look for information to undermine her?'

'I did.'

'You acted in a wilfully blind manner by not making any inquiry at all to test her allegation?'

'I disagree.'

'And that wasn't limited to Ms Stewart. The entirety of your investigation was conducted on the basis, from your perspective, when it came to claims made by sources of "don't ask, don't tell"?'

'That's not true.'

'Generally, you sought corroboration?'

'Of course, yes.'

'But you never sought to make inquiries that might contradict what you were being told?'

'That's completely not true.'

That afternoon, by this time my third consecutive day in the box, the questions turned to the degree Dr Al Muderis was responsible for his patients' problems. Chrysanthou argued the multidisciplinary team meant others, like pain specialists, also held responsibility. The questions echoed the doctor's 'I'm just a carpenter' mantra. I said I understood how the team was structured but, 'These were his patients. He was responsible for all aspects of their care.'

She thought this was ludicrous. She asked for my definition of 'responsible' and then, with a facial expression that looked exasperated by my apparent stupidity, asked if I expected Dr Al Muderis to treat a 'gynaecological emergency' for one of his patients, should one occur. The sick, dark comedy went on.

'Obviously not,' I said. 'He was responsible for all aspects of their care. Sorry I should have been more clear, I thought it was obvious, for osseointegration.'

She accused me of having 'no idea' of how medical specialists operate and said my view was 'utterly incorrect'. I disagreed.

'Ms Grieve, you are of the view, are you, that because my client had carried out a surgery, he was responsible for every aspect of the medical care forever after associated with that surgery?'

'Yes. That's what other surgeons have described their role and their duty to me as being. Once you perform the operation on the patient, you are responsible for that patient and how they deal with the consequences of that surgery for the rest of their life.'

She kept going; I stood firm.

'I maintain what I said before. They're his patients. They're his responsibility.'

By 4.15 pm that afternoon, we were still only a fraction of the way through my affidavit.

'The cross-examination will not finish tomorrow,' Chrysanthou said.

'Shocked, I say,' the judge replied.

Over the entire cross-examination, Chrysanthou described my work as 'wholly discreditable', 'utterly disgraceful', 'wholly dishonest' and 'utterly false'. She said I 'ambushed' Dr Al Muderis with 'stunts', gave 'absurd', 'dishonest' evidence that was 'made up as you sit here'. She accused me of 'tricking' sources, 'misleading them', of giving answers that were 'utterly absurd', an 'utter exaggeration' or 'wholly misdescribed'. She called me 'highly unethical', 'wholly incompetent', said I had 'deliberately concealed' documents, was 'merely a mouthpiece' for patients, and was 'so determined to malign' her client.

I was accused of not asking enough questions, asking too many questions, speaking to some people *too* much, others not enough. She chastised me for not answering her questions, then accused me of using the witness box as a 'soapbox' or giving a 'little speech'. She repeatedly called my sources 'unhinged' and even took aim at patients who praised Dr Al Muderis. She called Cindy Asch-Martin 'the loon who followed god'.

Then there were the bizarre moments. Like when she asked me why I didn't print out my Google searches. Whether I knew whether maggots were babies or could breed. Or whether I structured my affidavit to make it as 'confusing' for her team as possible. Or when she used her powers as a barrister to 'call' for a copy of the article, which was publicly accessible online. Or when she asked me: 'You speak English and you write in English?'

By 10 May, the fourth consecutive day, I was tired of going round in circles. I started shooting off the answer my father had used in his cross-examination, 'The records speak for themselves.' We laughed about this together later.

She asked whether a doctor had specifically described Dr Al Muderis's practice as 'dangerous' or 'unethical'. I said that was the substance of our conversation.

'He never said any such thing to you, did he?'

'Those two words?' I asked.

'Any such thing even resembling those words?'

'Well, I consider it dangerous to be conducting clinics in hotel rooms without proper sterilisation policies.'

'Ms Grieve,' Chrysanthou replied, like an angry schoolteacher scolding a petulant child. 'Are you deliberately choosing not to answer my question?'

'No.'

'And to make a speech which you think suits you?'

'No. You're asking me the same question over and over. I'm doing my best to answer your questions.'

'The question is, who are the surgeons who described to you his practice as "unethical at best, dangerous at worst"?'

'If you do a Control F in my notes document, those words will pop up. They popped up routinely. If you want me to describe, you know, individual situations that were described as "dangerous" or "unethical", I can go into that. I'm just not sure of what – how you want me to answer that question.'

I was dismissed at 4.17 pm on Friday. I had to come back on Monday, meaning the whole weekend was spent trapped under the rules of giving evidence. My sister had come over for dinner each night that week to be the 'evidence police', cutting off conversation any time it strayed anywhere near the day's events. In some respects, I had come to enjoy being prohibited from discussing what unfolded in court. I didn't want a running commentary on my performance. There was something about just trusting my gut and telling the truth that felt simpler, and less stressful. But as the days passed, I grew tired and frustrated by the unreasonable length of defamation lawsuits. I spent a total of six days in the witness box by the end of the trial, across the public interest defence and confidential source application. Chrysanthou remarked this was the longest she had ever cross-examined a journalist. I later learned it was the longest any journalist in Australia had ever been in the box.

It seemed disproportionate, and a waste of the court's time and everyone's money. I struggled to understand the point at times. I genuinely did not feel that Chrysanthou was achieving anything. In the breaks, she kept making remarks about how tired she was, and I think it showed. Her questioning felt unfocused, and while I understand barristers structure questions in ways that are foreign to journalists, I couldn't see a plan. The more it dragged on, racking up monster legal fees every hour of every day, the more it cemented the reality that this law – defamation – is reserved exclusively for the wealthy.

Finally, it was Monday – the final day of cross-examination. Chrysanthou began the day by accusing me of not giving Dr Al Muderis the proper right of reply. It was true that he never responded to the claims made by individual patients, but that wasn't due to lack of trying. We filmed Mark Urquhart, Brennan Smith and Chris Bruha giving consent for the doctor to discuss their cases. When Dr Al Muderis said that wouldn't do, I got Mark to send an email and showed it to him. He wouldn't budge during the interview and then he denigrated his patients off-camera. I gave him my mobile and asked for him to find a way so he could respond. I formed the view it was his privilege, so I put the ball in his court to get his patients' consent to discuss their treatment. There were weeks between the interview date and when we published, and in that time, he never did.

Chrysanthou returned to the conversation with Dr Al Muderis after the interview. She asked about topics that were discussed, and then appeared to quote, almost verbatim, something I had said. It was after Dr Al Muderis had spun a theory about his enemies being behind the story.

'And you said: *Yeah, I don't think that's what's going on. I mean, I appreciate you think there's a bit of, sort of, you know, a conspiracy against you, but this is journalism.* Do you remember saying that?'

'Is this ... Was this a recorded conversation?'

'I'm putting to you what I say happened during that conversation?'

'Yes. I'm asking for the basis of it.'

'You don't have a right to ask me for what's in my brief, Ms Grieve!'

'Okay.'

'It's up to you to remember?'

'I don't recall the specific words, but the substance of that sounds right.'

Later, Chrysanthou said it was 'wholly misleading' for us to have broadcast the line saying AHPRA's 'silence speaks volumes'.

'No. I stand by that completely,' I said.

'And you are of the view, are you, that you know more about AHPRA's role than AHPRA does?'

'No.'

Her questioning became more aggressive as the day wore on. 'You've continued to malign my client, haven't you, for months and months in new publications after the publications you've been sued over?'

'No.'

'You wanted to utterly destroy him, didn't you?'

'No.'

'You wouldn't let it rest. You published dozens and dozens of publications about him, didn't you?'

'I don't recall the total figure, but we were contacted by enormous amounts of people, so, you know, yes, we chose the ones which only went to systemic issues to publish.'

Later, she asked why I didn't tell Tom Steinfort that my father was the starting point of the investigation and suggested I'd withheld this because I knew it was a conflict of interest.

'No. I didn't think it was a conflict. I just didn't want to bring my family into it.'

'Did you disclose it to Ms Clancy?'

'The person I disclosed it to, who I thought was the only necessary person to disclose it to, was my editor, Michael Bachelard, at the time.'

There was a list of allegations in my affidavit about claims we didn't publish. I didn't know it at the time, but Dr Al Muderis's lawyers had specifically asked us to write this. The list included claims that the doctor was reported to the regulator for sexual relationships with his staff, and details of a toxic workplace culture. This was information we had but was never published because we felt it could distract from the main public interest of the story – patient care. If we were going to 'tip a bucket' on Dr Al Muderis, as Chrysanthou had said, these are the gruesome details we could have poured out.

Chrysanthou asked if I thought I should 'get some sort of credit' for not publishing these claims. She accused me of only including the list in my affidavit so it would be 'reported by media companies'. I said no, again and again.

'These claims would remain, you know, in the depths of nowhere if it weren't for this case. I was simply asked to dictate my steps,' I said.

She later went through each of the patient-witnesses insisting their experiences were 'wholly positive' – listing Kerry Ford, Rachael Ulrich, Iraqi patient Karar Hydar Yusur, and Fred Hernandez as some examples. I knocked each assertion back, but reading the transcript of this exchange more than a year later, I still find it shocking. It was a stark reminder that we really were living in parallel universes. Had she read their affidavits? Had she forgotten their evidence? After all that we had been through, how could she still think nothing had gone wrong for these people? Because in the real world, Kerry was dead, Rachael almost died, Karar was bed-bound and Fred was in prison.

She then turned her attention to my beliefs, which were set out in a 'very long list'. She said I didn't hold those opinions.

I disagreed. She then said my opinions were based only on what patients had told me. Again, I disagreed.

She put to me, one last time, that the stories were one-sided. 'No,' I said.

'I suggest to you that in relation to what you assert there about patients having no recourse, that was utterly baseless?'

'No.'

She said this answer couldn't be true because I knew about Leah Mooney and Kim Gollan, who had both been paid settlement sums. Once again, it was Chrysanthou who was wrong.

'I only became aware of that after publication,' I said.

She went through specific parts of the stories, saying they weren't in the public interest. I denied each proposition. I was using every ounce of my energy to concentrate, but the reality was, by this point, I was totally worn down.

It was nudging 4.13 pm when finally, after a week of giving evidence, of not being able to speak with anyone about this wild ride, she finished.

'No further questions, your Honour.'

As soon as I heard those words, it felt like the handbrake had been pulled on a speeding car. My bones and muscles suddenly felt slack, the tightness wound up inside me released. It was like I'd been in some kind of trance, concentrating intently on the exact wording of each question, on the lookout for traps, in a constant state of hypervigilance.

Collins said the re-examination would take about 15 minutes. Lawyers privately told me this was embarrassingly short for a cross-examination that had lasted so long.

Collins first asked how I reconciled Shona's ongoing friendly relationship with Dr Al Muderis while at the same time harbouring serious concerns. I explained she was still processing the traumatic experience of working for him. 'She was trying to put it behind her,' I said, 'and trying to maintain good relations with him as part of that.'

Collins asked me to expand on Dr Horst Aschoff's concerns. I explained that he believed amputees should try sockets first, whereas Dr Al Muderis believed everyone should have osseointegration. Dr Al Muderis portrayed socket prostheses as antiquated, outdated, when the reality is very different, I said. Amputees can have full lives using sockets.

There were a few more questions, but the lawyers remarked I looked completely spent. It was 4.27 pm when it was officially over. 'Nothing further, your Honour. Might Ms Grieve be excused? Well, not excused, she's a party, but excused from the witness box?'

The judge looked at me with the slightest hint of a smile. 'Yes. You're free. Thank you. You can finish.'

We shuffled out of the courtroom and into a small conference room, where Collins delivered his assessment. He said he thought I was one of the best three journalists he'd ever seen in the witness box, that it was a masterclass and I should be very proud. I was worried I waffled on at points, but he said my extended answers gave the court an insight into the depth of the reporting, the consideration behind it. This clearly wasn't the hit piece the doctor so badly wanted it to be, he said.

Collins said I had done a great service to my sources, particularly the confidential ones. I hadn't wavered in my duty to protect them, which would have lasting impacts, he said. Kiah said she wished the whole thing could have been filmed so she could show it to journalists preparing for court. Everyone said I couldn't have done any better. That was a huge relief to hear.

Afterward I met JP for a beer at a pub nearby, and we rehashed some of the stand-out moments from the case to date. He apologised for some parts of the cross-examination that got me into hot water, like the Facebook messages from Shona that hadn't been properly handed over.

'Sorry for putting you in that position,' he said.

None of that mattered. I was glad it was over, and so pleased they thought it had gone well. Over the record-breaking stint in the witness box, Chrysanthou didn't ask any of the questions I'd most feared – nothing about underwear-gate or even a single accusation of racism. Sam McGeoch joined us, and I thanked them both for everything. We joked about some of the tense points we'd had preparing for trial. Sam's first child was born at the beginning of this case and was now a toddler walking around. It was a reminder of how long the litigation had dragged on. Sam joked that she would feel a little lost once it was finished, and there was a sincerity in her voice that reminded me just how much this legal team cared about the case. And that's what mattered to me most.

***

The next day, it was time for Tom Steinfort to get in the box.

Tom studied journalism at RMIT in Melbourne in the early 2000s and got his start working in the WIN News bureau in Ballarat as a general news reporter. Tom quickly excelled, and in 2006 joined the 9News team. He was awarded Young Journalist of the Year for his coverage of the Black Saturday bushfires in 2009. The job took him around the world, where he was on the ground for many of the world's major events, from natural disasters to terror attacks, murder trials and US presidencies. He's a published author, a Walkley Award winner and nowadays, an encouraging mentor to younger journalists.

Tom had never heard of Dr Al Muderis before *60 Minutes'* chief of staff Stefanie Sgroi told him about what looked like a 'controversial investigation' in mid-2022.

I read Tom's affidavit the night before he took the stand, and saw how he had taken responsibility for the story. He'd done his own research, wanting to make sure everything stacked up for himself. Tom needed to be certain these patients were for real, and the more people he spoke to, the more convinced he was of the public interest of the investigation. He stated that he thought Dr Al Muderis didn't listen to his patients and placed profits over people. He agreed the regulators should have done more, and knew the media could play an important role in warning the public.

The next morning, I woke up exhausted. Court was the last place I felt like going. I put on my court clothes and headed to the Thomson Geer office, large coffee in hand. Tom was already there, dressed in a freshly pressed suit and surrounded by lawyers. I'd been told he was nervous, but he didn't give anything away. He'd re-read the material on the plane, had a good sleep and was in a good mood. I thought to myself about how this must all feel like a distant memory coming back to haunt him. He'd since left *60 Minutes* to become the co-news anchor for Nine's 6 pm Melbourne news. He was a 'Melebrity', as Kirsty described him, wearing a fabulous red suit that day.

Everyone kept saying how relieved I must feel now that my cross-examination was over. But in reality, I almost felt more nervous for Tom and Natalie. I knew Chrysanthou would encourage them to throw me under the bus, or try to spin them into making admissions that could harm the case at the eleventh hour. Once again, I felt my control over the situation slipping.

I walked over to the court building with Tom and kept the conversation light. I asked about his new role, and his new life in Melbourne. The ratings had skyrocketed since he and Alicia Loxley took over, and he was enjoying the more reliable hours and reduced travel, which allowed him to be more present as a father to his two children. Tom is a kind person, modest yet confident with good manners. I was certain the judge would see this.

In the courtroom, I sat in the back with Natalie, Kirsty and Kiah. The barristers arrived shortly afterward and Sandip looked at me with an expression of horror and surprise. 'What on earth are you doing here?' I smiled and shrugged.

In the witness box, Tom poured a glass of water, adjusted his tie and placed his hand on his chin as the questions began.

'Mr Steinfort, you accept, don't you, as a journalist, it's your responsibility to understand the subject matter of a topic that you're publishing about before [you] publish?'

'I do.'

Tom agreed that he had to be personally satisfied the serious allegations about Dr Al Muderis were true, and accepted that he did not 'merely rely on Ms Grieve' for that.

'She was certainly a very big part of the team, yes. But I, of course, did my own research,' he said.

Chrysanthou's tone was much less accusatory than it had been with me. She tried to get Tom onside, encouraging him to distance himself from me, to say I was a terrible journalist. He didn't bite. He stood by me, and even went the extra mile. He said he'd never received such detailed briefing notes, such extensive research, and that he considered me diligent, hard-working, detail-oriented and, importantly, objective.

Tom and I had worked on one other joint investigation together, a story about an elaborate fraud against Westpac, that I'd pitched when I was still a business reporter. 'Now, other than that, did you have any knowledge of what her experience and background was?' Chrysanthou asked.

'I knew that she had been with the publisher for some time, and had clearly impressed her bosses there, because you don't get a job in the investigations team at *The Age* and the *Sydney Morning Herald* without getting some significant runs on the board.'

Tom said his role was a little bit like Chrysanthou's, in that other people in the team do the background work, and he turns up on the day and pulls it all together. This was a useful theme that Tom would return to, his answers getting stronger and clearer each time.

Chrysanthou went through other media stories about Dr Al Muderis that she said Tom must have read or watched, including a previous *60 Minutes* episode about a soldier Dr Al Muderis had operated on. Each time, she said these journalists, his colleagues, were not the types of people to have the wool pulled over their eyes, were they? Tom politely said no, but offered an explanation.

'I would say that, often with those kinds of articles, they're feel-good stories. And I felt that the majority of stories, not the majority, I must say, all the stories that I saw, really pointed to this halo effect of a man who was performing miracles. And there seemed to be little to no – I guess, insight what happens when it goes wrong.'

Every time it felt like she was going nowhere, Chrysanthou tried to lure Tom into criticising me again.

'Now, having regard to your experience and interaction with Ms Grieve, you understood, didn't you, despite what you've said earlier this morning, that she had very little experience as a journalist?'

'Absolutely disagree,' Tom said.

Chrysanthou asked about everything from the technicalities of osseointegration surgery to the differences between current affairs shows at Channel Nine. All throughout, Tom was steady, clear and polite. He gave quick-witted, insightful, easy-to-follow answers. When the questions about maggots became convoluted, Tom reminded the court: 'We're talking about maggots in someone's legs here.' When Chrysanthou drilled into the cash commissions paid to Fred Hernandez, she suggested these were legal in America. Tom pushed back, saying any commissions were 'extremely inappropriate' and 'unethical' for a surgeon.

'It's perfectly legal to walk down the street with an AR-15 assault rifle in America. We are a different country, thankfully,' Tom said.

At times, Tom said Chrysanthou's questions were 'ridiculous' and began deploying our now-favourite response: 'The transcript speaks for itself.'

Then, Chrysanthou used Dr Al Muderis's line: 'There's a difference between facts and feelings?'

Tom said 'of course' before expanding. He talked about how these patients had dealt with a lot in life, and it was up to them to decide whether the surgery was successful or not. 'Sure, a doctor might tell you, "Well it did go well." You know who matters? The patient. The patient is the one who decides whether it went well or not, because if they're not happy with the operation, then as far as I'm concerned, that's not overly successful.'

Chrysanthou tried to ask about infection rates from a specific medical paper but again Tom brought the court back to the bigger picture, making a comparison to the fine print on a mobile contract. He said most people don't read the 'little Ts and Cs', just as patients don't read dense medical literature. Instead, he said, they'd have watched Dr Al Muderis's TEDx Talk or the Anh Do interview, which has a 'halo effect' on his work. Tom said we did include patients who celebrated the doctor's work, and gave him the opportunity to speak about his good deeds.

'But that being said, important journalism is highlighting a story that perhaps hasn't received the attention that it needs, and perhaps that others have made an effort to make sure doesn't get that much of a look-in. And so that is why this was so important. Yes, we tried to show that he had been celebrated in the past and the present, but there was a significant cohort – this wasn't just one voice. There was a significant cohort of people that thought that they had been let down by Dr Al Muderis and his surgery or rehabilitation processes.'

Decades of television experience had trained Tom in how to distil the most important parts of a complex story and express it in a way that makes sense. He nailed these answers, one after the next.

By 10.38 am on the second day, JP sent a text: *Tom doing so well. She needs to get him out of the box.*

Chrysanthou asked why *60 Minutes* didn't interview Dr Al Muderis a second time, as he had requested. Tom said there would have to be the most 'extraordinary extenuating circumstances' to consider that.

'Why?' Chrysanthou asked.

'Well, the simple fact is that you would come back with scripted answers to all of the questions. And again, you wouldn't cross-examine me and then two days later say, "Come back. Let's do it all again … Here, you can have another go at it." He had ample time, endless time, limitless, to answer on the day all of these issues. The idea that he would then get to come back four days later and have thought up a perfectly worded answer to everything … it's just fanciful to suggest that's how it would work.'

She accused Tom of 'gotcha journalism' and said we had 'no interest' in allowing Dr Al Muderis a fair right of reply. Tom responded that the doctor was a 'man of great intellect' and there were no questions he couldn't answer. 'We spent hours with him.'

The longer it went on, the more confident I felt. Even if the judge ruled that I was biased and inexperienced, it didn't matter. In the comparatively short time Tom had spent in the box, he totally demolished Chrysanthou's key arguments – including when she tried to defend her client's decision to amputate Mark Urquhart's 'useless' legs.

'What, so we just chop off everyone's legs who don't have function in them?' Tom said.

By early afternoon, the judge was already looking at the clock. *She's bored. We're all bored*, I wrote in my notes.

Chrysanthou claimed Tom had 'no basis' to make the final point in his affidavit:

I formed the opinion that Dr Al Muderis was a classic A-type personality with narcissistic traits. He is the type of ego and success-driven person who surrounds himself with yes men and sycophants such that he is incapable of admitting he could ever do something wrong.

'Unfortunately, in my line of work, you cover a lot of A-type personalities with narcissist traits, and as I've described there, Dr Al Muderis ticked many, many of the boxes of that type of person,' Tom said.

Finally, Chrysanthou suggested Tom didn't really hold beliefs that the stories were in the public interest.

'I did hold them, I remain holding them and I hold them very strongly.'

'And I want to suggest to you the last answer you gave is just not true, is it?'

'It is 100 per cent the truth.'

'No further questions.'

Collins had no re-examination. Another blow.

* * *

Next up was Natalie Clancy. She walked up to the box and sat down, her back straight, glasses on, and made the oath to tell the truth. A whip-smart producer, Natalie had been with Nine since 2016 and, like Tom, had quickly risen through the ranks. In her short career, Natalie had worked with some of the country's most well-known television journalists – Liz Hayes, Tara Brown and Sarah Abo – and won several awards. She had first become aware of Dr Al Muderis while working for *A Current Affair* sometime in 2019, when the show received an anonymous tip-off that he was mistreating his staff and allegedly improperly billing. Natalie and another journalist, Dimity Clancey, investigated the case – speaking to a handful of the same people who later ended up becoming my sources.

What do you think we do??? Dimity wrote to Natalie in April 2019. *He will be very difficult to deal with, but I feel like this is a battle we should fight. I fear he will make my life hell, but hey, journalism takes guts.*

Not enough people were prepared to go on the record, so they never ran the story. But when *60 Minutes* needed a producer for a joint investigation on the same topic a few years later, it only made sense Natalie was assigned.

Chrysanthou picked through parts of Natalie's affidavit, probing her knowledge of my experience, before criticising the 'rags to riches' line used to describe Dr Al Muderis's rise.

'You understood, didn't you, that although he was a refugee who was in detention for ten months, my client, in fact, came from quite a privileged background in Iraq?'

'Yes.'

'And you agree, don't you, that describing my client's life as a rags-to-riches tale was inaccurate?'

'I disagree,' Natalie said. 'Because I think that rags-to-riches isn't necessarily just financial. It can also be about lifestyle, and it can also reflect his journey as a refugee.'

Again, Natalie brought a refreshing clarity to the courtroom. When Chrysanthou asked whether Fred Hernandez's relationship with Dr Al Muderis went beyond a 'falling out' to an 'intense hatred', Natalie's answer came quickly and naturally.

'I don't know if I would go as far as intense hatred, but he didn't like the guy.'

Then, Chrysanthou returned to one of her favourite topics – how terrible I was. She asked if Natalie understood I was 'not balanced at all', had 'an axe to grind', 'exaggerated negative information' and 'lacked objectivity'. Natalie disagreed, again and again. Chrysanthou called me 'hateful and malicious', filled with 'ill will'. Again, Natalie calmly disagreed.

The cross-examination meandered around many of the same topics, but eventually petered out, finishing with one last stab.

'You did not have sufficient knowledge about Ms Grieve to trust her journalism?'

'I did.'

'And, in fact, the knowledge you had, as I've already put to you, would have made you be very wary about her approach to this particular story?'

'I disagree. I had full confidence.'

'And you didn't believe at the time of broadcast, did you, that that broadcast was in the public interest?'

'It was in the public interest.'

There was no re-examination from Collins.

That night, I had a shower, got changed and went to meet two old friends for dinner. I walked down Oxford Street, my headphones in, with what felt like a literal spring in my step. The night air was cool. I typed a note in my phone: *There's not an ounce in my body that makes me feel like we're going to lose this case. I feel fucking great.*

CHAPTER 20

Case Closed

The cross-examination and witnesses were over but the lawyers had another huge task ahead – submissions. This is where each side delivers oral and written arguments to bring the whole case into focus. If all the different types of evidence were pieces of a jigsaw puzzle, the submissions clicked them into one clear picture.

Justice Abraham ordered the submissions be no longer than 400 pages and set a strict deadline before the final hearing, ensuring each side had enough time to read, digest and prepare any responses. In the weeks leading up to the deadline, drafts had circulated within our team, who worked around the clock to debate certain words and phrases and make sure every single line was punchy and accurate. Our final submissions were handed in on time, within the word limit, and with a whole bunch of colour-coded flowcharts helpfully annexed to assist the judge in making her decision.

On the other side, it was a drastically different story. I heard they were looking for new barristers to help finish the job. They began filing partially submitted chunks at strange hours – 2.30 am, 4 am, 7 am, 8 am – in emails sent to the judge and our lawyers. In the end, their submissions were way over the word limit, riddled with typos, and late – all without any explanation to the court.

On 3 June 2024, the parties assembled before the judge. Chrysanthou walked into the courtroom, loudly disclosing personal details to anyone in earshot. 'I broke my arse,' she said, before pulling up copies of her X-rays and making jokes about ignoring her medical advice to sit on a 'whoopee cushion' in court. Chrysanthou's open musings had become a common occurrence throughout the trial – she often shared personal stories to no-one in particular. We'd heard about her appreciation of Seinfeld, how she used to listen to maths podcasts, stories about chess clubs, French pastry shops, zoos on mountains. People tuning into the YouTube stream also noticed these exchanges. 'The things you learn while court is coming back from lunch break,' one observer posted on social media. 'Sue Chrysanthou SC is going to see Seinfeld at some point this year and has front row seats. Her sister loves the show.'

When the judge entered, the cheery banter came to an abrupt end. Justice Abraham was furious. Chrysanthou tried to nip any criticism in the bud, starting with a grovelling apology. She said they had tried their best to meet the deadline but simply didn't have the resources. 'It's wholesale my responsibility,' Chrysanthou said. 'It's no excuse, but I kept my learned friend informed as best we could as to what we were up to.'

The judge didn't buy it. The deadline was a court order, she said, and if there was any risk of not meeting it, Chrysanthou should have filed an application for additional time, with an explanation. 'It's disrespectful to the court and it's disrespectful to the respondents,' the judge growled.

Chrysanthou kept trying to explain, only to be slapped down even harder. 'The order wasn't a suggestion. It was actually an order,' the judge said, her typical sternness now a full-blown rage. 'And orders of the court are to be followed except if there's a request for an extension. None of that was done.'

'I agree, your Honour,' Chrysanthou said.

I almost felt sorry for Chrysanthou. 'I don't,' a handful of the lawyers said in unison when I mentioned this later.

After the squabbling, Collins was up first to close our case. This was his moment to shine, the day his sparkling grand plan would finally be unfolded for everyone to see. Collins is the type of barrister who spends restless nights chewing over the precise words he wants to use, searching for the most accurate, most cutting, most persuasive. A perfectionist with a near-photographic memory, he deploys each line like a sniper, piercing his target right in the heart, shot after shot.

On his feet, Collins started by stating that his concern with Dr Al Muderis's submissions was not the length, but the 'various serious respects in which they are flatly wrong on matters of fact'. He was worried the judge could be led to error 'unless assertions of fact made in that document are very carefully reviewed'.

Collins then skilfully outlined our case, recounting the lines of attack offered by Chrysanthou only to pulverise them, one by one. He returned to what he'd said at the very beginning: that our investigation reported the lived experiences of a significant number of Dr Al Muderis's former patients – extremely vulnerable people, 'in most cases, amputees as a result of a catastrophe in each of their lives, who had come to see Dr Al Muderis, desperately seeking his help'.

'We told your Honour that we expected the stories of the patients to be harrowing, but the clear themes would emerge of risks being downplayed by Dr Al Muderis, or not mentioned at all, of medical records not accurately recording what was said in consultations, of alternatives to aggressive surgery not being explained or explored, of sales tactics and pressure undermining patients' ability to give informed consent.

'In some cases, of disastrous mistakes being made by Dr Al Muderis during surgery, and of post-operative care that was inadequate to non-existent, leaving patients feeling abandoned or worse off than before they were operated upon.

'We submit,' he said, 'that the evidence adduced in the course of the trial more than established the matters on which we open.'

Collins said Dr Al Muderis's claim that 'almost all' patients who dared to give evidence were 'lying in one way or another' was dead wrong. On the contrary, he said the remarkable feature of this case was that despite the extraordinary coercive powers of the court, the eye-watering costs involved, 'nothing emerged of substance, nothing, in our submission, to shake the fundamental accuracy' of the stories. The centrepiece of Dr Al Muderis's case, the concoction theory, was always factually wrong, Collins said, and 'now appears to have been essentially abandoned'.

He addressed Chrysanthou's efforts to paint the reporters as people who did not 'comprehend the meaning of truth' and published a 'terrible, terrible lie'. In reality, Collins said, we approached our jobs with an open mind, survived aggressive cross-examination and 'did a valuable public service'. He said I was the 'driving force' behind the 'major' investigation and was a 'tenacious, thoroughly professional, exhaustive, meticulous journalist of integrity'. Tom Steinfort showed an 'uncommon degree of emotional intelligence' and Natalie Clancy was 'very clearly telling the truth'.

Then, Collins turned his attention to Dr Al Muderis himself, noting he had a 'very complex personality'. Collins acknowledged the 'enormous amount of good' the doctor had done, and the many patients who consider him to be 'almost a god-like figure', but said there was another side, one thing that defines him: 'His inability, almost pathological inability to admit error. And it's a very strong feature of what has happened in this trial over the last 15 weeks.'

The barrister went through the 'glaring' examples of negligence that had 'catastrophic' results for patients, the ways in which Dr Al Muderis's actions had been 'appalling and beneath contempt', how he prioritised fame and money over his patients. He concluded such a surgeon does not deserve an unblemished reputation. 'And Dr Al Muderis *has* enjoyed an unblemished reputation.'

Collins said Dr Al Muderis could be forgiven for the occasional flash of anger over more than ten days of cross-examination, but described the surgeon's evidence as 'remarkable' as he gave 'wilfully false' answers that were 'just not credible', 'seriously dishonest' and showed a 'disturbing lack of insight'.

It was Dr Al Muderis's decision to bring this lawsuit, Collins reminded the court, based on the premise that everyone was lying but him. 'Dr Al Muderis elected to do this. He elected to make those assertions about all of his former patients, and it reflects some of the criticism in the broadcast that this is a man who, at times, is callous, arrogant, uncaring, lacking in empathy.'

Collins said the reporters were entitled to have a 'healthy scepticism' toward AHPRA's refusal to participate in an interview, where the regulator could have and should have faced up to questions about 'what appears, plainly, to be shortcomings in the regulation of this industry in this country'.

'But they chose not to,' Collins said.

Leah and Tim Mooney arrived at court the next day to see Collins' closing submissions in person, having caught the ferry into the city. 'Quite the little journey we've been on,' Tim said, with a twinkle in his eye, a nod to the wider meaning. Leah had left her hearing aid at home so asked the court staff if they could help. When the hammer knocked, the judge announced a request for hearing loops. Leah and Tim cautiously shuffled up to the front row, where the courtroom assistant helped plug the headphones in. Ever the team, Leah and Tim settled into their seats, their matching sets of headphones plugged in, as they listened intently to Collins guiding the judge through the legal histories underpinning the case.

Collins then returned to the Cambodian patients, who he said were among the 21 patients who did not provide informed consent to surgery with Dr Al Muderis. Collins said the language barrier for these patients only meant Dr Al Muderis should have gone to greater lengths to ensure they understood what they were signing up for. 'The day after the surgery, she asked to have it removed, as if that were a possibility,' Collins said of Eang Srey Da.

He spoke about Patient X, the woman with anorexia, noting that doctors had considered it a 'scandal that anyone would consider performing osseointegration on' her. There were cascading 'red flags' that should have caused any responsible surgeon to have 'grave doubts' about whether she consented to surgery. He went through patient after patient who felt Dr Al Muderis was too busy to help them.

Collins turned to his masterpiece – the colour-coded flowchart that forensically showed every piece of evidence and every defence for every imputation. Just as JP had assured me, Collins had a plan. And here it was. Like a captain steering a ship through wild seas, he navigated the complex legal intricacies to show the judge exactly how we should win.

'The man doesn't deserve the reputation he has enjoyed, and the publications are matters of substantial truth,' Collins said.

My father sent me a message during the hearing praising Collins' performance. *To my mind, he has left practically no room for doubt that this case has been misconceived from the outset.* Later that night, Dad told me it was one of the best closing submissions he had ever seen.

By that point, I felt extremely confident in the case, the team, the strategy, the story, the truth of it all. I put on a hoodie and walked through the winter's night to sit on the stairs underneath the Kings Cross Coca-Cola sign, overlooking the city. There, I typed out an email to Collins. I had been careful to maintain boundaries with everyone in the legal team, particularly Collins.

He was a fierce advocate, but also valued the ethics of barristers that demand impartiality and independence. But now, I felt compelled to reach out. The email was titled 'Brilliant day'. I thanked Collins for his advocacy and told him I was so proud to have him represent me. 'It was another brilliant day capping off an extraordinary effort over so many months and it's clear the judge trusts you immensely.'

The following day, it was time for Dr Al Muderis to close his case. He didn't turn up to court, and neither did his wife. One of our lawyers remarked how unusual that was, and said if their client didn't turn up for closings, they would have at least offered an explanation to the judge. When Chrysanthou stood, the change in the judge's demeanour was stark. With Collins, Justice Abraham barely said a word, engaged in an almost single continuous nod, removing her glasses to closely read the passages he took her to, scribbling notes as she hung on his every word. With Chrysanthou, her eyebrows rose. The judge tried to ask questions, but Chrysanthou talked over her, louder, faster, using more dramatic and emphatic language, only causing Justice Abraham's eyebrows to climb further and further up her forehead.

Chrysanthou tried to encourage the judge to look at the entire chronology for each patient, rather than 'piecemeal' examples that she said we had highlighted. With that approach, Chrysanthou argued that Dr Al Muderis had done everything he could for these patients, and that in many cases, patients had suffered a known complication of surgery that they *were* warned about. She argued that while surgeons are obliged to treat patients, they're also obliged not to 'over-treat' by over-prescribing antibiotics, or ordering tests that aren't necessary. The crux of Chrysanthou's case was that almost all of these patients, 'unfortunately for them', had so many health problems that along the way they had become confused, and blamed Dr Al Muderis for problems that he did not cause, or was not responsible for.

'Every single one of these patients was in a terrible situation when they came to see my client,' she said.

In an analogy that seemed to have a meta quality, Chrysanthou compared the risks of litigation with the risks of surgery, to explain how both lawyers and surgeons are not responsible if their clients or patients suffer bad outcomes. Barristers can lose a case, Chrysanthou said, then provide advice on appeal, but the client's response might be: 'I hate you. I hate courts. I'm not appealing.'

'Well, that doesn't mean the barrister who ran the case was negligent in the first place,' Chrysanthou said.

The judge interjected. 'They may have been.'

Feisty to the bitter end, Chrysanthou pushed back. 'That means 50 per cent of barristers are negligent because they lost. It's a known complication of litigation that 50 per cent of people lose. I don't know if there's any barrister that boasts of 100 per cent victory rate.'

'I am sure there is,' the judge said again.

'We all lose cases, but does that mean in every case we lose we were negligent? Of course not. Because like medicine, law is a matter of judgment.'

She concluded the day by saying if the stories were true, 'my client is some sort of Dr Frankenstein' who leaves people 'permanently and violently scarred and disfigured'. As soon as those words left her mouth, I knew they would be written up in the newspapers. For a lawyer with such a keen eye on the press, this metaphor seemed like a disastrous trap to lay for her client.

Like clockwork, at 6.12 pm that night, the *Sydney Morning Herald*'s article was published under the headline 'Surgeon Al Muderis was presented as "some sort of Dr Frankenstein", his lawyer says'.

Over three days, Chrysanthou accused our team of cherrypicking documents 'wholly out of context' to falsely accuse her client of negligence in a 'bucket-tipping exercise'. She said

Dr Al Muderis 'freely tells' patients of 'shocking complications' with 'utter bluntness' and 'doesn't try and sugar-coat it'. She said patients lied, got things wrong, as did our experts. She spoke about the virtue of Dr Al Muderis giving his mobile number to patients and said it was 'so hurtful' to say he 'dumps these people'.

She said it was 'ridiculous' to suggest that patients didn't provide informed consent, because most were subject to advice from a multidisciplinary team and Dr Al Muderis wasn't so 'charming' that he could overrule them. She said it was 'utterly absurd' that he shouldn't have operated on Lisa Calan, a young woman, 'because he can't perfectly attend to her'. She again openly asked, 'How was he to know that she had an aversion to Iraq, which, from his perspective, was unreasonable and illogical?' She delivered these arguments with such intensity that it was like method acting: the barrister had become the surgeon.

She flew from one patient to the next, and back again, moving rapid-fire through cases, experts. She denied that Carol needed a wheelchair. She denied that Dr Al Muderis ignored the maggots in Mark's legs. She said some patients were lying, others were 'poor historians' and confused. She branded the patients with positive experiences referenced in the story as 'unhinged' or 'irrational people who are part of some sort of cult'.

She accused me of destroying evidence in a 'calculated way' to conceal 'lies', saying I then 'engaged in subterfuge' when asked about it, and that I had failed to verify basic facts. 'It is an utter and disgraceful failure of a person calling herself a journalist, let alone an investigative journalist.'

The judge pushed back on one of Chrysanthou's claims that American patient Lisa Schaeffer had flown halfway across the world to lie in court about Dr Al Muderis calling her fat. 'You think she would manage to come up with some more,' the judge said.

Toward the end, Chrysanthou turned her attention to my father. She said it makes 'no sense' Dr Al Muderis told my father he would soon be in a wheelchair and then sent a letter to his GP stating that he didn't need the surgery. She went round and round, claiming no-one ever told him he needed the surgery urgently. 'Mr Grieve's evidence is false,' she said, in open court.

The judge asked why he would make this up, and what it meant for Dr Al Muderis's allegation that I had a conflict of interest. Chrysanthou said I didn't 'necessarily know' what really happened.

'So he has made it up to her?' the judge asked. 'At the time?'

As Chrysanthou clambered for an explanation, the judge only had more questions.

'It would be a rather bizarre thing to do when you've been told you don't need it to then say to a family member, "I've been there. They said I needed it. I needed it now",' the judge said.

I heard one of the juniors whisper a suggestion to Chrysanthou that she repeated verbatim.

'He has a motive to be dishonest, because he's here to assist his daughter,' Chrysanthou declared.

She said it was 'ridiculous' that my father's initial appointment lasted ten minutes, and accused him of fabricating their conversation at The Australian Club about phantom pain.

'He was adamant about it, even though he didn't have a problem with phantom pain. His phantom pain never needed medication. He was a very lucky amputee. Every now and then he had it, but it wasn't particularly problematic.'

This showed just how far Dr Al Muderis's position had strayed from reality. All my life I had seen my father struggle with phantom pain. To say that it wasn't a problem was an outright lie.

'So he has made that part up, as well?' the judge said.

Chrysanthou doubled down and described other parts of his evidence as a 'recent invention'. She said she regretted having to make that submission, but insisted 'there's no other available finding'.

This whole charade was extraordinary. Chrysanthou never put any of these theories to my father. Barristers have enormous power to raise serious allegations under the total privilege of court. With this enormous power comes enormous responsibility. Barristers must have a proper basis to make allegations, and the accused must have a fair opportunity to respond. None of these things happened when Chrysanthou savaged my father's reputation. Responsible barristers think deeply about how to raise serious charges, and rehearse the exact delivery to ensure fairness and accuracy. But in her typical style, Chrysanthou roamed from one allegation to the next. To accuse anyone of lying in court, committing the crime of perjury, is huge. To accuse a fellow King's Counsel, who is duty-bound to uphold the principles of justice, is even bigger.

Collins was furious, and eventually got to his feet.

'Quite scandalous allegations were made under absolute privilege about a member of the bar,' he said. 'We have been sitting at the bar table, reviewing the cross-examination of Mr Grieve, and we can see nothing – nothing that was fairly put to Mr Grieve that would warrant the attack that was made from the bar table.'

Collins invited her to reflect and then formally withdraw the comments. A more muted Chrysanthou thanked him for raising it and, after lunch, agreed he was right.

'I didn't intend to go beyond what I put to Mr Grieve,' she said. 'I accept that if I went beyond that this morning, I shouldn't have.'

Chrysanthou walked back her prior fury and said the judge doesn't need to make a finding of dishonesty. 'I did go beyond that,' she said. 'I didn't intend in my submissions this morning to go beyond what I had given him the opportunity to respond to. And I apologise for doing that.'

Finally, she tried to revive the smoking ashes of the concoction theory. Like a conspiracy theorist with a corkboard of tangled strings, she said various people had commercial interests and were trying to bring down her client. The judge tried to help Chrysanthou articulate exactly what she was trying to allege, but the more questions were asked, the vaguer it became. 'You made the submission that the journalists, knowing that or believing that your client is litigious, have knowingly published false material?'

'Yes,' Chrysanthou said.

'What's the motive?' the judge asked.

'I'm not ...' the barrister said, looking around.

'I know you don't have to. Are you putting one?'

'No, your Honour. I mean, journalists publish lies all the time. That's why defamation cases win. I can't go into their minds as to what their motives are and I wouldn't try ... People lie for many reasons, and often, you can never discern their motive. People just lie.'

It was a fitting end to the chaotic performance. Another vague, wild conspiracy, stated without a shred of evidence.

That week, the entire legal team went out to an Italian restaurant for a lavish feast in the heritage-listed Queen Victoria Building in George Street. It was incredible to see just how many lawyers had worked on this case, at various points, over the years-long ordeal. Before the food arrived, Collins stood and commanded the room once more. He talked about how this was the third-longest trial in Australian history, noting how difficult it was, not just because of the length, but the complexity, and praised everyone in the team for the way they had cared for the vulnerable patients who were witnesses.

He said there were other marks of success in a case than the outcome itself. 'Have we honoured the quality of the journalists whose work we are entrusted to defend? Have we been faithful to the ethics of our profession? If we had our time again, would we really do anything differently? I really think, on all those measures, this is a stunning exemplar.'

Collins singled out Issy Gwinner and Sophie Meixner as the 'smiling solicitors', JP and Marlia as 'the captains on our ship', Lyndelle who 'had a baby to get out of the case', 'amazing' juniors Claire Roberts, Melissa Marcus and Sandip Mukerjea. 'The amount of work you have all done on this case is just astonishing,' he said.

Then, he turned to our in-house lawyers Kiah Officer and Larina Alick, thanking them for the trust they put in the team, saying he could not imagine the internal conversations that went on behind the scenes. 'Best not to!' one yelled out, to laughter.

Collins said the media industry's business model had radically changed over the past 25 years, with fewer resources available for litigation like this. 'The easy course is not to fight these cases,' he said. 'But sometimes it's really important. In the right cases, to be able to back your journalists, back your lawyers, and take the fight – it's actually really important for the health of Australian democracy. Because without it, stories the rich and powerful prefer never see the light of day, would never see the light of day.'

Finally, he turned his attention to me. 'It's been an honour to stand up in court and defend journalism that we all believe was actually really, really important,' he said. 'This was an important story. It's a story that needed to be told. And it's actually a really important test for Australian defamation law. A surgeon shouldn't get away with a curated reputation that he had for so long ... I believe your journalism will be vindicated. Your preparation and dedication to defending the journalism was exemplary.'

It was a proud moment, for me, and everyone on the team. 'At the end of the day today,' Collins continued, 'as we were leaving the courtroom, Leah Mooney grabbed me by the arm, looked me in the eye, and just said "thank you". She wasn't thanking me. She was thanking all of you. I think we owe a toast to the patients.'

PART FOUR

CHAPTER 21

The Long Wait for Judgment

Two months after the court hearings officially wrapped, my father turned 80. We hosted a birthday party at The Australian Club, where almost 100 of his friends, colleagues and family gathered to celebrate the milestone – coincidentally in the very same room where my father first met Dr Al Muderis all those years ago.

At the same podium the doctor addressed club members, my brother Hugo started the speeches that night. An English teacher and brilliant wordsmith, Hugo interspersed poetry with childhood memories of Dad providing tactical advice from the sidelines of the soccer field, their father–son trip to Morocco, growing up living in a converted police station in the heart of Sydney's CBD, going on road trips with the radio on full blast, and learning how to use a chainsaw. 'Thank you for just being Dad,' he said.

It was a tough act to follow. I started with an anecdote about my sister and me as toddlers, rushing through the house to announce we had discovered the 'fucking' washing machine had broken. 'Shouting at inanimate objects is one lesson I have learnt from my father,' I said. The room laughed as I then turned to some of his more practical lessons. My father taught me to drive, to never stop learning, to always be curious, to stand up for myself, to take risks, to be bold and fearless in all pursuits.

'The last two years, as some of you would know,' I went on, 'Dad and I have been embroiled in a bit of a lawsuit together.' Many of the guests were lawyers. I confessed that growing up with my mother, father and sister all lawyers, my ears often glazed over the moment dinner conversation strayed to legal chat. But the process of being sued had given me a newfound appreciation for the law, and particularly what makes a good barrister. While there are rules and codes of ethics in place, I had come to learn that ultimately a good barrister is one who values truth, integrity and fairness. A good barrister treats people with respect and puts the pursuit of justice above all else. What makes someone a good barrister is not so different to what makes a good person, a good journalist, a good doctor. The experience of the trial had reaffirmed what I had long known. My father is a good barrister, a good person – one lesson I will keep learning. His sister Christine spoke about how he was always considered 'wise counsel' by their parents, and his university friend Steve Siebert recounted my father's favourite Winston Churchill line, 'You tell lies about me, I'll tell the truth about you.'

That night, like every other day, my father walked in and out of the club like he always had – unaided. This simple fact proved wrong Dr Al Muderis's warning that he would be in a wheelchair by 80 unless he underwent osseointegration surgery. Dr Al Muderis's prediction turned out to be false.

The next 12 months waiting for the judgment felt like an eternity. JP took bets on when everyone on the team thought it might arrive. As each date came and went, it started to feel like the day might never come. As time passed and the wait dragged on, I received calls and text messages from patients, surgeons or other sources, asking for updates. I didn't have any answers, other than to say it was a big case and a new defence, and these things take time.

Every now and then, I received an email from a new person detailing fresh problems within AHPRA. I noticed new court cases filed against Dr Al Muderis alleging medical negligence. In October 2024, Seven News broadcast an 'exclusive' television program that featured Dr Al Muderis and his life-saving surgery. No mention of risks. No mention of the defamation case in which dozens of his patients had testified about their suffering. A keyboard war erupted over Dr Al Muderis's Wikipedia page as new information about his scandals was added by members of the public, only to be deleted or softened by a user linked to an IP address at Macquarie University Hospital. A warning was splashed across the top of the page: 'This article contains promotional content'.

When people asked me about the case in the first few months, I was confident of victory. 'I may regret saying this but I will be shocked if we lose,' I said over and over. But, as time passed and no judgment came, nerves crept in. I found myself asking lawyers I met at pubs or parties what they thought the delay could mean. They told me it didn't mean anything, and although I knew they were right, it became harder to sit in the uncertainty.

Finally, the day did come: Monday 4 August 2025. I was sitting in Melbourne's beloved Cinema Nova in Carlton watching a terrifying zombie thriller, *28 Years Later*, when my phone lit up. It was JP. *Al Mud judgment Friday!* My heart skipped a beat. It had been more than a year since the trial had wrapped up, and I had somehow convinced myself that the judgment would most likely arrive the following year. Propelled into a moment of sheer avoidance, I tried to keep watching the movie for a few seconds until my phone started flashing and buzzing. This time it was my boss, Mathew Dunckley, calling. I rushed out of the cinema to take the call. 'Oh my god, oh my god, oh my god,' he said. 'How do you feel?'

The reality of the amount of work that lay ahead suddenly dawned. 'I'll put together a list of stories in the event of a positive judgment,' I told him.

It was too late in the evening to call my sources, so I sent text messages to Mark, Brennan, Carol, Leah and a few others to tell them the judgment was coming, before speaking with JP. 'I'd still much prefer to be on our side of the bar table than theirs,' he said. 'But as the week goes on, we'll probably all start feeling more nervous.'

The next day I spoke with sources over the phone. Leah and Tim Mooney told me the New South Wales healthcare regulator had officially closed their complaint. It was the end of a long quest for justice for them, and they just couldn't understand how Dr Al Muderis could hurt Leah so badly, but no action be taken. Their concerns had been vindicated in the Supreme Court of NSW, and they were awarded a significant payment, but the healthcare institutions designed to protect the public seemed totally uninterested.

In the months since we last spoke, Tim had been diagnosed with pancreatic cancer and had undergone emergency surgery to remove the tumour. A remarkably strong man, he cracked jokes about how much weight he'd lost from the removal of the organs and surrounding tissue. Despite Tim's recent surgery, he and Leah immediately said they would be in the courtroom for the judgment. They had watched almost every day of the trial and had no intention of missing the grand finale. I said I'd look forward to seeing them there.

In the next call, I spoke with Rowena, whose bad situation had continued to worsen. The pain she suffered in her leg had become even more excruciating. Rowena's implant had been removed, and she underwent several further surgeries, amputating the leg higher each time. In the last operation, surgeons had performed a hip disarticulation – a complete amputation of the leg at the hip. Nothing had worked, and now she was in more pain than ever.

As I spoke to more patients, they were just as rattled as I was by the news that judgment day had finally arrived. *Wow, I thought that would never happen. I'm glad you will be there,* Carol texted from Queensland.

I spent the week trying to focus on work, finishing off projects to clear my schedule. I knew there would be a wild storm if we won. I tried to stay as calm as possible, but found it difficult to concentrate or think straight. The stakes felt unimaginably high.

Defamation cases are almost always a 'winner takes all' outcome. Either we win, and the patients, whistleblowers, surgeons and public interest journalism more broadly are vindicated, or we lose, and suffer the consequences, costing Nine huge sums of money, removing the stories, and having a chilling effect on investigative journalism.

This lawsuit was huge, 68 trial days in total, and there was a hefty legal bill attached. Our side had spent more than $10 million by that point, hiring 14 solicitors and ten barristers over the three-year period. We estimated Dr Al Muderis had spent $8 million – and the battle was far from over. Lawyers would be kept on retainer to squabble over costs, and any potential appeal, which would send the already eye-watering bill climbing even higher.

In 2024, *The Age* and *Sydney Morning Herald* had a redundancy round that saw some of the country's best journalists leave the company. It was devastating to see that much experience and talent walk out the door, and a terrible outcome for journalism and Australian democracy. At a time when newsroom budgets had never been under more pressure, to sit in the reality that I might have cost the company $20 million felt like a crippling burden.

While colleagues and managers continued to assure me that everyone was with me, win or lose, I couldn't shake the feeling that losing was simply not an option. How could dozens of patients and their families testify and not be believed? How could the judge believe expert reports from people so obviously conflicted? How could she deny these stories were in the public interest? I couldn't bring myself to imagine what losing would mean for the patients who had trusted me to tell their story. What it would mean for healthcare regulation reform, the need to ensure people are put before profits, and patients have access to basic information about the people who operate on them.

The night before the judgment, I flew to Sydney. Word was circulating that neither Dr Al Muderis or Sue Chrysanthou was going to be in court. Nicholas Pullen would be there, the solicitor who had refused to settle two years ago, on his client's instructions, before any of this had unfolded.

I struggled to sleep that night but woke to a text message from Mark Urquhart: *Charlotte well today's the day. Super excited for us all. But I just wanted to say one thing before it all went down. No matter what happens today I am super proud of you for standing up in front of the world and calling this to their attention. I just want to say thank you from the bottom of my heart for the opportunity to speak within all that you've done. Words could not portray the amount of gratitude I have to you.*

When I read these words, I cried. Despite everything Mark had been through, the stomach-churning cross-examination and everything in between, that he felt this way meant the world. It suddenly felt that this really was all worth it. Mark deserved to be heard. Other patients texted too: *Fingers crossed today mate. May justice be served,* Brennan Smith wrote. With these final blessings, I felt I could now walk into the court with my head held high.

Justice Abraham's judgment was scheduled for 2 pm. I met JP in the Thomson Geer offices just before, in the same conference room we'd met in so many times. When I walked in, he was pacing quickly, and a smile flashed across his face. 'How many pages, you reckon?' he said, tapping answers into his phone, the latest round of bets – this time for the number of pages the judgment would run to. While JP had remained positive and calm throughout the whole ordeal, I could tell even he was feeling anxious at this point.

We walked together with barrister Claire Roberts to face the music. Kirsty and Natalie got ready to tune in from the *60 Minutes* office in North Sydney, and my editors watched from Melbourne online, along with so many of the witnesses. My father, mother, partner, my parent's friend Elizabeth, as well as Leah and Tim and their son Paul were already seated in the back row when I arrived. I nodded at my family and walked over to say hello to the Mooneys. Everyone was on edge, but relieved the moment had finally arrived.

I sat between Larina Alick and Monique Farmer, *The Age* and *Herald*'s managing editor, who had accompanied me for cross-examination and encouraged me with snacks and smiles throughout. As the minutes ticked by, I watched the clock – time had never gone so slowly. I dug my fingernails into my arm as we waited in silence, staring at the door where the judge would soon emerge. My heart thumped against my rib cage again. Eventually, the court staff announced the hearing was in session. Everyone stood as Justice Wendy Abraham appeared. Her steely demeanour had not changed, as she started delivering her judgment.

'It is not disputed that at the time of publication, Dr Al Muderis had a high profile,' she said. 'The respondents had described his reputation as "glittering".'

Over the next few minutes, Justice Abraham summarised the seven stories that conveyed 75 defamatory imputations, and the legal strategies we had deployed to defend them. There was dense legal-speak before, finally, she arrived at what mattered.

'I have found the respondents have established the contextual truth defence.'

It felt like time itself had stopped. My phone lit up with a text from my partner. *TRUTH!!!!!!!* More messages started flowing in from friends, colleagues, patients, surgeons. Then Justice Abraham turned to the public interest defence. Again, she found in our favour.

'The positive media coverage his practice had enjoyed needed correcting, and the investigation revealed another side of his practice,' the judge said.

'Patients should be making their decisions with both sides of the story.'

It was over. We had won. Almost three years after the stories were published, truth had prevailed. Public interest had prevailed.

Justice Abraham dismissed Dr Al Muderis's case. I was shocked almost to the point of disbelief, as huge smiles splashed across almost every face in the courtroom. I felt outside of my body. Pullen leaned over to JP and stated that his client would be appealing immediately.

I walked over to the Mooneys and hugged each of them. Paul Mooney's eyes welled with tears as he talked about how important this moment was, for all the patients, his parents, for the public, for journalism, for accountability and the need for change. It had been a long road for the Mooneys, a never-ending battle, but now, at last, some form of justice had finally been served.

Tim and Leah were interviewed by Nine News on the steps of the court building. 'The smiles say it all,' reporter Alison Piotrowski said on the bulletin that night.

'I'm happy that he's not going to cause damage to people anymore. No-one's going to suffer,' Leah told the camera crew.

'It's so wonderful to finally get some justice,' Tim said.

A photographer from the *Sydney Morning Herald* captured Tim and Leah embracing, and another with JP and me beside them, smiling, happy, relieved. I went back to Thomson Geer's offices with the lawyers, and we started poring over the judgment – 771 pages in total. I never found out who won that bet, but it was a monster of a document.

I skimmed the pages for the different findings. One after another, Justice Abraham found the patients, my father, me, Tom, Natalie, our experts, whistleblowers, surgeons, to be credible, honest people. Mark's surgery *was* experimental. Dad *was* pressured into surgery. I had no conflict of interest. Carol *did* need a wheelchair. 'Mutilated' *was* accurate. Ignoring Lisa Calan *was* callous. Shona *was* honest. Dr Al Muderis was a liar. He was callous and his conduct in some cases was cruel. He pressured vulnerable patients into high-risk surgery. He abused his staff and neglected his patients. It was a comprehensive evisceration of Dr Al Muderis's arguments, and a thumping endorsement of the journalism, the case, the truth.

As JP cracked a bottle of champagne, my phone lit up with a call from Mark Urquhart. I ducked into another room to take it. His voice was wavering as he choked back tears. 'I'm speechless,' Mark said. 'It's good. It's so good. It's all over. My story is recognised as true. If you ever need me for anything ...' he said, voice trailing off. I thanked Mark once again for his courage. This victory was his.

My phone was exploding with messages.

Congratulations you guys. That is a magnificent and comprehensive victory! the newspapers' national editor, Luke McIlveen, wrote.

Arrrghhh!!! Well done! I'm shaking and I have goosebumps, Kiah wrote.

Well done. Your court experience was a lot tougher than mine and Her Honour believed you, Dr John Anstee wrote.

Huge congrats on today, vindication of your tireless and fearless work, Tom Steinfort said.

So proud of you champion, Nick McKenzie wrote.

Karma and justice is served. Bloody stoked, Brennan Smith wrote.

Thanks for your tenacity, wrote one confidential surgeon.

You are saving lives with your journalism. It is not often one can say that, wrote another confidential surgeon.

JP said he'd received so many messages that it felt like we'd won a Logie.

I caught an Uber to Nine's office to say a few words for the 6 pm news package, and then joined the lawyers back in the city. That night I went out for margaritas with the legal team, where discussion swirled about the judgment and what it meant. I couldn't shake the feeling that we had been gaslit for three years, having been told over and over again that everyone was lying, when it was so obvious the opposite was true. My partner took me out for a late dinner in Surry Hills afterward. We drank nice wine and ate rich food. Our quick-witted friend Thomas Mitchell posted a photo of me to social media, holding the printed judgment with a huge grin, under the caption 'Not guilty!'. It was bliss but the celebration was short-lived. I spent the rest of the weekend ploughing through the judgment, before launching into the next two weeks of intensive reporting.

As I read more and more of Justice Abraham's ruling, I was astounded at the depths of her findings against Dr Al Muderis. She made it clear that this trial was *not* a medical negligence case, but that, based on the evidence, she was satisfied Dr Al Muderis had failed his patients in so many different ways. She separated her judgment into nine key defamatory stings – improper sales tactics, misleading osseointegration patients about risks, poor patient selection, negligent post-operative care, illegal surgery in America, prioritising money, fame, reputation and numbers over patients, bullying of staff, lying to journalists, unethical practice. While she wasn't satisfied there was enough evidence to say Dr Al Muderis performed 'surgery' in America, she did rule that he performed medical services from hotel rooms, which she found was unethical. All the other stings were true.

As for Dr Al Muderis, she ruled 'he was not always honest in the answers he gave'. She said he was evasive and argumentative at times, that he was disrespectful and that he had paid callous disregard to his patients. She said, for example, his description of throwing food at his employee as 'passionate banter' was not just wrong, but showed he 'fails to appreciate the nature of his conduct'.

'He gave the very strong impression that he considered his answers and opinions were unchallengeable,' she said. 'Dr Al Muderis also gave speeches justifying the importance of what he did and stressing the importance of his experience … to bolster his evidence.'

She had seen exactly what I had seen, and even gone further. She found his boat trips and dinner outings with patients had altered the normal patient-doctor relationship. She criticised him for cultivating dependence among his patients, by giving out his mobile number, saying they were family, pledging a lifelong relationship, only to drop them. This really was a man living in his own world. He blocked out the bad and put a shining light on the good. As his star rose, he left a trail of suffering in his wake, of human beings discarded, forgotten, ignored, rotten, maggot-infested. It was a cult-like, out-of-control, dangerous halo that surrounded him, and I was so thankful the judge could see that.

I stayed up past 2 am most nights that week, reading the judgment and doing my best to distil it into plain English for readers. I worked 18-hour days as I pumped out story after story. Having been restrained from reporting on Dr Al Muderis during the trial, there were so many untold stories that could now be published. My inbox exploded again with emails from people all over the world, thanking us for having the courage to defend the stories, and raising new, fresh allegations about Dr Al Muderis. The amount of new information coming in reminded me of the aftermath of the initial investigation. It was overwhelming.

I was staying in Sydney at the time, and my mother noticed my grooming standards had given way to the endless deadlines. *Keep writing and make sure you brush your hair!* she texted. *And get some sleep.*

The emails, calls and texts kept piling up. Among them was an email from a person who had recently held a senior position at AHPRA. 'It never acts in a timely manner, always after the death and destruction and abuse, it bullies the Board and Board members, removing those who speak up … AHPRA somehow answers to no-one. Millions are wasted on failed UK consultants, lavish dinners, business class flights, forays to other countries to extend its reach. It's a waste. It's useless. It's inept. It's a rort.'

The emails came from new sources in the medical industry too, saying every surgeon in Sydney was aware of Dr Al Muderis's 'unethical and egregious' practice, that Macquarie University Hospital and Medibank were negligent in not acting sooner. 'It's a pity that it takes an investigation such as yours to expose his misdeeds.'

One surgeon drew my attention to a private emergency facility where Dr Al Muderis works and orders expensive scans on machinery he part-owns 'regardless of their injury'. 'The vertical integration of his practice and businesses is something to behold. Once again, congratulations on your reporting.'

Ashley Gollan, widower of Kim Gollan, emailed me too. 'Spoke to the girls this morning after reading your *Age/SMH* story we all shed a tear and [gave] three cheers for you … Thanks again on behalf of Kim in heaven.' Ashley emailed the NSW Australian of the Year awards, which refused to comment publicly on the judgment. Ashley couldn't understand how this award was not immediately taken away. He kept emailing them with links to my articles and to the judgment. 'Please read this and let me know and others why his Award should not be REVOKED??'

As I fielded more phone calls and messages from every direction, I started approaching some of the organisations Dr Al Muderis had claimed to represent for comment. The results were disturbing. Despite Dr Al Muderis stating in his sworn affidavit that he was an ambassador for Amnesty International Australia, the organisation was the first to deny this was true. Dr Al Muderis was not, and never had been, an ambassador for Amnesty International. In fact, Amnesty International had never had any ambassadors and a spokesperson said they were concerned vulnerable patients may have trusted him because of false claims. They issued a public statement correcting the record.

Red Cross Australia, another charity Dr Al Muderis had claimed to represent, said he stopped being an ambassador in 2019, years before the ambassador role was listed as current in his affidavit. They said any relationship was historic and 'very limited in nature'. Other smaller charities he claimed to represent said they had either never heard of him or had only fleeting interactions many years ago. Sue Hallam, who runs Sanctuary Australia Foundation, said she had approached Dr Al Muderis by email in early 2016 and he agreed they could use his image on their website to promote his advocacy of refugees. She invited Dr Al Muderis to a fundraising concert at the time, but he was too busy, so never came. 'Apart from that, we don't know him,' she said. No-one from her charity had ever met Dr Al Muderis face-to-face. She was alarmed to read the judgment, and quickly removed him from their website.

The executive director of another charity that Dr Al Muderis listed in his affidavit, Multicultural Disability Advocacy Association, called me in a panic. She did not know Dr Al Muderis and had no idea why he had claimed to be an ambassador for her organisation. 'Why is he claiming to represent us? This is really concerning,' she said.

Next, I contacted the University of Sydney. After all, his affidavit stated he was an honorary associate there and had ongoing, collaborative research relationships. Surely, this was true? Again, the university denied what was written in his affidavit. The unpaid position had finished years ago, a spokesperson said, and there was no ongoing affiliation, despite the prestigious institution's name being splashed across his promotional websites. 'We welcome the opportunity to correct the record,' the university said. Everything was starting to feel frighteningly dishonest.

The depths of his deception grew deeper and deeper. His lawyers denied any deliberate misrepresentation, but once someone is found by the Federal Court to be a liar, each new denial becomes harder to swallow. When I asked each of these organisations to respond to the judgment, I expected them to decline to comment, or issue a vague statement about reviewing the findings. I could never have imagined they would deny that these affiliations existed.

I contacted Saxton Speakers, the speakers' agency that promoted Dr Al Muderis's alleged affiliations with the Red Cross and Amnesty International, charging tens of thousands of dollars for speeches that were sometimes as short as ten minutes. They said they no longer represented him and swiftly deleted his profile from their website. It was a spectacular unravelling of the image he presented to the public, and to his patients.

In the eye of this storm, I attended the Kennedy Awards at Randwick Racecourse, where Kirsty Thomson was awarded for being an outstanding mentor and delivered a speech: 'If you haven't read the landmark judgment and seen what Justice Abraham had to say about the journalism and evidence of Charlotte Grieve, Natalie Clancy and Tom Steinfort, I urge you to. It's only 770 pages, an absolute page turner!' she told the room. 'It was such a bright moment in what is not an easy time for our industry. The very idea of journalism, truthful, independent, fearless reporting, is being tested from every direction. Now, more than ever, we need unity, not petty takedowns, not cynicism. What's at stake is too important.'

The following week, the Australian Orthopaedic Association held a late-night board meeting and decided to remove Dr Al Muderis from its membership. This is the country's peak professional association that is responsible for setting standards for orthopaedic surgeons. Dozens of complaints had been filed with the AOA, from surgeons and patients warning that his ongoing membership risked causing harm to the wider fraternity's reputation. One surgeon told me the decision to remove him was a big step that exposed the association to risk, but that so many members felt it was the right course of action. 'The standard you walk past is the standard you accept.' I was thrilled that after so many confidential calls from surgeons all around the country, expressing concerns behind the scenes, now finally the profession was standing up. This could no longer be dismissed as 'trial by media'.

Macquarie University Hospital initially stood by him, but then announced he had taken indefinite leave. We published a story about this, and I received a panicked phone call from the hospital's media representative. He wanted to make it crystal clear that it was Dr Al Muderis who 'has elected to take leave from the hospital', rather than being pushed. Medibank, the country's largest healthcare insurer, which part-owns a short-stay hospital with Dr Al Muderis, said they were 'very concerned' about the judgment, and pledged to cooperate with any regulatory investigations. Other hospitals, including Norwest and East Sydney Private, stood by him.

Sadly, what was entirely missing was any commitment from the healthcare regulators to do anything beyond look at the judgment. No investigation was called. No patients were contacted. Both the HCCC and AHPRA declined interviews, and issued hollow statements pledging to protect the public. From my vantage point, it seemed not a single course of action was put into place, despite what had to be one of the most damning public findings about a high-profile doctor still operating on vulnerable patients, both around the country and around the world.

CHAPTER 22

What Next?

After two weeks of non-stop calls, meetings and reporting, I had done my best to respond to every message, publish every breaking story. At last, I took a few days to collapse into a heap. It was only then that I fully appreciated the magnitude of what we had achieved. The judgment could not have been a bigger vindication of this journey we had all chosen to embark on. As Dr John Anstee had told me, it's what we ought to have done. And I did feel proud.

But beneath that, there was a gnawing sense of unease and frustration. There were hundreds upon hundreds of solid-gold, cast-in-stone Federal Court findings about how Dr Al Muderis had failed his patients, failed to uphold his duty of care, his duty to warn. While the AOA's decision to revoke his membership was historic, it was also entirely symbolic. Dr Al Muderis immediately lawyered up, sued the AOA and got a court order to overturn his expulsion. 'He's got deep pockets,' one surgeon told me.

In a statement posted on social media, Dr Al Muderis said he was 'disappointed' by the defamation judgment and intended to appeal. He said his intention in suing 'was not about avoiding transparency' but to 'protect my reputation … from what I believed to be unfounded and inaccurate representations' of his practice. Missing from his statement was any apology to the people he had failed. Dozens of his supporters commented underneath, praising his work. I noticed some less flattering comments were swiftly deleted. US surgeon Solon Rosenblatt posted: *Time to get back to work and put this behind you. Take a course on yoga and introspection.*

Dr Al Muderis continued promoting himself on social media, in wildly misleading ways. He shared old clips from the ABC's *Foreign Correspondent* program, saying he wanted to 'set an example for people to follow' as both the doctor and journalist cried. Two weeks after the University of Sydney denied any affiliation with the surgeon, he claimed in a video posted online that he was a 'professor in orthopaedics' at three universities in Sydney. He continued to post videos stating 70 per cent of osseointegration patients never get any infection. It seemed clear to me that he was still living in his own fantasy world.

On paper, Dr Al Muderis's national healthcare record remained completely clean. This allowed him to claim innocence while working to rehabilitate his reputation through aggressive social media posting, glowing media interviews with foreign journalists, and threats of further legal action.

I tracked court listings and saw that over the past two years alone, six medical negligence lawsuits had been launched against him in Australia, most of which were quietly settled behind closed doors. I had seen for myself complaints to the regulators, where errors and lies had been found, yet these also had again been handled without a trace. There were cascading failures with this surgeon's care – that the courts, regulators, and now the Federal Court of Australia all knew about, yet his public profile on the national healthcare register remained entirely clear.

The only organisations that could do anything – HCCC and AHPRA – seemed uninterested at best, obstructive at worst. The organisations in charge of informing the public of dangerous doctors were failing to do the very basics of their job. After we published the first investigation into Dr Al Muderis, I became determined to understand the structural factors at play, so I began investigating AHPRA itself. By that point, it seemed there had been non-stop medical scandals, from Adele Ferguson's investigation into cosmetic cowboys to Kate McClymont's exposé of neurosurgeon Charlie Teo. I thought there must be a missing link. Over months, I spoke with dozens of people working inside AHPRA – investigators, board members, compliance officers – and a picture emerged of a toxic organisation battling a huge work backlog, and serious cases falling through the cracks.

The entire regulatory model as enshrined by the national law relies on members of the public submitting complaints, meaning the vast majority of doctor misconduct goes unreported. When it is reported, any investigation is plagued by delays, a lack of resources and poorly trained staff. Through this process, doctors like Al Muderis are represented by well-resourced insurers and backed by powerful hospitals that throw significant money and pressure at keeping doctors' records clean.

At the very core of the national law is a non-punitive approach. The intention is to keep doctors in the workplace, not take them out. Many of the battles AHPRA are willing to pursue are low-hanging fruit – doctors who are poor note-takers, or have weak insurance policies. They clock up enforcement actions on easy targets as a shield to deflect accountability from their neglect of the systemic, longstanding problems forever consigned to the too-hard basket. Doctors without the power, prestige and deep pockets of Dr Al Muderis contacted me over and over again with stories of unfounded complaints that dragged out for years, destroying their careers and mental health in the process. The system was failing both patients and doctors.

Even more disturbingly, my dealings with AHPRA revealed an entrenched desire to protect the organisation's reputation over the public's right to know. In one example, I was investigating an optometrist in a suburban mall in Western Australia who touched the thigh of a teenage girl while she was having her eyes tested. This practitioner commented on the girl's breasts and body, in a clear abuse of his position that seemed to breach not only medical ethics, but also the law. When I called the clinic, a receptionist said this particular optometrist was known for his inappropriate comments about women.

AHPRA took almost two years to investigate the girl's complaint. They declined to report the matter to the police, declined to temporarily suspend him and eventually requested he undertake training and mentorship. Temporarily, a dense legal notice was published on his profile with no details of his offending, but today, this has been deleted and his profile is again entirely clear. Incensed by the regulator's response, the young woman, Cate, had the courage to share her story publicly, calling for change. When I spoke with AHPRA, they defended the regulator's actions. I was told 'on background' that touching a teenage girl like this was on the lower end of offending for healthcare practitioners, and they couldn't see why the girl was dissatisfied, nor the public interest in reporting the story.

As I continued reporting on the rotten core of Australia's healthcare system, I was contacted by a woman named Suzanne Hogan. She had been operated on by podiatric surgeon Paul Bours in 2014, who, over a series of operations, had caused serious disfigurement, leaving her with different-sized feet, crippling pain and permanent disability. Little did she know, the entire time Bours was operating on her, he was under investigation for seriously harming several other patients. He was eventually suspended by the Health Care Complaints Commission for a year, and subjected to a range of other sanctions but, for Suzanne, it was too late.

She later discovered podiatric surgeons like Bours were a small profession that were legally allowed to perform invasive, high-risk foot surgeries without even a medical degree. Many in this niche profession had been trained at an obscure college where even the college president had once been suspended from operating. It was an unbelievable scenario, and one that neatly exposed how the regulator was failing across multiple fronts. When Suzanne first contacted me, I knew this would be a difficult story to tell. I pitched another joint investigation with *60 Minutes*, and the end result was a shocking exposé that prompted AHPRA to commit to a regulatory review.

The reviewer, after a few months, made a series of recommendations about podiatric surgeons, but also about the broader regulatory framework. Among these, the reviewer argued, there needed to be far greater transparency regarding the track records of doctors with a history of complaints, rather than being scrubbed after they are deemed to have expired. He said negligence cases should also be listed on doctors' AHPRA profiles, but that the political will was lacking.

'Many registered health practitioners believe that the right to privacy and the protection of their professional reputation and livelihood means that their regulatory history should not be visible to the public. Ultimately ministers did not amend the National Law to expand the information about a practitioner's disciplinary history on the register.'

The reviewer said the public should know if a healthcare practitioner has been found to fall below an acceptable standard of care so patients can ask questions and make informed choices about who cuts them open. 'At present,' he wrote, 'the community is denied access to such information.'

In short, when it comes to dangerous doctors, the public is flying blind.

* * *

When I pressed AHPRA for answers about what was being done about Dr Al Muderis following the defamation judgment, the new media manager called me for an 'off the record' chat. I was told the HCCC was responsible for investigating complaints for practitioners based in New South Wales. I explained that I understood this, but AHPRA was responsible for policing national guidelines, such as bans on patient testimonials. The social media pages for Dr Al Muderis's osseointegration business were plastered with videos of patients sharing wholly positive experiences to the backdrop of inspirational music. 'I'd recommend it to anybody,' one man said from a hospital bed the day after osseointegration surgery. 'It's been life-changing,' said another.

Dr Al Muderis was doing this in broad daylight, and none of the authorities seemed to give a damn. It was mind-bending, and I couldn't help wondering – will the court case really change anything? If this level of exposure hasn't forced the regulators to act, what will?

I came to realise that Dr Al Muderis is merely a symptom of a much larger disease, where dangerous doctors are protected by useless regulators and profit-driven hospitals, and are able to hire lawyers to protect their reputation if there's any whiff of scandal (whether or not they have a strong case). The public should be entitled to know the track records of doctors they put their trust in. This should be uncontroversial. The medical industry should want this. The regulators should too. Politicians should see greater transparency of dangerous doctors as an easy path to win votes. Basic policy reforms to better arm the public with such vital information have already been debated, then sidelined and forgotten about. Reports with overdue recommendations gather dust, while politicians just order new reviews. The whole charade shows just how captured decision-makers are by the medical industry, so fearful to put a foot wrong that change is now seen as unattainable. As medical care in Australia becomes more expensive, and less transparent, this lack of political will shows how spineless, visionless and uncaring the world we live in really is. If our political leaders cannot guarantee that dangerous doctors are not cutting people open, how can we trust them with anything else? If they don't resist the private takeover of Australian healthcare, what *will* they fight?

Australians rightly take pride in our public health system. Ensuring that everyone has the right to free healthcare is a sign of a country that cares about its people. However, laws and policies over the years have slowly but surely nudged Australian healthcare into an increasingly privatised model. In this model, celebrity surgeons reign supreme and the public suffers. There is a reason that surgeons are Australia's highest-paid profession.

I do not pretend to have all the answers to the complex, intersecting problems plaguing our healthcare system. But I do want readers to finish this book armed with the courage to always seek a second opinion, to ask questions about your doctor's record, to demand evidence that suggested treatments will work, and to always explore alternatives. I want readers to call on their political leaders to act now to reform healthcare regulation in this country, so we have watchdogs with teeth that *can* punish poor behaviour, so that doctors *are* stopped from harming people before it's too late. There should be far greater transparency on the AHPRA register so patients can make up their own minds. It should not take a three-year-long, $20 million defamation trial to put the findings about Dr Al Muderis on the record. Doctors should not be able to delete their past mistakes.

The doctor's duty to warn is enshrined in law. Journalists, too, have a duty to warn. While our trade doesn't deal with life or death, the media is trusted to warn the public about the dangers of society, the failures of institutions. This book has laid bare the failure of separate professions to deploy this duty. Dr Al Muderis failed to warn patients of the risks of his controversial surgery. The uncritical media coverage failed to warn the public by turning him into a celebrity. The legal system allowed him to sue, spending millions of dollars trying to prevent the public from knowing the truth.

This is a book about the duty to warn, what it means, and when it fails. It's a story about the cost of a good reputation and the battle for the truth. And it's a story about the people who risked everything to speak out in the public interest. Thanks to them, the truth won, and now it's up to everyone else to demand change.

Author's Note

This book is based on the author's observations, reporting, court documents and original interviews. It is not a complete summary of the trial, with much of the evidence left out due to page constraints. Dr Al Muderis has appealed the judgment, which will be heard by the Full Court of the Federal Court of Australia in June 2026.

Acknowledgements

Thank you to everyone who has trusted me to tell their story. This includes all the patients, whistleblowers, experts and surgeons who had the courage to tell the truth, no matter the pressure to stay silent. To Mark Urquhart, Brennan Smith, Carol Todd, Blythe Warland, Chris Bruha, Rachael Ulrich, John Anstee, Shona, and Fred Hernandez who went on the record for the first investigation. The story would never have seen the light of day without your strength and conviction.

To everyone who took the stand, often pushing through unimaginable pain to be there. To Leah and Tim Mooney, for your pursuit of justice. To Jane Orford, who never got to see justice.

Thank you to Michael Bachelard, who backed this project from the beginning and encouraged me to stick with investigative journalism. Thank you to my colleagues, particularly Tom Steinfort and Natalie Clancy, who stood by me. To Nick McKenzie for paving the way and teaching me the ropes, along with invaluable mentorship from Richard Baker, Ben Schneiders, Sarah Danckert, Jo Chandler, Andrew Dodd, Lawrence Gibbons, Mathew Dunckley, Kirsty Thomson and many others over the years. To Larina Alick and Kiah Officer, for always having my back.

To *The Age* and Nine for trusting my work, and taking on the fight. To the camera operators and sound recordists at *60 Minutes*, and the photographers, digital producers and subeditors at *The Age* who brought the series to life.

Thank you to the Thomson Geer team, led by John-Paul Cashen and Marlia Saunders, who are the best lawyers I could have asked for. Your team went the extra mile and it showed every single day. Special thanks to Samantha McGeoch, Issy Gwinner, Sophie Meixner, and everyone who handled this case forensically and empathetically. To Matt Collins, whose integrity is second to none. To Declan Roche, Melissa Marcus, Claire Roberts, Renee Enbom, Lyndelle Barnett and importantly, Sandip Mukerjea, whose preparation was priceless.

To Monique Farmer, for coming with me to court. To Osman Faruqi, for everything. To Georgia Morgan and Kit Murphie, for your unconditional support, and all my friends, for putting up with my leaves of absence, and Sam Jonscher, for the photos. To Georgia King, for encouraging me to write this book. To my agent, Rachel Crawford, for believing in the project and going above and beyond. To everyone at Hachette, particularly Vanessa Radnidge, Katherine Hassett and Vanessa Lanaway.

Thank you to all the people who have got in touch with new information over the years, editors who encouraged me to keep writing, as well as the Australian Orthopaedic Association for pushing for higher standards. To Ange Bowne, Elizabeth Pakchung and Jane Barnett, for support during the trial and always.

And above all, to my family. To my aunt Jenny, for your archives, and Steve and Christine for sharing your memories. To my brothers Hugo and Fergus, and Azlifa, Natalie, Emma and Noah, and my sister Madeleine, who we all wish was still here today. To Tess, for always being there, and Laura, Lucy and John. To Mum and Dad, for your unflinching support and making me who I am today.

hachette
AUSTRALIA

If you would like to find out more about Hachette Australia, our authors, upcoming events and new releases, you can visit our website or our social media channels:

hachette.com.au

 HachetteAustralia

 HachetteAus

About the Author

Charlotte Grieve is an award-winning investigative journalist. She joined *The Age* and *Sydney Morning Herald* as a cadet in 2018 and worked for two years as a national business journalist, during which she was twice awarded Citi Young Business Journalist of the Year in 2022 and 2023. She joined *The Age*'s investigations team in 2022 and has since been awarded two Quill Awards, highly commended for the Grant Hattam Quill for Investigative Journalism, a Kennedy Award for Outstanding Reporting on the environment and nominated for a Walkley Mid-Year Prize for Environment Reporting. She was awarded the Michael Gordon fellowship in both 2021 and 2023 where she travelled to the outback to report regional investigations with an environmental focus. She has producer credits for five documentaries with *60 Minutes*, on topics ranging from white-collar crime to healthcare investigations.

Charlotte will join the ABC's national investigations team in 2026.